McGRAW-HILL

Spanish

saludos

first part

ANNOTATED TEACHER'S EDITION

Conrad J. Schmitt
Protase E. Woodford
Randall G. Marshall

Webster Division
McGraw-Hill Book Company

NEW YORK • ST. LOUIS • SAN FRANCISCO • ATLANTA
AUCKLAND • BOGOTÁ • DALLAS • HAMBURG
JOHANNESBURG • LONDON • MADRID • MEXICO • MONTREAL
NEW DELHI • PANAMA • PARIS • SÃO PAULO • SINGAPORE • SYDNEY
TOKYO • TORONTO

McGraw-Hill Spanish Saludos—first part

Teacher's Edition

ISBN 0-07-056243-1

3 4 5 6 7 8 9 10 DOCDOC 94 93 92 91 90 89 88 87

Contents

Introduction

The front matter of the Teacher's Edition of the *McGraw-Hill Spanish* **Saludos** program presents the following information:

- A description of *McGraw-Hill Spanish* **Saludos,** including the philosophy of the program and features and benefits of the program

- The organization of *McGraw-Hill Spanish* **Saludos,** which includes a description of the Teacher's Resource Kit, a description of the Student Text, and a description of all the ancillary materials

- How to use *McGraw-Hill Spanish* **Saludos,** with teaching suggestions for each lesson part, sample lesson plans, and a detailed table of contents

- Reference lists for *McGraw-Hill Spanish* **Saludos,** including Spanish names, useful classroom words and expressions, and answers to all exercises and activities in the Student Text

In addition to the front matter, the blue overprint on each page of the Student Text provides the following information:

- Teaching suggestions for specific exercises and activities

- Suggestions for expanding specific exercises

- Material considered optional

- Material recorded on the Cassette Program

In each lesson it is also noted for teachers when to include activities from the Cassette Program, when to assign specific exercises from the Workbook, and when to administer quizzes included in the Teacher's Resource Kit.

4

SECTION ONE
Description of *McGraw-Hill Spanish* **Saludos**

McGraw-Hill Spanish **Saludos**—*first part* and *second part* is a two-volume edition of *McGraw-Hill Spanish* **Saludos.** The **Lecciones Preliminares A–G** and **Lessons 1–12** comprise the text for the *first part.* **Lessons 13–24** and three new review lessons, **Repaso A–C,** which systematically reinforce and review the material presented in **Saludos**—*first part,* comprise the text for the *second part.* These split editions of the *McGraw-Hill Spanish* **Saludos** program allow for greater flexibility when using the program at the junior high school level or with slower learners.

The **Saludos**—*first part* program contains the following components: the Student Text, the Teacher's Edition, and the Workbook. The Cassette Program, Student Tape Manual, Tests, Overhead Transparencies, and Teacher's Resource Kit are also adaptable for use with this split edition.

Philosophy of the program

The main objective of the *McGraw-Hill Spanish* **Saludos** program is to enable students to attain a measurable degree of communicative competency and proficiency in each of the four language skills: listening, speaking, reading, and writing. Every effort has been made to present the language in an interesting and stimulating context so that the students' experience in acquiring a second language will be an enjoyable one.

Another equally important objective of the program is to allow Spanish teachers flexibility so that they will feel comfortable with the material. Every effort has been made to present the material in such a way that teachers can adapt the program to their own teaching styles and methodological preferences.

Features and benefits

• Flexibility

McGraw-Hill Spanish **Saludos** can be used in large or small group instruction, with slower or more-able students using a variety of teaching techniques. This flexibility is made possible through the wide range of exercises and activities provided within the Student Text, in the Cassette Program, and in the Workbook; and the multiplicity of teacher's aids available in the Teacher's Resource Kit and the range of optional materials presented in the Student Text.

• Logical organization

STRUCTURE   The material is logically sequenced and programmed to make the acquisition of the structure of the language as logical as possible. Simpler concepts are presented before more complex ones. Regular patterns are presented before irregular ones. Irregularities are grouped together to make them appear as regular and as logical as possible. In keeping with our major objective of communicative competency, more-frequently used (or needed) structures precede the introduction of less-frequently used ones. Each lesson presents from one to three structure concepts so that students will feel comfortable with the amount of grammar they must grasp in each lesson.

VOCABULARY A realistic amount of vocabulary is presented in each lesson— approximately ten to fifteen words per lesson. Words are "collocated" into logical communicative groupings. By this we mean that students are given the ten to fifteen words they would need in order to communicate effectively about a specific situation. The words presented in each lesson pertain to the particular communicative situation being developed in that lesson.

• Logical presentation

The **Vocabulario** section of each lesson presents the new words that should become an active part of the students' vocabulary. A large percentage of the words are presented in isolation accompanied by a concise drawing so that there is no confusion in meaning and so that students can easily study, learn, and review the new vocabulary on their own. These new words are immediately put into a situational context. In order to add variety, the new words are used in either sentences, short conversations, or short narratives—all of which hold to the particular situation of the lesson. The structure concepts to be taught in the lesson are also introduced in the **Vocabulario** section. The exercises in the **Vocabulario** section encourage students to use and to have fun with their new language. All new material appears in bold type so that both students and teachers will know exactly which words are new.

• Grammar presentation

The approach used in the teaching of grammar permits teachers to select the teaching technique with which they feel most comfortable. The new structures are introduced either through contextualized sentences, conversations, narratives, or activities in the **Vocabulario** section. Teachers who wish to use the discovery approach can have students explore the structure concept being introduced before they ever reach the grammatical explanation.

The grammatical explanations under **Estructura** that follow the **Vocabulario** are in English and are accompanied by many examples. Students can also come to their own conclusions if teachers wish to use a *deductive* approach. If teachers prefer to use an *inductive* approach, the grammar explanation can be given first. A variety of grammar exercises and activities follow the grammatical explanations. If teachers wish to have their students practice a grammatical point before going over the explanation, the additional supplementary oral drills provided in the Teacher's Resource Kit can be used.

This multiple approach to the presentation, learning, and teaching of grammatical concepts enables teachers to choose the method they feel best suits their needs and those of their students.

• Variety

*McGraw-Hill Spanish **Saludos*** offers a wide range of exercises and activities that lead students to communicative competency. At the same time, the wide variety of exercises and activities that are provided minimize the possibility of boredom. Some examples of the types of exercises the students will encounter are:

short conversations, short-story narratives, answering questions, answering personal questions, role playing (A new friend just arrived from Mexico; tell him/her how to get to your house to visit you.), conducting or taking part in an interview, etc. Many activities in the texts are based on authentic cultural realia. As students look at the realia in their texts, they will answer questions and talk about such real-life situations as buying a plane ticket, filling out a hotel registration form, reading a menu, following a recipe, reading an advertisement, etc. Many activities in the text are also based on illustrations that depict only the subject matter that students can truly talk about. Using these illustrations, students can answer questions, make up stories, ask questions of one another, and role play by pretending they are the people in the illustration.

To make the exercises and activities more valuable as teaching/learning tools, almost every exercise in *McGraw-Hill Spanish* **Saludos** progressively builds to tell a story. The eight or ten individual items of an exercise hold together to tell a new, complete story. Rather than present a series of isolated, nonrelated sentences, each exercise in its totality adheres to a communicative situation or context.

• Culture

McGraw-Hill Spanish **Saludos** is based on the premise that language cannot be separated from culture. Spanish is the language of culture groups consisting of millions of people living on several continents, including millions of people in our own country. In each lesson of *McGraw-Hill Spanish* **Saludos,** students will learn up-to-date, authentic information about the Spanish-speaking world. They will learn how people live, where they live, and what their customs and mores are. Most of the cultural information is found in the **Lectura cultural** section of each lesson. In addition, cultural information is given in the **Actividades** and **Revista** sections of each lesson of the Student Text and in the **Más Vocabulario y Cultura** section of the Workbook. After every four lessons there are additional *optional* cultural readings (**Lecturas culturales opcionales**) that teachers can either assign to groups, to individuals, to the entire class or that they can omit completely. All photographs in the program are authentic and contemporary and relate to the specific cultural theme of the lesson.

In order to be authentic in the presentation of culture, all areas of the Spanish-speaking world as well as all socio-economic groups are included. Stereotypes and broad generalizations have been avoided. Additional cultural information for each lesson is available in the Culture Booklet provided in the Teacher's Resource Kit. It is left to the discretion of the teacher to decide how much additional information he/she wishes to give the students.

• Natural language

One of the most difficult tasks in developing materials for beginning language learners is to keep the language simple but, at the same time, natural and realistic. *McGraw-Hill Spanish* **Saludos** has been able to bring these two worlds together through the inclusion of short sections within the text entitled **Expresiones útiles.** For example, in Lesson 1 students learn how to respond in a natural communicative or conversational sequence in Spanish when someone answers **No** to a question.

> ¿Es rubio Juan?
> No, no. Él no es rubio.
> Entonces, ¿qué es?
> Pues, es moreno.

Rather than merely explain to students that this is what Spanish speakers would say, a short exercise is included to permit students to use these useful expressions and communicate naturally.

Concerning the selection of words, we have at all times attempted to choose words that would be understood most universally throughout the vast Spanish-speaking world. Since it is often the most commonly used words that have the widest variety of usage, we have included alternates and regionalisms in the Culture Booklet provided in the Teacher's Resource Kit. Teachers are free to decide whether or not they wish to present the additional regional words and expressions to their students.

• Reinforcement and review

McGraw-Hill Spanish Saludos has a cyclical review built into the material. Each word or structural point is reintroduced and reinforced many times throughout the exercises in subsequent lessons. In addition to this type of re-entry, there is a review lesson—**Repaso**—after every four lessons. Also, at the beginning of *Saludos*—*second part,* there are three review lessons that cover all the important material presented in *Saludos*—*first part.* Because of this articulation between the two levels, second-year junior high school students who have not completed *Saludos*—*first part* or who have used other materials, can easily and smoothly begin the school year with the material in *Saludos*—*second part.*

Since every exercise of the text tells a story, the situations presented in some lessons are frequently reintroduced in a slightly different context in the exercises of subsequent lessons.

• Productive and receptive skills

The major goal of *McGraw-Hill Spanish Saludos* is to enable students to attain a measurable degree of communicative competency in the language. Accepting this as our major goal, we recognize the need to differentiate between *productive* and *receptive* skills, once referred to as active and passive skills. What students should be able to do or to produce is included in each lesson of the Student Text. However, we have presented material that will train students not to fear any new or unfamiliar vocabulary and structure they may encounter. Students can receive more information passively than they can produce actively. Nonetheless, students need assistance in acquiring the receptive skills, just as they need assistance in acquiring the productive skills. Each lesson of the Cassette Program includes two parts. The first part **(Primera parte)** of each lesson provides practice in the *productive* skills. The second part **(Segunda parte)** includes real announcements, conversations, advertisements, etc. which use words or expressions that students have *not* yet learned to produce. Nonetheless, students should, from the viewpoint of communicative competency, be able to receive and understand at least the basic message from what they have just heard. This enables students to experience the realities of using and understanding a foreign language in a natural setting, within the classroom. Although students may not have understood every single word, they got the main idea!!!

The **Más Vocabulario y Cultura** section of the Workbook that accompanies the text enables students to read material that contains some words and structures they cannot produce actively. Nonetheless, they should be able to understand or receive the essence of the selection. Word studies are also included to help students guess the meanings of words based on some previous knowledge of the language.

McGraw-Hill Spanish **Saludos** considers *receptive* skill development an important aspect of language acquisition, since communicative competency is the major goal.

• **Youth-oriented**

McGraw-Hill Spanish **Saludos** deals specifically with topics of interest relevant to teenagers today. The young people the program presents are the youth of Spain and Latin America and the Hispanics living within the continental United States. The situational topics of each lesson deal with themes and life-styles that young people can relate to. They learn about their peers in a Spanish-speaking environment. However, it must be stated that to deal solely with youth-oriented topics in a secondary school language program would, in our estimation, be ultimately detrimental to most language learners. Most students, except the fortunate few, will reap the benefits of their language learning at a later age. *McGraw-Hill Spanish* **Saludos** has addressed this problem. In one lesson students will learn to communicate about such adult topics as taking a plane trip. The vocabulary in the lesson deals with airline travel, but the situation or reason for the air travel focuses on a group of young people flying off to the slopes to ski. Thus, the interests of the young are incorporated with the needs of adults. These needs are the needs that our youngsters will experience tomorrow. Let's make their language study interesting to them today but still useful to them tomorrow. «¡**Bienvenidos a bordo!**»

SECTION TWO
Organization of *McGraw-Hill Spanish* **Saludos**

The following pages describe *McGraw-Hill Spanish* **Saludos**—*first part;* the **Saludos**—*second part* program has a similar organization with some slight modifications. Also included here is a description of the Overhead Transparencies, Cassette Program, Tape Activities, Test Package, and Teacher's Resource Kit. These components were originally designed to supplement the Student Text of *McGraw-Hill Spanish* **Saludos.** However, they can also be successfully used with **Saludos**—*first part* and **Saludos**—*second part*. Lessons 1–12 of these components correspond to the material in the *first part*. Lessons 13–24 of the components correspond to the material in the *second part*.

Teacher's Resource Kit

To assist teachers in adapting the material of *McGraw-Hill Spanish* **Saludos** to their own teaching styles and to the needs of their individual classes, the following aids are provided in the Teacher's Resource Kit:

- A Teacher's Edition of the Workbook containing all the answers to the exercises and activities in the student Workbook.
- A booklet with cultural information for each lesson of the Student Text. This booklet also contains alternate regional words and expressions.
- A booklet of optional supplementary oral drills for every structure point presented in the Student Text.
- Blackline masters, for easy duplication, containing a detailed explanation in English of any grammatical term used in the Student Text.
- The Tape Script for all the recorded material in the Cassette Program, including the answers to all the recorded activities.
- Blackline masters containing quizzes for every part of every lesson.
- A booklet with the answers to all the quizzes.
- Blackline masters containing a list of all the new words in each lesson accompanied by the English definitions.

Student Text

The Student Text of *McGraw-Hill Spanish* **Saludos**—*first part* is divided as follows:

Lección preliminar A
Lección preliminar B
Lección preliminar C
Lección preliminar D
Lección preliminar E
Lección preliminar F
Lección preliminar G
Lección 1
Lección 2
Lección 3
Lección 4
Repaso
Lecturas culturales opcionales
Lección 5
Lección 6

Lección 7
Lección 8
Repaso
Lecturas culturales opcionales
Lección 9
Lección 10
Lección 11
Lección 12
Repaso
Lecturas culturales opcionales
Appendix
Verb Charts
Spanish-English Vocabulary
English-Spanish Vocabulary
Index

McGraw-Hill Spanish **Saludos**—*second part* begins with three review lessons covering all the important material presented in **Saludos**—*first part*. Any material taught in Lessons 9 through 12 of *McGraw-Hill Spanish* **Saludos**—*first part* is retaught in the beginning lessons of **Saludos**—*second part*. It is not necessary to complete or to teach the final unit of the *first part* in order to make a smooth transition to the *second part*.

Lecciones preliminares

The seven preliminary lessons of *McGraw-Hill Spanish* **Saludos**—*first part* give students the opportunity to say those things beginners like to and want to say immediately. The topics covered are:

A greetings, salutations, and peoples' names
B farewell expressions
C numbers, counting, telephone numbers
D expressions of courtesy, ordering food
E giving dates
F telling time
G describing the weather

The preliminary lessons include many activities that permit students to use these new expressions in realistic situations. No grammar is taught in the preliminary lessons. The emphasis is on useful expressions and on the use of cognates. Structures that will serve only to confuse students prior to learning anything about the structure of the language have been purposely avoided in these lessons.

Organization of a lesson

Each lesson of *McGraw-Hill Spanish* **Saludos** is divided into the following parts:

• Vocabulario
• Estructura
• Pronunciación
• Expresiones útiles
• Conversación
• Lectura cultural
• Actividades
• Revista

VOCABULARIO The **Vocabulario** section presents all the important new words of the lesson. Almost all words are first presented in isolation accompanied by a precise illustration that depicts the meaning of the word. This permits students to learn, study, and review the new words on their own.

The new words are immediately used in context to make them more meaningful. To add variety, words may be used in sentences, definitions, short conversations, or narratives—all of which pertain to the communicative situation of the lesson. The new structure point of the lesson is introduced in these contextualized segments. The contextualized segments are also accompanied by illustrations or photographs to reinforce meaning.

All new words are highlighted in bold type so that both students and teachers will know exactly which words are new in each lesson.

The **Vocabulario** section will sometimes contain a **Nota,** explaining the formation of cognates and word derivations. The **Nota** will also deal with false cognates when necessary.

Vocabulary exercises are interspersed throughout the **Vocabulario** section. Students learn a few new words and are encouraged to put them to use immediately. Teachers do not have to wait until all the vocabulary has been presented before they assign or go over an exercise. The exercises also deal with the particular communicative situation of the lesson.

ESTRUCTURA   The **Estructura** section immediately follows the vocabulary presentation and opens with a detailed grammatical explanation in English. The explanation is accompanied by many examples and charts to facilitate the students' learning of the grammatical concept.

The grammar exercises that follow the grammatical explanation are extremely varied to prevent boredom. Almost all exercises tell a story on their own. The story of the exercises may deal with the new communicative situation of the lesson, review the information learned in a previous lesson, or present a new interesting cultural point.

The exercises in the structure section are of the following types: answering questions, talking about yourself by answering personal questions, interviews, forming questions, making up statements, short conversations, discussions concerning the conversations, and short narratives. Each exercise, of course, deals only with the new structure or grammar point being taught. Some exercises are based on a visual cue such as an illustration, photograph, or cultural realia.

PRONUNCIACIÓN   The **Pronunciación** section gives a brief explanation in English of the sound or sounds being studied. When appropriate or necessary, suggestions are given as to the correct position of the tongue or lips needed to pronounce each sound correctly.

Each sound is followed by a series of words to enable students to practice the new sound. Groups of words containing the sound or sounds are given in the **Trabalenguas y dictado** section. Dictations are also provided in the Cassette Program.

EXPRESIONES ÚTILES   The **Expresiones útiles** section presents common, everyday expressions that are frequently used in natural speech. An example is **¡Ay de mí!, ¡Qué pena!,** or **¡Qué lástima!**

The placement of the **Expresiones útiles** section varies from lesson to lesson. The expressions are introduced as needed to give a natural flavor to whatever aspect of the language is being learned. In all cases, students are given the opportunity to spice up their language by using these natural and authentic expressions.

CONVERSACIÓN   The **Conversación** section of each lesson reincorporates the vocabulary, structure, and useful expressions taught in the lesson and enables students to discuss the new situation they have learned in the particular lesson. Each conversation is followed by one or more communicative exercises that stimulate discussion.

LECTURA CULTURAL   The **Lectura cultural** section in each lesson is a short reading selection that takes the communicative situation of the lesson and puts it into a cultural setting. Most selections deal with everyday life situations in the Spanish-speaking world. Some examples are: shopping customs, school life, afterschool activities, family celebrations, **la quinceañera,** housing accommodations, leisure time activities, the **abrazo** and **besito,** Hispanic groups in the continental United States, etc. Through these reading selections, students acquaint themselves with the culture of the people who speak the language they are learning.

   The **Lectura cultural** is followed by a series of exercises that encourage students to talk or to write about what they have just read. There are many different types of exercises included, such as answering questions, correcting false statements, completing statements, matching columns, and multiple-choice exercises.

ACTIVIDADES   The **Actividades** section of each lesson of *McGraw-Hill Spanish Saludos* encourages and enables students to use on their own, but with the necessary guidance, the core of all the language and information they have acquired to date. Every effort has been made to make these activities real and authentic. Students are encouraged to use the language in natural, real-life situations. Students prepare conversations and reports. They write postcards and letters, address envelopes, prepare their autobiography. Heavy use is made of interviews (**Entrevista**) in which students can work in small groups and truly personalize the language. Much realia is included in the **Actividades** section. Students look at plane tickets, theatre tickets, advertisements, magazine or newspaper articles—all of which are accompanied by activities that permit students to use the language they have learned in real-life settings. The use of realia as an integral part of the text frees teachers from the burden of having to find their own realia to enliven the lesson. Whenever appropriate, artwork and photographs have been included to assist students in using the new language on their own.

REVISTA   Each lesson concludes with a **Revista** section. The magazine section includes photographs and realia that once again bring to life the cultural content of the lesson. They serve as the students' vicarious voyage into the real Spanish-speaking world. To increase the enjoyment that students will get from these **Revista** sections, there are no "exercises" provided. Each photograph or piece of realia is accompanied by a small amount of information in Spanish that students can easily read. The commentary purposely imbeds several questions that students can either think about or actually respond to.

REPASO   After every four lessons there is a **Repaso** unit that reviews all the material presented in the previous four lessons. There are three **Repaso** units included within the entire *first part* text.

LECTURAS CULTURALES OPCIONALES   After every **Repaso,** there are several optional reading selections that give an in-depth view of life-styles within specific areas of the Spanish-speaking world. Some optional readings also deal with literary themes. The optional reading selections contain only previously learned structures. Any new vocabulary is presented or footnoted. Vocabulary from the optional readings is never incorporated into the basic lessons without being completely retaught.

Description of the ancillary materials

Following is a description of each of the ancillary materials included in the *McGraw-Hill Spanish* **Saludos** program.

Overhead Transparencies

A set of overhead transparencies—in color—is provided to assist teachers in presenting the new vocabulary of each lesson. A transparency is available for every new vocabulary item taught in the **Vocabulario** section of each lesson. The overhead transparencies can also be used to introduce and reinforce grammatical concepts.

Cassette Program

The Cassette Program that accompanies *McGraw-Hill Spanish* **Saludos** provides students with additional activities to improve both their productive and receptive aural/oral skills. Special features of the Cassette Program are:

- the use of native speakers from several Latin American countries to acquaint students with pronunciation differences.
- the use of sound effects with many of the activities to make them more lifelike and authentic.
- the use of songs throughout to help students enjoy the language.

All material is recorded at a natural rate of speed. The Tape Script for all recorded material, along with the answers to all the activities, is provided in the Teacher's Resource Kit that accompanies the program.

TYPES OF RECORDED ACTIVITIES   The recorded activities for each lesson are divided into two parts—**Primera parte** and **Segunda parte.**

The **Primera parte** includes the following types of activities:

Repeat   All vocabulary words presented in isolation in the **Vocabulario** section are recorded and students are told to repeat each word after the model speaker. This activity assists students in developing good pronunciation habits.

Listen   Students listen to an uninterrupted, lively recording of the contextualized material in the **Vocabulario** section. In some lessons, students also listen to a lively recording of the **Conversación,** complete with realistic sound effects.

Listen and repeat   Students listen to the sounds, words, and the sentences in **Trabalenguas y dictado** from the **Pronunciación** section and repeat after the model speaker.

Listen and answer   The types of activities under the *Listen and answer* category are quite varied. Some types of activities are: 1) students listen to a question and answer it; 2) students take part in an interview; 3) a speaker on the cassette instructs students as to what type of response they are to give to the particular stimulus; 4) the speaker gives the students a personal type of question and students respond with an open-ended answer. Most of the exercises in the *Listen and answer* category are different from those in the Student Text.

Listen and choose   The speaker gives the students an oral stimulus—a word, a sentence, a question, an extremely short conversation, etc.—and students are given an activity to do in their Student Tape Manual. This may consist of writing a letter over an illustration, circling a response, checking A or B on their activity sheet. Most of the exercises in the *Listen and choose* category are also different from those that appear in the Student Text. At times, students listen to a somewhat longer passage in the form of a conversation or narrative. They are then given various types of exercises in their Tape Manual to determine if they understood the passage.

Discrimination The speaker gives the students directions as to what they are to listen for. The speaker then gives an oral stimulus and students check the correct information on their activity sheet in the Student Tape Manual. These exercises train students to listen for grammatical cues such as singular/plural; masculine/feminine; present/past, etc.

Listen and write This is a dictation. The speaker gives the students material from the **Pronunciación** section and students are to write what they hear on their activity sheet in the Tape Manual. This activity consists of three parts: 1) known words given in isolation; 2) sentences using known words; 3) new words in isolation. The new words in isolation contain the particular sound being studied. Both students and teachers can then determine whether or not the students are able to give the correct printed representation of a known sound in an unfamiliar word.

Songs Each unit contains a song that can be enjoyed and sung by the class. The words to the songs are printed in the Tape Script in the Teacher's Resource Kit.

The **Segunda Parte** of the recorded material for each lesson is optional, but it introduces an aspect of language learning that is extremely important in the development of communicative competency. In this section, students hear announcements, conferences, lectures, conversations, advertisements, broadcasts, etc. Much of what they hear contains language they already know, but unlike the recorded material in the first part, students will hear some new words and some unfamiliar structures. These passages are intended to give students training in the development of receptive skills—since listening comprehension itself is a receptive skill. Although students may not understand every word they hear, they should be able to get the basic idea or the essence of what they just heard. A series of activities such as those described above accompany each passage in the **Segunda Parte.**

The complete Tape Script of the recorded program is included in the Teacher's Resource Kit. The script also includes the answers to all tape activities.

All activities to which students must respond orally are four-phase: stimulus, pause for response, recording of the correct response, pause to make correction. The only exception to this is in the case of activities that have open-ended responses.

Workbook

The Workbook that accompanies the **Saludos**—*first part* program has been adapted from the Workbook for *McGraw-Hill Spanish Saludos.* It contains a multitude of written exercises to supplement the material presented in the Student Text.

CONTENT OF THE WORKBOOK To prevent boredom, a wide variety of exercises is provided in the Workbook. Examples are: 1) fill-in-the-blank; 2) answer a question; 3) give a synonym; 4) give an antonym; 5) match Column A with Column B; 6) multiple choice; 7) form a question; 8) complete a statement; 9) complete a narrative; 10) rewrite a paragraph changing the subject; 11) rewrite a paragraph changing the tense.

The Workbook also contains many exercises based on visual cues such as illustrations, realia, and photographs. These exercises lead students to self-expression such as 1) writing original sentences, 2) writing original questions, 3) writing original paragraphs.

In developing self-expression, students are also given postcards and letters to read. They are then told to respond to the postcard or letter.

Throughout the Workbook, the students are told to write their autobiography. After every few lessons, they are given instructions to add to their autobiography based on the content of the lessons they have just learned. Most exercises in the Workbook require students to work with the language on their own rather than to have them give fixed, mechanical responses. As in the Student Text, almost all exercises in the Workbook tell a story so that upon completion of a given exercise, students can read it in its entirety to receive a complete situational narrative or dialogue. The exercise in its totality conveys a coherent message rather than being made up of a series of isolated sentences.

Más Vocabulario y Cultura   Each lesson of the workbook contains a **Más Vocabulario y Cultura** section which gives students additional interesting cultural information based on the cultural theme of the lesson they have just learned. This section includes explanations and exercises that help students expand and enrich their vocabulary. Particular emphasis is placed on cognates and word development (making a noun from a verb). Students are also shown the similarities between the Romance languages. This will show them how learning Spanish will assist them in understanding and acquiring another language.

Another objective of the **Más Vocabulario y Cultura** section is to train students in the development of their receptive skills. Realia from newspapers and magazines are included. Although students cannnot understand every word, they are shown how they can get the main message from what they are reading. Exercises to help them do this accompany each piece of realia.

Games and puzzles   Every lesson of the Workbook contains a game or puzzle in Spanish so that students can enjoy and have fun with their new language. The inclusion of games and puzzles rids the teachers of the burden of having to make up their own. Following are additional suggestions for some games that students may enjoy:

1. Bring six people to the front of the room. Divide the six into two teams of three. Call on another person to serve as master of ceremonies. The master of ceremonies either makes up his/her own statement or reads one prepared by the teacher. The statement contains a blank to be filled in with any appropriate completion. (Example: **Los estudiantes bajaron _____.**) If two members of the same team write the same answer, that team receives a point. (Example: If two members of the same team say **del autobús,** the team receives a point. If each member of the team, however, gives a different response, the team receives no points.) Give each team six to eight items, add up the score, and decide the winning team.

2. Give students a ditto sheet containing a series of simple drawings. Let them look at the drawings for two minutes. On a separate sheet of paper have them write as many items as they recall. The person who writes the most correct items wins.

3. After several lessons of the book have been completed, students can play **¿Quién soy yo?** Call one student to the front of the room or permit him or her to speak from his or her seat. The student gives a statement and calls on an individual to guess who he or she is. If the other person cannot guess, the original student gives another statement or clue and calls on another individual.

This game can be played in the reverse. One student decides who he or she is. Another student asks questions such as **¿Eres de España?,** and so forth. The original student answers **sí** or **no** until the questioner guesses who he or she is. Set a time limit of approximately 90 seconds.

4. Have a student give a brief description of a classmate. Other members of the class guess who is being described.

5. Quiz Game: Two teams of three students each come to the front of the room. The teacher gives the master of ceremonies a series of questions based on information learned in the text. The first student from either team who rings a bell is called upon to respond. Each correct answer is worth 5 points. If the student answers incorrectly, five points are deducted. The team receiving more points in 5 minutes wins.

6. The teacher may wish to obtain a copy of *Games for Second Language Learning* by Gertrude Nye Dorry, McGraw-Hill, 1966 (Code 0-07-017653-1) for additional suggestions for games that can be used in the classroom situation.

Repaso/Self-test   For each **Repaso** unit (one after every four lessons), the Workbook provides a **Prueba** or **Self-test** for students. Answers to the Self-tests are provided at the end of the Workbook. After students correct their own tests, they are told which page or pages they should review in the Student Text if they have missed particular items on the Self-test. The purpose of this activity is to help students prepare for the Unit Test that appears in the Test Package.

A Teacher's Edition of the Workbook containing answers to all the exercises appears in the Teacher's Resource Kit. If teachers prefer that students correct their own exercises, the Workbook answers can be easily duplicated and distributed to students.

Test Package

In addition to the quizzes in the Teacher's Resource Kit, *McGraw-Hill Spanish Saludos* offers a complete Testing Program. The Test Package consists of:

- A Reading and Writing Test for each lesson of the Student Text.
- A Reading and Writing Unit Test to accompany each **Repaso** unit (after every four lessons).
- A Listening-Comprehension Unit Test for each **Repaso.**

The Reading and Writing tests and the student answer sheets for the Listening Comprehension tests are provided on blackline masters for easy duplication in the test booklet. The Listening Comprehension tests are recorded on the cassette provided within the Test Package.

The exercises on the tests contain a variety of formats to account for all teaching/learning modalities. Exercises include: fill-in-the blank, completion, answer questions, multiple choice, matching columns, visual stimuli, and recorded stimuli.

Each test includes exercises that test vocabulary, structure, reading, and culture. The answers to the tests appear in the front of the Test Booklet.

Computer Software

McGraw-Hill Spanish **Saludos** offers two computer software programs. One program provides for reinforcement of vocabulary, grammar concepts, and culture and the other program includes a presentation of a series of simulations and games.

Program One gives practice in and immediate correction on vocabulary, grammar concepts, and culture taught in the program. This computer program can act as reinforcement of previously taught concepts as well as preparation and review for a test.

Program Two allows students to "play" with the language they have learned through an interesting series of simulations, activities, and games. The rewards are built directly into the program so that students are encouraged to pursue each simulation and activity to its conclusion.

SECTION THREE
Using *McGraw-Hill Spanish Saludos*

Suggestions for teaching each lesson part

One of the major objectives of the *McGraw-Hill Spanish Saludos* program is to enable teachers to adapt the material of the program to their own methodological philosophy, teaching styles, and students' needs. As a result, we offer a variety of suggestions for the teaching of each lesson part.

Vocabulario

GENERAL TECHNIQUES The **Vocabulario** section always contains some words in isolation accompanied by an illustration or photograph that depicts the meaning of the new word. In addition, new words are used in contextualized sentences. These contextualized sentences appear in the following formats: 1) one to three sentences accompanying an illustration or photograph, 2) a short conversation, 3) a short narrative or paragraph. In addition to teaching the new vocabulary, these contextualized segments of sentences introduce, but do not teach, the new structure point of the lesson.

A series of color transparencies is available. These transparencies contain all the artwork necessary to teach the new vocabulary. They can easily be projected as large visuals in the classroom for those teachers who prefer to introduce the vocabulary orally with books closed.

All the vocabulary in each lesson is recorded on the Cassette Program. Students are instructed to repeat the isolated words after the model speaker. Students listen to a lively, uninterrupted recording of the contextualized segment but do not repeat.

A vocabulary list for each lesson appears in the Teacher's Resource Kit on blackline masters for easy duplication. These vocabulary lists are divided by parts of speech and contain the English translation of each word. There are varying opinions among foreign language teachers today concerning the use of vocabulary lists. Some teachers prefer to give them to students as soon as they present the new vocabulary. Others prefer to give them to students as they are completing the lesson for review purposes prior to a final test. Other teachers prefer not to use such a list because they prefer that students learn vocabulary without reliance on an English translation. Teachers should feel free to use these lists based on their own preferences and based on the needs of their own students.

SPECIFIC TECHNIQUES

Option 1 Option 1 for the presentation of vocabulary probably best meets the needs of those teachers who consider the development of oral skills a prime objective.

- While students have their books closed, project the transparencies. Point to the item being taught and have students repeat the word after you or the cassette several times. After you have presented several words in this manner, project the transparencies again and ask questions such as:

> ¿Es la panadería?   (Lección 7)
> ¿Qué es?
> ¿Es el panadero?
> ¿Quién es?

- To teach the contextualized segments, project the transparency in the same way. Point to the part of the illustration that depicts the meaning of any new word in the sentence, be it an isolated sentence or a sentence from a conversation or narrative. Immediately ask questions about the sentence. For example, the following sentence appears in **Lección 7.**

> **Juanito va de compras.**
> **Va de compras por la mañana.**

Questions to ask are:

> **¿Va Juanito de compras?**
> **¿Quién va de compras?**
> **¿Adónde va?**
> **¿Va de compras por la mañana?**
> **¿Cuándo va de compras?**

- Dramatizations, in addition to the illustrations, can also help convey the meaning of many words such as **canta, baila,** etc.
- After this basic presentation of the vocabulary, have students open their books and read the **Vocabulario** section for additional reinforcement.
- Go over the exercises in the **Vocabulario** section orally.
- Assign the exercises in the **Vocabulario** section for homework. Also assign the vocabulary exercises in the Workbook. If the vocabulary section should take more than one day, assign only those exercises that pertain to the material you have presented.
- The following day, go over the exercises that were assigned for homework.
- Give the vocabulary list provided in the Teacher's Resource Kit after presenting the new vocabulary or as the lesson is being completed. If you prefer that your students not have the English translations, before duplicating you can cover the right-hand column containing the English definitions.

Option 2   Option 2 will meet the needs of those teachers who wish to teach the oral skills but consider reading and writing equally important.

- Project the transparencies and have students repeat each word once or twice after you or the cassette.
- Have students repeat the contextualized sentences after you or the cassette as they look at the illustration.
- Open books and have students read the **Vocabulario** section. Correct pronunciation errors as they are made.
- Go over the exercises in the **Vocabulario** section.
- Assign the exercises of the **Vocabulario** section for homework. Also assign the vocabulary exercises in the Workbook.
- The following day, go over the exercises that were assigned for homework.
- Give the vocabulary list provided in the Teacher's Resource Kit after presenting the new vocabulary or as the lesson is being completed. If you prefer that your students not have the English translations, before duplication you can cover the right-hand columns containing the English definitions.

Option 3   Option 3 will meet the needs of those teachers who consider the reading and writing skills of utmost importance.

- Have students open their books and read the vocabulary items as they look at the illustrations.

- Give students several minutes to look at the words and vocabulary exercises. Then go over the exercises.
- Give students the vocabulary list from the Teacher's Resource Kit. Have them study the list for homework and write the vocabulary exercises from the Student Text and the Workbook.
- Go over the exercises the following day.

EXPANSION ACTIVITIES   Teachers may use any one of the following activities from time to time. These activities can be done in conjunction with any of the *Options* previously outlined.

- After the vocabulary has been presented, project the transparencies or have students open their books and make up as many original sentences as they can, using the new words. This can be done orally or in writing.
- Have students work in pairs or small groups. As they look at the illustrations in the book, have them make up as many questions as they can. They can direct their questions to their peers. It is often fun to make this a competitive activity. Let's see which person or team can make up the most questions in three minutes. This activity provides the students with an excellent opportunity to use interrogative words.
- Call on one student to read to the class one of the vocabulary exercises that tells a story. Then call on a more-able student to retell the story in his/her own words.
- With slower groups you can have one student go to the front of the room. Have him/her think of one of the new words. Let classmates give the student the new words from the lesson until they guess the word the student in the front of the room has in mind. This is a very easy way to have students recall the words they have just learned.

Estructura

GENERAL TECHNIQUES   The **Estructura** section of the lesson opens with a grammatical explanation. The grammatical explanation is always in English. Each grammatical explanation is accompanied by many examples. With verbs, complete paradigms are given. In the case of other grammar concepts such as object pronouns, many examples are given with noun vs. pronoun objects. Irregular patterns are grouped together to make them appear more regular. For example, **ir, dar,** and **estar** are taught together in Lesson 7. Since the only irregular form of these verbs is the first-person singular—**estoy, voy, doy**—these forms appear in bold type in the paradigm so that students can focus their attention on them.

Whenever the contrast between English and Spanish poses problems for students in the learning process, a contrastive analysis between the two languages is made. An example of this is the reflexive construction in *McGraw-Hill Spanish* **Saludos**— *second part.*

Certain structure points are taught more effectively in their entirety and others are more easily acquired if they are taught in segments. An example of the latter is the direct and indirect object pronouns. In one lesson we present **lo, la, los, las,** immediately followed by **me, te, nos** (as direct or indirect), immediately followed by **le, les.** After the three segments are presented, they are put together and reviewed in their entirety in the **Repaso** unit.

The structure or grammar exercises that follow the grammatical explanation are plateaued or graded to build from simple to more complex. In the case of verbs with an irregular form, for example, emphasis is placed on the irregular form, since it is the one students will most often confuse or forget. However, in all cases, students are given one or more exercises that force them to use all forms at random. The first few exercises that follow the grammatical explanation are considered learning exercises because they assist the students in grasping and internalizing the new grammar concept. These learning exercises are immediately followed by test exercises—exercises that make the students use all aspects of the grammatical point they have just learned. This format greatly assists teachers in meeting the needs of the various ability levels of students in their classes.

These days students have a rather limited grasp of grammatical terminology. We have attempted to make the grammatical explanations as succinct and as complete as possible. We have purposely avoided extremely technical grammatical or linguistic jargon that most students would not understand. Nonetheless, it is necessary to use certain basic grammatical terms. In the Teacher's Resource Kit, there are blackline masters that explain every grammatical term used in the *McGraw-Hill Spanish Saludos* program. The terms are presented in the order in which they appear in the Student Text. If teachers have students who need additional help in this area, the blackline masters can be easily duplicated and distributed to students.

Some of the grammar exercises from the Student Text are recorded on the Cassette Program. Whenever an exercise is recorded, it is noted in the blue print annotations next to the particular exercise. Many other grammar activities are included in the Cassette Program. It is annotated throughout the Teacher's Edition when a specific recorded activity can be administered.

The exercises in the Workbook also parallel the order of presentation in the Student Text. The teacher annotations indicate when certain exercises from the Workbook can be assigned.

There exists among foreign language teachers a great deal of controversy concerning the amount of drill work that should be provided, particularly in the area of structure. Some teachers feel that drill has been completely overdone and others feel that there is never enough drill and practice. In order to meet the needs of all teachers in this area, we have provided in the Teacher's Resource Kit a series of supplementary oral drills for every grammar point presented and taught in the Student Text. Teachers can use these drills at their own discretion depending upon the needs of their individual classes and their own teaching styles and preferences.

SPECIFIC TECHNIQUES FOR PRESENTING GRAMMAR RULES

Option 1   Some teachers prefer the *inductive* approach to the teaching of grammar. When this is the preferred method, teachers can begin the **Estructura** part of the lesson by presenting the grammatical rule to students or by having them read the rule in their books. After they have gone over the rule, have them read the examples in their books or write the examples on the chalkboard. Then proceed with the exercises that follow the grammatical explanation.

Option 2   Other teachers prefer the *deductive* approach to the teaching of grammar. If this is the case, begin the **Estructura** part of the lesson by writing the examples that accompany the rule on the chalkboard or by having students read them in their books. Let us take, for example, the direct object pronouns **lo, la, los, las.** The examples the students have in their books are:

Elena compra el boleto.	**Elena lo compra.**
Elena compra los boletos en la boletería.	**Ella los compra en la boletería.**
Elena pone la bota en la maleta.	**Ella la pone en la maleta.**
Elena conoce a Roberto.	**Ella lo conoce.**

Elena conoce a Roberto y a su hermano.	Ella los conoce.
Roberto conoce a Elena.	Él la conoce.
Roberto conoce a Elena y a su hermana.	Él las conoce.

In order to teach this concept *deductively*, teachers can ask students to do or answer the following:

- Have students find the object of each sentence in the first column. Say it or underline the object if it is written on the board.
- Have students notice that these words disappeared in the sentences in the second column. Have students give (or underline) the word that replaced each one.
- Ask students what word replaced **el boleto, los boletos, la bota, las botas.**
- Ask: What do we call a word that replaces a noun?
- Ask: What direct object pronoun replaces a masculine noun? A feminine noun, etc.?
- Have students look again. Ask: What word replaces **a Roberto? A Elena?**
- Ask: Can **lo** or **la** be used to replace a person or a thing?
- Ask: Where do the direct object pronouns **lo, la, los, las** go? Before or after the verb?

By answering these questions, students have deduced, on their own, the rule from the examples. To further reinforce the rule, have students read the grammatical explanation and then continue with the grammar exercises that follow. Suggestions for the deductive presentation of the grammatical points are given in the Teacher's Edition annotations.

Option 3 Some teachers prefer to have students do some oral drill work before they learn the grammatical rule. In this case, teachers can do all the drills or select some of the supplementary oral drills in the Teacher's Resource Kit before presenting the grammatical explanation. Upon completion of the drill work, teachers can present the explanation inductively or deductively as outlined in *Options 1* and *2*. Then continue with the grammar exercises in the Student Text.

SPECIFIC TECHNIQUES FOR TEACHING GRAMMAR EXERCISES In the development of the *McGraw-Hill Spanish Saludos* series, we have purposely provided a wide variety of exercises in the grammar section so that students can proceed from one exercise to another without becoming bored. The types of exercises they will encounter are: short conversations, answering questions, conducting or taking part in an interview, making up questions, describing an illustration, filling in the blanks, multiple choice, completing a conversation, completing a narrative, etc. In going over the exercises with the students, teachers may want to conduct the exercises themselves or they may want students to work in pairs. The structure exercises can be gone over in class before they are assigned for homework or they may be assigned before they are gone over. Many teachers may want to vary their approach.

All the exercises in the Student Text can be done with books open. Many of the exercises—question, interview, and ask question—can also be done with books closed.

EXPANSION EXERCISES

- *Question exercises* The answers to the question exercises that have a title, which is almost every exercise in the program, build to tell a complete story. Once you have gone over the exercises by calling on several students (Student 1, numbers 1,2,3; Student 2, numbers 4,5,6 etc.), you can call on one student to give the answers to the entire exercise. Now the entire class has heard an uninterrupted story. Students can ask one another questions about the story, give an oral synopsis of the story in their own words, or write a short paragraph about the story.

• *Personal questions or interview exercises* Students can easily work in pairs or teachers can call a moderator to the front of the room to ask questions of various class members. Two students can come to the front of the room and the exercise can be performed—one student takes the role of the interviewer and the other takes the role of the interviewee.

• *Completion of a conversation* See Exercise 7, page 85 as an example. After students complete the exercise, they can be given time either in class or as an outside assignment to prepare a skit for the class based on the conversation.

Pronunciación

SPECIFIC TECHNIQUES Have the students read on their own or go over with them the short explanation in the book concerning the particular sound that is being studied. For the more difficult sounds such as the **d, t, r, rr, b, v, g, j,** etc. teachers may wish to demonstrate the tongue and lip positions. Have students repeat the words after you or the model speaker on the cassette. Then let the students have some fun with the **Trabalenguas.** Inform students that they will be responsible for spelling each word correctly for a dictation.

Conversación

SPECIFIC TECHNIQUES Teachers may wish to vary the presentation of the **Conversación** from one lesson to another. In some lessons, the **Conversación** can be presented thoroughly and in other lessons it may be presented quickly as a reading exercise. Some possible options are:

• Have the class repeat the conversation after you twice. Then have students work in pairs and present the conversation to the class. The conversation does not have to be memorized. If students change it a bit, all the better.
• Have students read the conversation several times on their own. Then have them work in pairs and read the conversation as a skit. Try to encourage them to be animated and to use proper intonation. This is a very important aspect of the **Conversación** part of the lesson.
• Rather than read the conversations, students can work in pairs, having one make up as many questions as possible related to the topic of the **Conversación.** The other students can answer his/her questions.
• Once students can complete the exercise(s) that accompany the **Conversación** with relative ease, they know the **Conversación** sufficiently well without having to memorize it.
• Students can tell or write a synopsis of the **Conversación.**

Lectura cultural

SPECIFIC TECHNIQUES
Option 1 Just as the presentation of the **Conversación** can vary from lesson to lesson, the same is true of the **Lecturas culturales.** In some lessons the teachers

may want the students to go over the reading selection very thoroughly. In this case all or any combination of the following techniques can be used.

- Give students a brief synopsis of the story in Spanish.
- Ask questions about the brief synopsis.
- Have students open books. Have students repeat several sentences after you or call on individuals to read.
- Ask questions about what was just read.
- Have students read the story at home and write the answers to the exercises that accompany the **Lectura cultural.**
- Go over the exercises in class the next day.
- Call on a student to give a review of the story in his/her own words. If necessary, guide students to make up an oral review. Ask five or six questions, the answers to which review the salient points of the reading selection.
- After the oral review, the more-able students can write a synopsis of the **Lectura cultural** in their own words.

It should not take more than one class period to present the **Lectura** in the early lessons. In later lessons, teachers may wish to spend two or three days on those reading selections they want students to know thoroughly.

Option 2   With those **Lecturas culturales** that teachers wish to present less thoroughly, the following techniques may be used:

- Call on an individual to read a paragraph.
- Ask questions about the paragraph read.
- Assign the **Lectura cultural** to be read at home. Have students write the exercises that accompany the **Lectura.**
- Go over the exercises the following day.

Option 3   With some reading selections, teachers may wish to merely assign them to be read at home and then go over the exercises the following day. This is possible since the only new material in the **Lecturas culturales** consist of a few new vocabulary items that are always footnoted.

Actividades

SPECIFIC TECHNIQUES   The **Actividades** section presents activities that assist students in working with the language on their own. All the activities are optional. In some cases, teachers may want the whole class to do all the activities. In other cases, teachers can decide which activities the whole class will do. Another possibility is to break the class into groups and have each group work on a different activity.

Revista

SPECIFIC TECHNIQUES   The purpose of the **Revista** section is to permit students to look at the authentic photographs and realia from the Spanish-speaking world and acquaint them with the many areas that speak the language they are learning. As already stated, the **Revista** section contains no exercises. The purpose of this section is for students to enjoy the material as if they were browsing through pages of a real magazine. Items the students can think about are imbedded in the commentary that accompanies the photographs or realia. Teachers can either have students read the material in class or students can go over the material on their own.

Lecturas culturales opcionales

The optional cultural reading selections give students an in-depth knowledge of many areas of the Spanish-speaking world and an introduction to some of the great works of Peninsular and Latin American literature. Teachers can omit any or all these selections or they may choose certain selections that they would like the whole class to read. The same suggestions given for the **Lectura cultural** of each lesson can be followed. Teachers may also assign the reading selections to different groups. Students can read the selection outside of class and prepare a report for those students who did not read that particular selection. This activity is very beneficial for slower students. Although they may not read the selection, they learn the material by listening to what their peers say about it.

The **Lecturas culturales opcionales** and the exercises that accompany them can also be done by students on a voluntary basis for extra credit.

Teaching the preliminary lessons

The first day of class, teachers may wish to give students a pep-talk concerning the importance of the language they have chosen to study. Some suggested activities are:

- Show students a map (the maps on pages xiii, xiv, xv of the Student Text can be used) to give them an idea of the magnitude of the Spanish-speaking world.
- Have students discuss the areas within the United States in which there is a high percentage of Spanish speakers.
- Go over place names such as Los Ángeles, San Antonio, Arizona, Colorado that are of Spanish origin.
- Explain to students the possibility of using Spanish in numerous careers such as: health services, social work, teaching, economics, law, sales, merchandising, engineering, social services.
- The first day teachers will also want to give each student a Spanish name. In the cases of students with names such as Kevin and Erica, teachers may want to give them a Spanish nickname.

The preliminary lessons are designed to give students useful, everyday expressions that they can use immediately. Each lesson is designed to take one or two days. With the lesson on numbers (**Lección preliminar C**), teachers may wish to concentrate on the numbers 1 through 50 first and continue to reinforce the remainder of the numbers throughout the first two months of instruction.

The **Lecciones preliminares** present students with easily learned expressions such as **¿Qué tal?, ¡Hola!, ¡Hasta luego!, ¡Adiós!, Por favor, Gracias, ¿Cuánto es?,** etc. but do not confuse the students by expecting them to make structural changes such as the manipulation of verb endings. Formal grammar begins with **Lección 1.** No grammar is taught in the **Lecciones preliminares.**

Using the ancillary materials

The ancillary materials are described in Section Two of this Teacher's commentary. All ancillaries are supplementary to the Student Text. Any or all parts of the ancillaries can be used at the discretion of the teacher.

Overhead Transparencies

Purpose   To present new vocabulary

The overhead transparencies can be used for the initial presentation of new vocabulary in each lesson. The overhead transparencies can also be reprojected to review vocabulary from previous lessons.

With more-able groups, teachers can show the transparencies from previous lessons and have students make up original sentences using a particular word. These sentences can be given orally or they can be written.

Cassette Program

Purpose   To reinforce productive and receptive oral skills

The Cassette Program contains activities for each lesson part. It is indicated in the annotations of this Teacher's Edition when to use each cassette or recorded activity. The Student Tape Manual accompanies the Cassette Program.

Workbook

Purpose   To reinforce productive and receptive reading and writing skills

The exercises in the Workbook are presented in the same order as the presentation of the material in the Student Text. It is indicated in the annotations when each exercise of the Workbook can be assigned. The Workbook contains exercises for the **Vocabulario, Estructura** and **Lectura cultural** section of each lesson in addition to the **Más Vocabulario y Cultura** section. The Workbook also contains Self-tests for the students. The Self-tests appear after every **Repaso** (after every four lessons).

Tests

Purpose   To test the acquisition of concepts and content in each of the four languages skills

The Lesson Tests can be administered upon the completion of each lesson. The Reading-Writing and Listening Comprehension Unit Tests can be administered upon the completion of each **Repaso** unit (after every four lessons).

In addition to the testing program, there are quizzes for each lesson provided in the Teacher's Resource Kit.

Sample lesson plans

McGraw-Hill Spanish **Saludos**—*first part* has been developed so that it may be completed in one school year. However, it is up to the individual teacher to decide how many lessons will be covered. Although completion of the book by the end of the year is recommended, it is not necessary. Most of the important structures of *McGraw-Hill Spanish* **Saludos**—*first part* are reviewed in a different context in the first three lessons of **Saludos**—*second part*. Also, it is not necessary to complete the last unit (the last four lessons) of the *first part* in order to make a smooth transition to the *second part* since many of the important structures in the *first part* are retaught once again as new concepts in *McGraw-Hill Spanish* **Saludos**—*second part*.

Lesson plans help the teacher visualize how a lesson can be presented. However, by emphasizing certain aspects of the program and deemphasizing others, the teacher can change the focus and the approach of a lesson to meet students' needs and to suit his/her own teaching styles and techniques. Sample lesson plans for Lessons 7 and 11 are provided below. They include some of the suggestions and techniques that were described on pages 19 through 26 of this teacher's insert.

Lección 7	
Day 1	Present **Vocabulario,** page 80 Go over vocabulary exercises 1–2, page 80
Day 2	Present **Vocabulario,** page 81 Go over exercises 3–5, page 82
Day 3	Review **Vocabulario,** pages 80–82 Do Workbook exercises A–D, pages 35–36
Day 4	Present the verbs **ir, dar, estar,** page 83 Go over structure exercises 1–7, pages 83–85
Day 5	Review verbs **ir, dar, estar,** pages 83–85 Present **al,** page 85 Go over structure exercises 8–9, page 86
Day 6	Present **del,** page 86 Go over structure exercise 10, page 86 Present **hay,** page 87 Go over structure exercise 11, page 87
Day 7	Review **ir, dar, estar** Review **al, del, hay,** pages 85–86 Do Workbook exercises E–M, pages 37–40
Day 8	Go over **Pronunciación,** page 87 Present **Expresiones útiles** and **Conversación,** pages 88–89
Day 9	Review **Pronunciación** and **Conversación,** pages 87–89 Go over exercise, page 89

Lección 7—*continued*
Day 10   Present **Lectura cultural** Go over questions concerning **Lectura** Review lesson in general
Day 11   (optional) Review lesson in general Do as much of the **Actividades** and **Revista** sections as you wish.

Lección 11
Day 1   Present **Vocabulario,** page 146 Go over vocabulary exercise 1, page 146
Day 2   Present **Vocabulario,** page 147 Go over exercises 2–3, pages 147–148
Day 3   Present **Vocabulario,** pages 148–149 Go over exercises 4–5, pages 148–149
Day 4   Review **Vocabulario,** pages 146–149 Do Workbook exercises A–C, page 61–63
Day 5   Present **ir a** + infinitive, page 150 Go over structure exercises 1–2, page 150
Day 6   Present the **a personal,** page 150 Go over structure exercises 3–4, page 151
Day 7   Review **ir a** + infinitive, page 150 Review **a personal,** page 150 Do Workbook exercises D–I, pages 63–67
Day 8   Go over **Pronunciación,** page 151 Present **Expresiones útiles** and **Conversación,** page 152
Day 9   Review **Pronunciación** and **Conversación,** pages 151–152 Go over exercise, page 153
Day 10   Present **Lectura cultural,** page 155 Go over questions concerning **Lectura** Review lesson in general
Day 11   (optional) Review lesson in general Do as much of the **Actividades** and **Revista** sections as you wish.

Detailed listing of contents

The following detailed table of contents for each lesson is included to enable teachers to determine at a glance the exact material they will be covering in each lesson of *McGraw-Hill Spanish* **Saludos**—*first part.*

The following abbreviations are used in this listing: **V = Vocabulario, E = Estructura, C = Conversación, LC = Lectura cultural.**

Correlation: Student Text with ancillary materials

This section contains a listing of the activities in the Cassette Program, the exercises in the Workbook, and the quizzes in the Teacher's Resource Kit that can be used with each lesson part of *McGraw-Hill Spanish Saludos—first part.* You will find these charts useful in preparing lesson plans or additional tests and study guides for your students. However, note that all this information is also provided in the blue overprint throughout each lesson of this Teacher's Edition. Below we have listed the lesson part of the Student Text and cross referenced each part to the related exercises in the Tapescript, Workbook, and Quizzes. For those teachers who wish to do all the activities and exercises by lesson section, these charts provide a quick and easy reference check.

The following abbreviations are used throughout this list: **Segunda = Segunda parte** (Tapescript Activities) and **Más = Más Vocabulario y Cultura** (Workbook Exercises).

	Tapescript Activities	Workbook Exercises	Quizzes
Lección 1			
• Vocabulary	1–9	A–G	1
• Structure	10–11	H–L	2–4
• Pronunciation	12		
• Expansion	**Segunda**		
Lección 2			
• Vocabulary	1–5	A–C	1
• Structure	6–8	D–H	2–3
• Pronunciation	9–10		
• Conversation	11–12		
• Expansion	**Segunda**	**Más**	
Lección 3			
• Vocabulary	1–6	A–D	1
• Structure	7–11	E–I	2–4
• Pronunciation	12–13		
• Expansion	**Segunda**	**Más**	
Lección 4			
• Vocabulary	1–2		1
• Structure	3–8	A–E	2
• Pronunciation	9–10		
• Reading	11		
• Expansion	**Segunda**	**Más**	
Repaso		Self-test	
Lección 5			
• Vocabulary	1–4	A–D	1
• Structure	5–11	E–G	2–3
• Pronunciation	12–13		
• Conversation	14–15		
• Reading		H–K	
• Expansion	**Segunda**	**Más**	

	Tapescript Activities	*Workbook Exercises*	*Quizzes*
Lección 6			
• Vocabulary	1–4	A–C	1
• Structure	5–9	D–F	2
• Pronunciation	10–11		
• Reading	12–14	G	
• Expansion	**Segunda**		
Lección 7			
• Vocabulary	1–5	A–D	1
• Structure	6–9	E–J	2–3
• Pronunciation	10–11		
• Conversation	12–13	K	
• Reading		L–M	
• Expansion	**Segunda**		
Lección 8			
• Vocabulary	1–7	A–C	1
• Structure	8–11	D–G	2–3
• Pronunciation	12–13		
• Conversation	14–15		
• Reading		H–I	
• Expansion	**Segunda**	**Más**	
Repaso		Self-test	
Lección 9			
• Vocabulary	1–4	A	1
• Structure	5–15	B–I	2–4
• Pronunciation	16–17		
• Conversation	18–19		
• Reading		J	
• Expansion	**Segunda**		
Lección 10			
• Vocabulary	1–4	A–C	1
• Structure	5–12	D–J	2–3
• Pronunciation	13–14		
• Conversation	15–16		
• Expansion	**Segunda**	**Más**	
Lección 11			
• Vocabulary	1–7	A–C	1
• Structure	8–12	D–E	2–3
• Pronunciation	13–14		
• Conversation	15–16	F	
• Reading		G	
• Expansion	**Segunda**	**Más**	
Lección 12			
• Vocabulary	1–4	A–B	1
• Structure	5–9	C–J	2
• Pronunciation	10–11		
• Conversation	13–14		
• Reading	15–16	K–O	
• Expansion	**Segunda**	**Más**	
Repaso		Self-test	

SECTION FOUR
Reference Lists for
*McGraw-Hill Spanish **Saludos**—first part*

The following reference lists are included to give teachers a general idea or overview of the vocabulary topics, structure items, pronunciation areas, and cultural content that are presented in the Student Text.

Vocabulary topics

Preliminar A	Greetings, salutations, and people's names
Preliminar B	Farewell expressions
Preliminar C	Numbers, counting
Preliminar D	Polite expressions
Preliminar E	Dates
Preliminar F	Telling time
Preliminar G	Weather expressions
Lección 1	Describing physical attributes
Lección 2	More physical attributes and telling where you are from
Lección 3	Describing yourself
Lección 4	Talking about your Spanish class
Lección 5	Classroom activities
Lección 6	After-school activities
Lección 7	Shopping for food
Lección 8	Family-oriented daily activities
Lección 9	Family members and family celebrations
Lección 10	Talking about your health
Lección 11	Shopping for clothing; colors
Lección 12	Sports

Structure items

Lección 1	Definite articles—singular
	Indefinite articles
	Agreement of nouns and adjectives—singular
Lección 2	Present tense of the verb **ser**—singular
	Agreement of nouns and adjectives (Consonant and **-e**)
Lección 3	Nouns and articles—plural
	Subject pronouns
	Agreement of nouns and adjectives—plural
Lección 4	Present tense of the verb **ser**—all forms
Lección 5	Present tense of regular **-ar** verbs—singular forms
	Tú vs. **Ud.**
Lección 6	Present tense of regular **-ar** verbs—plural forms
	Present tense of regular **-ar** verbs—review of all forms

Structure items

Pronunciation areas

Cultural themes

Lección 1	colegio vs. high school
Lección 2	colegio vs. high school
Lección 3	students at a colegio in Bogotá, Colombia
Lección 4	a postcard from a student in Guadalajara, México
Lección 5	school schedules in the United States and in most Spanish-speaking countries
Lección 6	after-school jobs in U.S. and in Spanish-speaking countries
Lección 7	shopping for food; individual stores such as **carnicería, panadería,** etc. in comparison to **el mercado** or **el supermercado**
Lección 8	some differences between the cities and suburbs of Spain and Latin America and the United States
Lectura opcional	where and under what conditions bargaining is possible and permissible in Spanish-speaking areas
Lectura opcional	the popularity of and the activities in the beautiful parks of Spain and Latin America
Lectura opcional	the life of a teenage Indian girl in a small village of Guatemala
Lección 9	family relationships and family celebrations in Hispanic societies
Lección 10	history and contributions of the Hispanic population within the continental United States
Lección 11	the celebration for a girl's fifteenth birthday in Spanish-speaking countries
Lección 12	differences between the football played in the United States and in Spanish-speaking countries
Lectura opcional	serenades in Spanish-speaking countries
Lectura opcional	the touching life story of **El Cordobés**

Common Spanish names

For your reference, below is a list of the most frequently used names in Spanish. You may wish to use these lists as a quick and easy reference on the first day of class when you assign each student in class a Spanish name.

Boys' names

Alberto	Eduardo	Ignacio	Miguel
Alejandro	Emilio	Jaime	Pablo
Alfonso	Enrique	Jesús	Patricio
Alfredo	Ernesto	Jorge	Pedro
Andrés	Esteban	Juan	Rafael
Antonio	Federico	Julio	Ramón
Armando	Felipe	Leonardo	Raúl
Arturo	Fernando	Luis	Ricardo
Carlos	Francisco	Manuel	Roberto
Daniel	Gregorio	Marcos	Salvador
David	Guillermo	Mario	Tomás
Diego	Héctor	Mateo	Víctor

Girls' names

Adela	Cristina	Julia	Paula
Alicia	Clara	Linda	Pilar
Ana	Diana	Laura	Rita
Ángela	Dolores	Leonor	Rosa
Amelia	Elena	Lucía	Rosario
Anita	Emilia	Luisa	Sara
Antonia	Éster	Lupe (Lupita)	Soledad
Bárbara	Eva	Margarita	Sonia
Beatriz	Francisca	María	Susana
Carmen	Guadalupe	Marta	Teresa
Carolina	Inés	Mercedes	Verónica
Catalina	Irene	Mariana	Victoria
Cecilia	Isabel	Nora	Virginia
Concepción	Josefina	Norma	Yolanda
Consuelo	Juana	Patricia	

Useful classroom words and expressions

Below is a list of the most frequently used words and expressions needed in conducting a Spanish class.

Words

el papel	paper	la cesta	waste basket
la hoja de papel	sheet of paper	el pupitre	student desk
el cuaderno, el bloc	notebook	la fila	row
el cuaderno	workbook	la silla	chair
la pluma	pen	la pantalla	screen
el bolígrafo	ballpoint pen	el proyector	projector
el lápiz	pencil	el cartucho	cassette
la tiza	chalk	el libro	book
la pizarra	blackboard	la regla	ruler
el borrador	eraser		

Expressions (commands)

Both the singular and the plural command forms are provided.

Ven.	Vengan Uds.	*Come.*
Ve.	Vayan Uds.	*Go.*
Pasa.	Pasen Uds.	*Enter.*
Sal.	Salgan Uds.	*Leave.*
Espera.	Esperen Uds.	*Wait.*
Pon.	Pongan Uds.	*Put.*
Dame.	Denme Uds.	*Give me.*
Dime.	Díganme Uds.	*Tell me.*
Tráeme.	Tráiganme Uds.	*Bring me.*
Repite.	Repitan Uds.	*Repeat.*
Practica.	Practiquen Uds.	*Practice.*
Estudia.	Estudien Uds.	*Study.*
Contesta.	Contesten Uds.	*Answer.*
Aprende.	Aprendan Uds.	*Learn.*
Escoge.	Escojan Uds.	*Choose.*
Prepara.	Preparen Uds.	*Prepare.*
Mira.	Miren Uds.	*Look at.*
Describe.	Describan Uds.	*Describe.*
Empieza.	Empiecen Uds.	*Begin.*
Pronuncia.	Pronuncien Uds.	*Pronounce.*
Escucha.	Escuchen Uds.	*Listen.*
Habla.	Hablen Uds.	*Speak.*
Lee.	Lean Uds.	*Read.*
Escribe.	Escriban Uds.	*Write.*
Pregunta.	Pregunten Uds.	*Ask.*
Sigue el modelo.	Sigan Uds. el modelo.	*Follow the model.*
Haz el papel de ...	Hagan Uds. el papel de ...	*Take the part of ...*
Saca.	Saquen Uds.	*Take out.*
Abre.	Abran Uds.	*Open.*
Cierra.	Cierren Uds.	*Close.*
Dobla la página.	Doblen Uds. la página.	*Turn the page.*
Borra.	Borren Uds.	*Erase.*
Continúa (Sigue).	Continúen Uds. (Sigan Uds.)	*Continue.*
Siéntate.	Siéntense Uds.	*Sit down.*
Levántate.	Levántense Uds.	*Get up.*
Levanta la mano.	Levanten Uds. la mano.	*Raise your hand.*
Cállate.	Cállense Uds.	*Be quiet.*
Presta (Pon) atención.	Presten (Pongan) Uds. atención.	*Pay attention.*

Atención.		*Attention.*
Su atención, por favor.		*Your attention, please.*
Silencio.		*Quiet.*
Cuidado.		*Careful.*
Otra vez.		*Again.*
Una vez más.		*Once again.*
Uno(a) a la vez.		*One at a time.*
Todos juntos.		*All together.*
En voz alta.		*Out loud.*
En español.		*In Spanish.*
En inglés.		*In English.*
Para mañana.		*For tomorrow.*
¿Comprendes?	¿Comprenden Uds.?	*Do you understand?*
¿Me oyes?	¿Me oyen Uds?	*Can you hear me?*
¿Hay preguntas?		*Are there any questions?*

Answer Key for *McGraw-Hill Spanish* **Saludos**

For your convenience, answer keys are provided on the following pages for all the exercises that appear in the Student Text. Ambiguity of response has, as much as possible, been avoided in the exercises but individual classroom procedures do give rise to the possibility of acceptable alternate answers. In these cases, we have provided one response but have also indicated that "answers will vary" in some exercises. The teacher is free, of course, to decide if an alternate response is or is not acceptable.

Ejercicio 1 *(page 16)*
1. Sí, Lupita es mexicana.
2. Sí, ella es alumna.
3. Sí, ella es alumna en un colegio mexicano.
4. Es alta.
5. Es rubia.
6. Ella es una muchacha lista.

Ejercicio 2 *(page 16)*
1. Lupita es mexicana.
2. Lupita es alumna en un colegio mexicano.
3. Lupita es alta.
4. Lupita es rubia.
5. Lupita es lista.

Ejercicio 3 *(page 17)*
1. Sí, Roberto es un muchacho americano.
2. Sí, él es alumno.
3. Sí, es alumno en una escuela secundaria.
4. Roberto es alto.
5. Es moreno.
6. Él es listo.

Ejercicio 4 *(page 17)*
1. Es alto.
2. Es moreno.
3. Es listo.

Ejercicio 1 *(page 18)*
1. El	6. El, la
2. El	7. La, el
3. El	8. El
4. La	9. La
5. El, la	

Ejercicio 2 *(page 18)*
1. un	5. una
2. una	6. una
3. un, una	7. un
4. un	

Ejercicio 3 *(page 19)*
1. Lupita es mexicana.
2. Él es americano.
3. Lupita es alta.
4. Es alto.
5. Lupita es rubia.
6. Roberto es moreno.
7. Lupita es alumna en un colegio mexicano.
8. Roberto es alumno en una escuela secundaria americana.

Ejercicio 4 *(page 19)*
1. mexicana	5. listo
2. americano	6. rubio, moreno
3. lista	7. alta, alto
4. rubia	

Ejercicio *(page 22)*
1. a	4. c
2. a	5. b
3. b	6. b

Actividad 3 *(page 23)*
Es Gloria.
No, no. Es mexicana.
Ella es una muchacha muy lista. Ella es rubia y alta.
Sí, ella es alumna en un colegio mexicano.

Ejercicio 1 *(page 27)*
1. Sí, Marisa Jiménez es colombiana.
2. Sí, ella es de Bogotá.
3. Sí, ella es una amiga de Elena Ochoa.
4. Elena es guapa y divertida. (*Any descriptive adjectives from the vocabulary section are acceptable.*)
5. Sí, es guapa también.
6. Sí, ella es una persona divertida.

Ejercicio 2 *(page 27)*
1.–3. (*Answers will vary.*)
4. alumno(a)

Ejercicio 3 *(page 27)*
1. Marisa es de Bogotá.
2. Roberto es de Miami.
3. Lupita es de México.
4. Carlos es de San Juan de Puerto Rico.

Ejercicio 2 *(page 28)*
1.–4. Soy . . . . (*Answers will vary.*)
5. Soy alumno(a) en una escuela americana.

Ejercicio 3 *(page 29)*
1. No, no soy colombiano(a).
2. No, no soy de Bogotá.
3. No, no soy alumno(a) en un colegio colombiano.
4. No, no soy amigo(a) de Cervantes.

Ejercicio 4 *(page 29)*
2. Enrique, ¿eres rubio?
3. Enrique, ¿eres alumno?
4. Enrique, ¿eres de Cali?
5. Enrique, ¿eres listo?

Ejercicio 5 *(page 29)*
1. Isabel, ¿eres de Puerto Rico?
2. Isabel, ¿eres alumna?
3. Isabel, ¿eres lista?
4. Isabel, ¿eres amiga de Enrique Figueroa?

Ejercicio 6 *(page 29)*
1. soy	3. Eres
2. soy	4. eres

5. soy   8. eres
6. es   9. es
7. es

Ejercicio 7 *(page 30)*
1. mexicana   5. colombiano
2. inteligente   6. inteligente
3. popular   7. divertido
4. mexicano   8. popular

Ejercicio 8 *(page 30)*
1. El, de   3. La, de
2. La, de   4. El, de

Ejercicio 1 *(page 31)*
1. Falso   4. Verdadero
2. Falso   5. Verdadero
3. Falso

Actividad 3 *(page 33)*
—Hola, (Pedro).
—Hola, (Juan).
—¡Oye! ¿Quién es la muchacha?
—¿Quién? ¿La muchacha alta?
—Sí, ella.
—Es (Teresa).
—¿Es americana ella?
—No, no es americana. Es cubana.
—Es guapa, ¿no?
—Es verdad. Es muy guapa. Y es también muy
  simpática y muy inteligente.

Ejercicio 1 *(page 36)*
1. Sí, Tadeo y Alfonso son amigos.
2. No, no son hermanos.
3. Sí, ellos son muy aficionados a los deportes.
4. Ellos son grandes.
5. Ellos son fuertes.

Ejercicio 2 *(page 37)*
1. Tadeo y Alfonso son amigos.
2. Tadeo y Alfonso son muy aficionados a los
   deportes.
3. Tadeo y Alfonso son muy atléticos.
4. Tadeo y Alfonso son fuertes.

Ejercicio 3 *(page 37)*
1. No.   3. No.
   ¿Entonces?   ¿Entonces?
   Pues, son altos.   Pues, son aburridos.
2. No.   4. No.
   ¿Entonces?   ¿Entonces?
   Pues, son fuertes.   Pues, son rubios.

Ejercicio 4 *(page 37)*
1. Las dos muchachas son amigas.
2. Sí, ellas son aficionadas a los deportes.
3. Ellas son altas.

4. Ellas son fuertes.
5. Sí, son atléticas.

Ejercicio 1 *(page 38)*
1. Los   4. Los, los
2. Las   5. Los
3. Las

Ejercicio 2 *(page 39)*
Las, Ellas, son, los, Ellas
ellos, son, Los, Ellos, los, Los, son

Ejercicio 3 *(page 40)*
1. No, los dos muchachos son morenos.
2. Sí, ellos son americanos. (No, ellos no son
   americanos.)
3. Sí, los dos amigos son atléticos.
4. Son fuertes.
5. Sí, los dos muchachos son populares.

Ejercicio 4 *(page 40)*
1. Sí, las dos muchachas son morenas.
2. Sí, ellas son americanas. (No, ellas no son
   americanas.)
3. Sí, las dos amigas son atléticas.
4. Son fuertes.
5. Sí, las dos muchachas son populares.

Ejercicio 5 *(page 40)*
 1. mexicanas
 2. aficionadas
 3. inteligentes, simpáticas
 4. atléticas
 5. débiles, fuertes
 6. mexicanos
 7. colombianos
 8. aficionados
 9. fuertes, débiles
10. inteligentes, divertidos, atléticos
11. fantásticos
12. populares

Ejercicio 6 *(page 41)*
1. Sí, son atléticos.
2. Son fuertes.
3. Sí, son aficionados a los deportes.
4. Sí, son simpáticos.
5. Son altos.
6. Son (inteligentes, divertidos, fantásticos,
   populares).

Ejercicio 7 *(page 41)*
1. Sí, son atléticas.
2. Son fuertes.
3. Sí, son aficionadas a los deportes.
4. Sí, son simpáticas.
5. Son altas.
6. Son (inteligentes, divertidas, fantásticas,
   populares).

Ejercicio *(page 42)*
1. Marisa y Elena son colombianas.
2. Ellas son de Bogotá, la capital de Colombia.
3. Las dos muchachas son alumnas en un colegio en Bogotá.
4. Ellas son altas.
5. Ellas son muy aficionadas a los deportes.

Actividad 1 *(page 43)*
Diego y Federico
Diego y Federico son dos muchachos colombianos. Ellos son de Bogotá, la capital de Colombia. Ellos son alumnos en un colegio en Bogotá. Los dos amigos son muy inteligentes. ¿Son ellos pequeños? No, ellos no son pequeños. Entonces, ¿cómo son? Ellos son altos. Ellos son muy atléticos. Los dos muchachos son muy aficionados a los deportes. Y además, son muchachos sinceros y simpáticos. Ellos son muy populares.

Ejercicio 1 *(page 46)*
1. Sí, los alumnos son americanos.
2. Sí, ellos son alumnos de español.
3. El español es bastante fácil. (No es difícil.)

Ejercicio 2 *(page 46)*
1.–3. *Answers will vary.*
4. español
5. bastante fácil
6. bastante listos

Ejercicio 2 *(page 48)*
1. Sí, somos alumnos.
2. Sí, somos americanos.
3. Sí, somos alumnos de español.
4. Sí, somos muy listos.
5. Sí, somos muy aficionados a los deportes.

Ejercicio 3 *(page 48)*
1. Pablo y Sandra, ¿son Uds. americanos?
2. Pablo y Sandra, ¿son Uds. alumnos?
3. Pablo y Sandra, ¿son Uds. alumnos de español?
4. Pablo y Sandra, ¿son Uds. amigos de José?
5. Pablo Y Sandra, ¿son Uds. aficionados a los deportes?

Ejercicio 4 *(page 48)*
1. (María y José), ¿son Uds. americanos o cubanos? Somos americanos.
2. (María y José), ¿son Uds. bajos o altos? Somos (altos/bajos).
3. (María y José), ¿son Uds. hermanos o amigos? Somos amigos.
4. (María y José), ¿son Uds. morenos o rubios? Somos (morenos/rubios).
5. (María y José), ¿son Uds. listos o tontos? Somos listos.

6. (María y José), ¿son Uds. guapos o feos? Somos guapos.
7. (María y José), ¿son Uds. divertidos o aburridos? Somos divertidos.
8. (María y José), ¿son Uds. fuertes o débiles? Somos (fuertes/débiles).

Ejercicio 5 *(page 48)*

1. soy	7. somos
2. es	8. son
3. eres	9. Son
4. somos	10. es, Es
5. somos	11. son
6. Son	

Ejercicio *(page 50)*
1. La tarjeta postal es de Marta Aguilar.
2. Marta es mexicana.
3. Ella es de Guadalajara.
4. Ella es alumna en un colegio privado en Guadalajara.
5. Carmen Salinas es la amiga de Marta.
6. Carmen es simpática, generosa y muy inteligente.
7. Sí, ellas son muy aficionadas a los deportes.
8. Las dos muchachas son bastante atléticas.

Ejercicio 1 *(page 54)*
1. Marisa Jiménez es de Bogotá.
2. Carlos Gutiérrez es un amigo de Marisa.
3. Él es de Cali.
4. Carlos es muy simpático y es un amigo muy sincero.
5. Sí, son atléticos Carlos y Marisa.
6. Carlos y Marisa son muy aficionados a los deportes.
7. Carlos es alumno en un colegio en Cali.
8. Ella es alumna en un colegio en Bogotá.

Ejercicio 2 *(page 54)*

1. es	8. soy, (Carlos)
2. es, es, es	9. somos
3. Eres	10. somos
4. eres	11. Son
5. eres	12. Son
6. soy	13. somos, (John F. Kennedy)
7. soy, (Chicago)	14. son, son

Ejercicio 3 *(page 55)*
el, El
la, La
la, la, el, Los, las, el

Ejercicio 1 *(page 57)*
1. Sí, la señora Mariscal enseña español.
2. Sí, ella habla con los alumnos.
3. Sí, habla español en la clase de español.
4. Sí, Carlos estudia mucho.

5. Sí, Rosita toma apuntes.
6. Sí, la profesora canta.
7. Sí, un alumno toca la guitarra.
8. Carlos saca buenas notas.

Ejercicio 2 *(page 57)*
1. La señora Mariscal enseña español.
   La señora Mariscal enseña español.
   Ella enseña español en la Escuela Thomas Jefferson.
2. Rosita toma apuntes.
   Rosita toma apuntes.
   Ella toma apuntes en la clase de español.

Ejercicio 3 *(page 57)*
1. La profesora de español habla con los alumnos.
2. Rosita toma apuntes.
3. La profesora canta en la clase de español.
4. Un alumno toca la guitarra.
5. Carlos saca buenas notas.

Ejercicio 2 *(page 59)*
1. Sí, estudio español.
2. Sí, hablo español.
3. Sí, hablo bien.
4. Sí, hablo español con el (la) profesor(a) de español.
5. Sí, en la clase de español tomo apuntes.
6. Sí, canto.
7. Sí, toco la guitarra.
8. Saco buenas notas en español.

Ejercicio 3 *(page 59)*
1. Sí, estudio matemáticas.
2. Sí, saco buenas notas en matemáticas.
3. Sí, estudio ciencias.
4. Sí, saco buenas notas en ciencias.
5. Sí, estudio historia.
6. Sí, saco buenas notas en historia.
7. Sí, estudio inglés.
8. Sí, saco buenas notas en inglés.
9. Saco buenas notas en (español, matemáticas, ciencias, historia, inglés).
10. Saco malas notas en (español, matemáticas, ciencias, historia, inglés).

Ejercicio 4 *(page 59)*
1. ¿Estudias?
2. ¿Cantas?
3. ¿Tomas apuntes?
4. ¿Hablas con el profesor?

Ejercicio 5 *(page 59)*
1. b   4. c
2. c   5. a
3. a

Ejercicio 6 *(page 60)*
(Carlos), (John F. Kennedy), estudio, hablo, enseña, enseña, tomo, canta, canto, canto, toca, toca, estudio, saco, estudias, cantas, Hablas, Sacas

Ejercicio 7 *(page 60)*
1. ¿Habla Ud. francés?
2. ¿Canta Ud. en clase?
3. ¿Toca Ud. la guitarra?
4. ¿Enseña Ud. historia?

Ejercicio 8 *(page 60)*
1. ¿Hablas tú?
2. ¿Toca Ud. la guitarra?
3. ¿Enseña Ud.?
4. ¿Estudias tú?
5. ¿Tomas tú apuntes?

Ejercicio *(page 62)*
1. Roberto habla con Antonio.
2. Sí, Roberto habla español.
3. Sí, Antonio habla español también.
4. No, Roberto no es español.
5. Estudia español en la escuela.
6. Sí, habla muy bien.

Ejercicio *(page 63)*
1. b   4. b
2. a   5. a
3. c

Actividad 4 *(page 65)*
La profesora enseña español.
La muchacha habla con el muchacho.
La muchacha (Ella) toma apuntes.
La muchacha (Ella) toca la guitarra.
El muchacho (Él) estudia mucho.

Ejercicio 1 *(page 69)*
1. Los alumnos llegan a casa.
2. Preparan una merienda en la cocina.
3. Miran la televisión en la sala.
4. Hablan por teléfono en la sala.
5. Escuchan discos en la sala.
6. Trabajan en una tienda.

Ejercicio 2 *(page 69)*
1. Qué   4. Qué
2. Dónde   5. Dónde
3. Quiénes

Ejercicio 1 *(page 71)*
1. Sí, los amigos preparan una merienda.
2. Sí, toman la merienda en la cocina.
3. Sí, después miran la televisión en la sala.
4. Sí, escuchan discos.
5. Sí, hablan por teléfono.

Ejercicio 2 *(page 71)*
1. Sí, estudiamos español.
2. Sí, estudiamos mucho.
3. Sí, sacamos buenas notas.
4. Sí, hablamos mucho en la clase de español.
5. Sí, después de las clases preparamos una merienda.
6. Tomamos la merienda en casa.
7. Sí, a veces miramos la televisión.
8. Sí, escuchamos discos.
9. Escuchamos discos de (rock).
10. Sí, hablamos mucho por teléfono.
11. Con los amigos hablamos inglés.

Ejercicio 3 *(page 71)*
1. ¿Estudian Uds.?
2. ¿Escuchan Uds. discos?
3. ¿Hablan Uds. con el profesor?
4. ¿Miran Uds. la televisión?

Ejercicio 4 *(page 72)*
1. Sí, estudio español.
2. Sí, hablo español con la profesora de español.
3. Sí, ella habla inglés también.
4. Sí, trabajo mucho en la clase de español.
5. Saco buenas/malas notas.
6. Sí, en la clase de español cantamos.
7. Sí, después de las clases los amigos toman una merienda.
8. Sí, escuchamos discos también.
9. Sí, miramos la televisión.
10. (Sara) trabaja después de las clases.
11. Sí, estudiamos en casa.

Ejercicio 5 *(page 72)*
estudia, trabaja, estudia, hablan, cantan
estudio, trabajo, saco, hablamos, cantamos, tocamos
toman, miramos, miramos, escuchamos, hablamos

Ejercicio 6 *(page 73)*
1. c   4. b
2. a   5. a
3. b

Conversación *(page 74)*
—Sí, nosotros tomamos una merienda.
—Nosotros escuchamos discos/miramos la televisión.
—Sí, a veces hablamos por teléfono.
—Hablamos con los amigos.
—Sí (No), (no) trabajamos después de las clases.

Ejercicio *(page 76)*
1. las clases   2. una tienda

3. hispánicos   6. cuatro, cinco
4. primaria   7. la escuela
5. todo el día

Actividad 1 *(page 77)*
Después de las clases, ¿preparan Uds. una merienda?
¿Toman Uds. la merienda en la cocina?
¿Trabajan Uds. después de las clases? ¿Dónde trabajan Uds.?
¿Hablan Uds. mucho por teléfono?
¿Miran Uds. la televisión?
¿Escuchan Uds. discos?
¿Estudian Uds. (mucho)?

Actividad 2 *(page 77)*
El muchacho (Él) mira la televisión.
Las muchachas (Las amigas) (Ellas) escuchan discos.
La muchacha (Ella) estudia (en casa).
El muchacho (Él) trabaja en una tienda.
El muchacho (Él) prepara una merienda.
La muchacha (Ella) habla por teléfono.

Actividad 3 *(page 77)*
Students will use the verbs from **Actividad 2**, but now the verbs should be in the **nosotros** form.

Ejercicio 1 *(page 80)*
1. Sí, Juanito va de compras.
2. Sí, va de compras por la mañana.
3. Sí, él está en la panadería.
4. Sí, compra pan en la panadería.
5. Sí, paga en la caja.
6. Sí, da el dinero al panadero.

Ejercicio 2 *(page 80)*
la mañana, panadería, caja, dinero

Ejercicio 3 *(page 82)*
1. pan   4. Ella compra pescado.
2. leche   5. Ella compra frutas.
3. compra carne

Ejercicio 4 *(page 82)*
1. lechería
2. a la frutería
3. va a la carnicería
4. Ella va a la panadería.
5. Ella va a la pescadería.

Ejercicio 5 *(page 82)*
1. ¿Ah, sí? ¿Adónde va ella?
   Pues, ella va a la lechería.
2. ¿Ah, sí? ¿Adónde va ella?
   Pues, ella va a la pescadería?
3. ¿Ah, sí? ¿Adónde va ella?
   Pues, ella va a la frutería.

4. ¿Ah, sí? ¿Adónde va ella?
   Pues, ella va a la pastelería.

Ejercicio 1 *(page 84)*
1. Sí, voy a la escuela.
2. Sí, voy a la escuela por la mañana.
3. Sí, estoy en la clase ahora.
4. Sí, estoy en la clase de español.
5. Sí, doy el cuaderno a la profesora.
6. Sí, a veces voy de compras.
7. Sí, voy de compras después de las clases.
8. Sí, voy al supermercado.
9. No, no estoy en el supermercado ahora.
10. Sí, en el supermercado doy el dinero al empleado en la caja.

Ejercicio 2 *(page 84)*
1. Sí, estoy bien.
2. No, no estoy enfermo(a).
3. Estoy bien.

Ejercicio 3 *(page 84)*
1. Sí, Juan va a la tienda.
2. Sí, va a la tienda con Teresa.
3. Sí, Juan está en la tienda ahora.
4. Sí, Teresa está también.
5. Sí, ellos están en la panadería.
6. Sí, ellos están en la caja.
7. Sí, ellos dan el dinero al empleado.

Ejercicio 4 *(page 84)*
1. Sí, vamos a la escuela por la mañana.
2. Vamos a la Escuela . . . .
3. Sí, estamos en la escuela ahora.
4. Estamos en la clase de español.
5. Sí, estamos con la profesora de español.
6. Sí, después de las clases a veces vamos a un café.
7. Sí, a veces vamos de compras.
8. Sí, vamos a un supermercado.
9. Vamos al supermercado . . . .

Ejercicio 5 *(page 85)*
1.–4. Perdón. ¿Adónde vas?

Ejercicio 6 *(page 85)*
1. ¿Va Ud. a la escuela por la mañana?
2. ¿Está Ud. en la escuela ahora?
3. ¿Da Ud. buenas notas?
4. ¿Va Ud. de compras después de las clases?

Ejercicio 7 *(page 85)*

va, va	están
vamos	estamos, está
voy, vas, voy	estoy
voy	da, dan
están, está	

Ejercicio 8 *(page 86)*
1. Sí, voy a la escuela por la mañana.
2. Sí, voy a la clase de español.
3. Sí, Marisol va al colegio por la mañana.
4. Sí, a veces voy al supermercado.
5. Sí, Marisol va al mercado.

Ejercicio 9 *(page 86)*

1. a la escuela	3. al mercado
2. a la pescadería	4. al supermercado

Ejercicio 10 *(page 86)*
1. Sí, la amiga del muchacho es argentina.
2. Sí, ella es de la Argentina.
3. Sí, ella es del continente sudamericano.
4. Sí, ellos son amigos de los hermanos de Lupita.

Ejercicio 11 *(page 87)*
1. Hay una televisión en la sala.
2. Hay frutas en la frutería.
3. Hay una caja en la tienda.
4. Hay apuntes en el cuaderno.
5. Hay pan en la cocina.

Ejercicio *(page 89)*
1. Pedro está muy bien hoy.
2. Él va al mercado.
3. Las habichuelas están a 50 pesos el kilo hoy.
4. Pedro compra medio kilo de habichuelas.
5. No, no compra nada más en el mercado.

Ejercicio *(page 90)*
1. Sí, hay supermercados en los países hispánicos.
2. No, la gente no va mucho a los supermercados.
3. No, no compran todo en la misma tienda.
4. Sí, van de una tienda a otra.
5. Compran carne en la carnicería.
6. Compran leche en la lechería.
7. Sí, van de compras casi todos los días.
8. Sí, la calidad de los productos en las tiendas pequeñas es buena (excelente).
9. Todo está muy fresco.
10. Los precios no son muy altos.
11. La gente compra alimentos enlatados, botellas de agua mineral, rollos de papel higiénico o cajas de jabón en polvo.

Actividad 1 *(page 91)*

la lechería	la pastelería
la pescadería	el supermercado
la frutería	la frutería
la panadería	la frutería
la carnicería	el supermercado

Actividad 2 *(page 91)*
Pasteles. Ah, ¿tú vas a la pastelería?
Carne. Ah, ¿tú vas a la carnicería?
Pescado. Ah, ¿tú vas a la pescadería?
Legumbres. Ah, ¿tú vas a la frutería?
Fresas. Ah, ¿tú vas a la frutería?

Actividad 3 *(page 91)*
Latinoamérica   Estados Unidos
Estados Unidos   Estados Unidos
Latinoamérica   Latinoamérica

Ejercicio 1 *(page 94)*
1. Sí, la familia Vázquez vive en un apartamento.
2. Sí, la familia come en casa.
3. Sí, ellos comen en el comedor.
4. Sí, después de la comida ellos ven una película.
5. Sí, ven la película en la televisión.
6. Sí, ven la película en la sala.

Ejercicio 2 *(page 95)*
1. carne   5. Él come pan.
2. come papas   6. Él come frutas.
3. Él come ensalada.   7. Él come pescado.
4. Él come helado.   8. Él come pasteles.

Ejercicio 3 *(page 96)*
1. Sí, en la escuela los jóvenes escriben mucho.
2. Sí, leen mucho también.
3. Sí, ellos aprenden mucho en la escuela.
4. Sí, ellos reciben (muy) buenas notas.

Ejercicio 4 *(page 96)*
1. cartas
2. escribe composiciones
3. Ella escribe apuntes.
4. Ella escribe tarjetas postales.

Ejercicio 5 *(page 96)*
1. un libro
2. lee un periódico
3. Él lee una carta.
4. Él lee una tarjeta postal.

Ejercicio 6 *(page 96)*
1. Los jóvenes escriben composiciones.
2. Los jóvenes escriben composiciones.
3. Escriben muchas composiciones.
4. Las composiciones son buenas.
5. Escriben las composiciones en la clase de español.

Ejercicio 2 *(page 98)*
1. Sí, Paco Machado vive en Costa Rica.
2. No, Enrique no vive en Costa Rica.
3. Sí, Enrique escribe una carta.
4. Enrique escribe la carta.

Ejercicio 3 *(page 98)*
1. Sí, en la escuela los alumnos aprenden mucho.
2. Sí, aprenden español.
3. Sí, leen mucho en la clase de inglés.
4. Sí, escriben mucho también.
5. Sí, reciben buenas notas.

Ejercicio 4 *(page 99)*
1. Vivo en . . . .
2. Vivo en . . . .
3. Sí, en casa como con la familia.
4. Como en . . . .
5. Sí (No), después de la cena (no) leo el periódico.
6. Sí (No), (no) leo el periódico en la sala.
7. Sí, a veces leo un libro.
8. Sí, a veces escribo una carta a un amigo o a una amiga.

Ejercicio 5 *(page 99)*
1. Oye, Catalina. ¿Qué comes?
2. Oye, Catalina. ¿Qué escribes?
3. Oye, Catalina. ¿Qué bebes?
4. Oye, Catalina. ¿Qué recibes?

Ejercicio 6 *(page 99)*
1. Vivimos en los Estados Unidos.
2. Sí (No), (no) vivimos en una casa particular.
3. Sí (No), (no) vivimos en un apartamento.
4. Sí, escribimos mucho en la clase de español.
5. Sí, en la clase de inglés escribimos mucho.
6. Sí, recibimos buenas notas en español.
7. Sí, aprendemos mucho en la escuela.
8. Sí, leemos muchos libros.
9. Sí (No), (no) comemos en la cafetería de la escuela.

Ejercicio 7 *(page 99)*
1. Y Uds. también viven en los Estados Unidos, ¿no?
2. Y Uds. también reciben el periódico todos los días, ¿no?
3. Y Uds. también leen el periódico todos los días, ¿no?
4. Y Uds. también aprenden mucho del periódico, ¿no?

Ejercicio 8 *(page 100)*
1. vive   8. comen
2. viven   9. comemos, comemos
3. viven   10. asisten
4. vivimos, . . .   11. asisten
5. Vives   12. asistimos
6. vivo, . . .   13. escriben, leen, aprenden
7. come   14. escribo, leo, aprendo

Ejercicio 9 *(page 100)*

1. veo
2. veo
3. vemos
4. Ves
5. Ven

Ejercicio 10 *(page 101)*

1. la facilidad
2. la mentalidad
3. la universalidad
4. la entidad

Ejercicio 11 *(page 101)*

1. las universidades
2. las responsabilidades
3. las oportunidades
4. las capacidades

Ejercicio *(page 103)*

1. Sí, Cristina vive en Madrid.
2. Sí, ella es madrileña.
3. Ella vive en la Calle Velázquez.
4. Sí, ella vive con la familia.
5. No, ellos no viven en la planta baja.
6. Viven en el segundo piso, derecho.

Ejercicio *(page 105)*

1. b
2. a
3. b
4. c
5. b
6. c

Actividad 1 *(page 106)*

Vivo en . . . .
Vivo en . . . .
Vivo en la Calle . . . .
Vivo en . . . .
Tomo el almuerzo (al mediodía).
Al mediodía como en (la cafetería de la escuela).
El almuerzo es una comida ligera.
Ceno a las . . . .
En muchos países de Latinoamérica cenan a (eso
    de) las ocho.
En España cenan a las nueve y media o las diez
    (de la noche).

Actividad 3 *(page 106)*

La familia come en el comedor.
Comen sopa, ensalada, papas y carne.
Sí, después de la comida van a la sala.
Sí, leen el periódico.
Sí, miran la televisión.
Sí, ven una película en la televisión.

Ejercicio 1 *(page 110)*

1. La familia Ureña vive en un apartamento.
2. Ellos viven en Caracas, la capital de
   Venezuela.
3. Ellos viven en el cuarto piso de un edificio alto
   en la avenida Simón Bolívar.
4. Isabel y Rafael asisten a un colegio privado en
   la capital.
5. En la escuela ellos toman muchos cursos y
   sacan muy buenas notas.

6. Ellos estudian inglés.
7. El profesor de inglés es de Chicago (pero
   ahora vive en Caracas).
8. Después de las clases, Isabel y Rafael van a
   un café (con los amigos).
9. Luego ellos van a casa donde cenan con la
   familia.

Ejercicio 2 *(page 111)*

1. Sí, estudio español.
2. Sí, en la clase de español, hablo. Sí, leo y
   escribo también.
3. Sí, a veces nosotros cantamos en la clase de
   español.
4. Sí (No), el (la) profesor(a) (no) toca la guitarra.
5. Sí, nosotros leemos y escribimos mucho en la
   clase de español.
6. Sí (No), después de las clases, (no) trabajo.

Ejercicio 3 *(page 111)*

1. tomamos, aprendemos, Leemos, escribimos
2. enseña, canta, toca, aprenden, reciben,
   trabajan

Ejercicio 4 *(page 111)*

estás	estoy, vas
Estoy	voy, vas
estás	voy

Ejercicio 1 *(page 113)*

1. a
2. c
3. b
4. b
5. c
6. c

Ejercicio 2 *(page 113)*

Sí, a veces compro comida.
Voy a un supermercado.
Voy al supermercado . . . . Está . . . .
No, no hay muchos puestos distintos en el
    supermercado.
No, en el supermercado no regateo.
Sí, pago un precio fijo.
No, los mexicanos no regatean en un
    supermercado.
Sí, ellos regatean en los mercados al aire libre.
Sí, yo regateo a veces.

Ejercicio *(page 115)*

1. El Retiro es el parque famoso de Madrid.
2. El Parque Palermo es el parque famoso de
   Buenos Aires.
3. El Bosque de Chapultepec es el parque
   famoso de México.
4. Los parques son muy populares.
5. Mucha gente va al parque los domingos.
6. Venden helados y otros refrescos en los
   puestos en el parque.
7. Los amigos toman una merienda.

8. Sí, a veces dan un paseo en el parque.
9. Hay un lago en el Bosque de Chapultepec, en el Retiro y en el Parque Palermo.
10. La gente alquila un barquito.
11. Reman en el lago.

Ejercicio 1 *(page 119)*
1. Sí, el señor y la señora Fuentes tienen dos hijos.
2. Sí, ellos tienen un perrito también.
3. Sí, Sarita y Pablo tienen primos.
4. Sí, ellos tienen abuelos.
5. Sí, Sarita tiene un hermano.
6. Sí, Pablo tiene una hermana.

Ejercicio 2 *(page 119)*
el marido = *the husband*
la esposa (la mujer) = *the wife*
los nietos = *the grandchildren*
los sobrinos = *the niece and nephew*

Ejercicio 3 *(page 119)*
el abuelo   los primos
la tía   los sobrinos
el tío

Ejercicio 1 *(page 120)*
1. Sí, los señores Fuentes tienen dos hijos.
2. Sí, Sarita tiene un hermano.
3. Sí, Pablo tiene una hermana.
4. Sí, ellos tienen un perrito.

Ejercicio 3 *(page 121)*
1. Sí (No), (no) tengo hermanos.
2. Tengo . . . hermanos.
3. Sí (No), (no) tengo primos.
4. Tengo . . . primos.
5. Tengo un . . . .
6. Tengo . . . años.

Ejercicio 4 *(page 121)*
1. ¿Tienes un hermano? Sí (No), (no) tengo un hermano.
2. ¿Tienes una hermana? Sí (No), (no) tengo una hermana.
3. ¿Tienes un primo? Sí (No), (no) tengo un primo.
4. ¿Tienes una prima? Sí (No), (no) tengo una prima.
5. ¿Tienes un perro? Sí (No), (no) tengo un perro.
6. ¿Tienes un gato? Sí (No), (no) tengo un gato.

Ejercicio 5 *(page 121)*
1. ¿Tiene Ud. hijos?
2. ¿Tiene Ud. hermanos?
3. ¿Tiene Ud. primos?
4. ¿Tiene Ud. un perro o un gato?

Ejercicio 6 *(page 121)*
1.–4. ¡Perdón! ¿Qué tienen Uds.?

Ejercicio 7 *(page (121)*
1. Sí (No), (no) tenemos una casa particular.
2. Sí (No), (no) tenemos un apartamento.
3. Sí (No), (no) tenemos un perro.
4. Sí (No), (no) tenemos un gato.
5. Sí (No), (no) tenemos una familia grande.

Ejercicio 8 *(page 122)*
tienen, tienen
tiene, tiene, tiene, tiene
tienes, tienes, Tienen, Tienen
tengo, tengo, tenemos, tenemos

Ejercicio 9 *(page 122)*
1. Sí, tengo que trabajar mucho en la clase de español.
2. Sí, tengo que hablar español en la clase de español.
3. Sí, tengo que estudiar mucho.
4. Sí, tenemos que leer mucho.
5. Sí, tenemos que aprender la gramática.
6. Sí, tenemos que escribir muchas composiciones.

Ejercicio 10 *(page 122)*
1. tenemos,-ar
2. tienen,-er,-ar,-er,-ir
3. tiene,-ar, tiene,-ar
4. tenemos,-er

Ejercicio 11 *(page 123)*
1. Aquí está mi amigo.
2. Aquí está mi amiga.
3. Aquí está mi libro.
4. Aquí están mis amigos.
5. Aquí están mis libros.

Ejercicio 12 *(page 124)*
1. Ricardo, ¿tienes tu cuaderno también?
2. Ricardo, ¿tienes tu disco también?
3. Ricardo, ¿tienes tu guitarra también?
4. Ricardo, ¿tienes tus libros también?
5. Ricardo, ¿tienes tus apuntes también?
6. Ricardo, ¿tienes tus cartas también?

Ejercicio 13 *(page 124)*
1. Sí, sí. Su primo está.
2. Sí, sí. Su amigo está.
3. Sí, sí. Su hermana está.
4. Sí, sí. Su amiga está.
5. Sí, sí. Sus primos están.
6. Sí, sí. Sus amigos están.

Ejercicio 14 *(page 124)*
1. Su amigo es muy simpático.
2. Su primo es muy simpático.

3. Su madre es muy simpática.
4. Su hermana es muy simpática.
5. Sus hermanos son muy simpáticos.
6. Sus amigos son muy simpáticos.

Ejercicio 15 *(page 124)*
1. Sí, hablamos con nuestro(a) profesor(a) de español.
2. Sí, leemos nuestro libro de español.
3. Sí, escribimos en nuestro cuaderno.
4. Sí, miramos nuestras notas.
5. Sí, hablamos con nuestros amigos en la clase de español.

Ejercicio 16 *(page 124)*
1. Sí, el apartamento de la familia Ochoa está en Madrid.
2. Sí, sus parientes viven en Madrid también.
3. Sí, a veces ellos van a la casa de sus parientes.
4. Sí, comen en su casa.
5. Sí, ellos hablan con sus parientes.

Ejercicio 17 *(page 125)*
Mis, mi, mis, sus, Mi, Su, mi, Mi, mi, Su, mi, Mis, mi, Mi, mi, Su, mi, Su, Nuestro
tu, tu, tus

Ejercicio *(page 126)*
1. Tadeo tiene dos hermanos.
2. Su hermano tiene dieciséis años.
3. Su hermana tiene dieciocho años.
4. Tadeo es el bebé de la familia.
5. Él tiene quince años.

Ejercicio *(page 128)*
1. La familia tiene mucha importancia en la sociedad hispánica.
2. No, cuando un joven hispano habla de su familia, no habla solamente de sus padres y de sus hermanos.
3. Habla de sus abuelos, de sus tíos y de sus primos.
4. Sí, muchas veces los abuelos viven con sus hijos y sus nietos.

Actividad 1 *(page 129)*
Hay . . . personas en mi familia.
Tengo . . . hermanos.
(Mi hermano tiene . . . años y mi hermana tiene . . . años.)
Yo tengo . . . años.
Nosotros vivimos en . . . .
Nosotros tenemos un . . . .
Sí (No), (no) tengo muchos primos.
Ellos viven en . . . .

Actividad 3 *(page 129)*
(Answers will vary.)

Ejercicio 1 *(page 132)*
1. La muchacha está contenta.
2. El muchacho está triste.
3. El muchacho está enfermo.
4. La muchacha está bien.
5. El muchacho está nervioso.

Ejercicio 2 *(page 133)*
1. Sí, Juanito tiene la gripe.
2. Sí, tiene fiebre.
3. Sí, tiene dolor de cabeza.
4. Sí, está en cama.
5. Sí, está en el hospital.

Ejercicio 3 *(page 133)*
1. Estoy de mal humor cuando estoy enfermo(a).
2. Estoy de buen humor cuando estoy contento(a).
3. Estoy de mal humor cuando estoy nervioso(a).
4. Estoy de mal humor cuando tengo catarro.
5. Estoy de mal humor cuando tengo la gripe.
6. Estoy de mal humor cuando tengo fiebre.
7. Estoy de mal humor cuando tengo dolor de cabeza.

Ejercicio 4 *(page 133)*
1.–5. ¡Ay de mí! ¡Qué lástima!

Ejercicio 1 *(page 134)*
1. Sí, el muchacho es de Cuba.
2. Sí, la muchacha es de Colombia.
3. Sí, el joven es de Guatemala.
4. Sí, la joven es de Puerto Rico.
5. Sí, la guitarra es de España.
6. Sí, la profesora es de Puerto Rico.
7. Sí, las fresas son de México.
8. Sí, las películas son de Venezuela.

Ejercicio 2 *(page 134)*
1. Mi abuelo es de . . . .
2. Mi abuela es de . . . .
3. Mi padre es de . . . .
4. Mi madre es de . . . .
5. Yo soy de . . . .

Ejercicio 3 *(page 134)*
1. Sí, Madrid está en España.
2. Sí, la calle Velázquez está en Madrid.
3. Sí, el apartamento está en la calle Velázquez.
4. Sí, el apartamento está en un edificio alto.
5. Sí, el apartamento está en la planta baja.
6. Sí, el hospital también está en la calle Velázquez.
7. Sí, el médico está en el hospital.
8. Sí, la consulta del médico está en el hospital.

Ejercicio 4 *(page 135)*
1. Sí, estoy en la escuela ahora.
2. Estoy en la clase de español.

3. Sí, estoy con mis amigos.
4. Mi escuela está en . . . .
5. Mi casa está en . . . .

Ejercicio 5 *(page 135)*
1. Rosita es de Puerto Rico.
   Rosita está en España ahora.
2. Jesús es de España.
   Él está en México ahora.
3. Inés es de Colombia.
   Ella está en los Estados Unidos ahora.

Ejercicio 7 *(page 135)*
1. Sí, el periódico es interesante.
2. Sí, la película es buena.
3. Sí, el deporte es popular.
4. Sí, el español es fácil.
5. Sí, la escuela es grande.

Ejercicio 8 *(page 136)*
1. Está cansado.
2. Está enferma.
3. Está contento.
4. Está triste.
5. Está nervioso.
6. Está de mal humor.

Ejercicio 9 *(page 136)*
1. El libro es interesante.
2. La joven está contenta.
3. Los muchachos son atléticos.
4. El señor está enfermo.
5. La ciudad es grande.
6. El edificio es alto.
7. Mi amigo está cansado.
8. Elena está triste.
9. La tienda es elegante.
10. El apartamento es pequeño.

Ejercicio 10 *(page 136)*
1. están   4. está
2. es   5. está
3. es   6. están, son

Ejercicio 11 *(page 136)*
es, es, Es, es, está, es, está, está, Está, está,
   Está, está
está, es, es, está, son, son, son, están, están, es,
   Está

Ejercicio 12 *(page 137)*
1. Sí, el libro es español.
2. Sí, los profesores son españoles.
3. Sí, la película es española.
4. Sí, las señoras son españolas.

Ejercicio 13 *(page 137)*
1. español   2. mexicanos

3. argentinos   6. irlandeses
4. portuguesa   7. americana
5. francesas   8. inglés

Ejercicio 14 *(page 138)*
1. Es verdad. Jesús es español.
2. Es verdad. Los jóvenes son mexicanos.
3. Es verdad. Colette es francesa.
4. Es verdad. Ellos son alemanes.
5. Es verdad. Los vestidos son ingleses.
6. Es verdad. Los muchachos son cubanos.
7. Es verdad. Elena es irlandesa.
8. Es verdad. Ellos son portugueses.

Ejercicio *(page 139)*
está, está, está, dolor, tiene, médico

Ejercicio *(page 141)*
1. Verdadero   6. Falso
2. Verdadero   7. Falso
3. Falso   8. Falso
4. Falso   9. Verdadero
5. Verdadero   10. Verdadero

Actividad 1 *(page 142)*
Nevada, Florida, Colorado, Arizona, Montana

Actividad 3 *(page 143)*
Tengo el pelo . . . .   Tengo una boca . . . .
Tengo ojos . . . .   Tengo los brazos . . . .
Tengo una nariz . . . .

Actividad 4 *(page 143)*
Es bajo.
Es pequeño.
Los ojos son azules.
La nariz es grande.
La boca es grande.
Los brazos y los pies son grandes. Las piernas
   son cortas. *(Answers will vary.)*

Ejercicio 1 *(page 146)*
1. Venden pantalones.
2. Venden zapatos.
3. Venden trajes.
4. Venden abrigos.
5. Venden camisas.
6. Venden corbatas.

Ejercicio 2 *(page 147)*
1. Venden faldas.
2. Venden blusas.
3. Venden sombreros.
4. Venden suéteres.
5. Venden vestidos.
6. Venden zapatos (de tacón alto).

Ejercicio 3 *(page 147)*
1. La blusa tiene mangas largas.
2. La camisa tiene mangas cortas.
3. No, la camisa no tiene rayas.
4. Los zapatos tienen tacones bajos.
5. El número de los zapatos es 37.
6. La talla del traje es 42.

Ejercicio 4 *(page 148)*
1. Clarita va a cumplir quince años.
2. Va a cumplir quince años mañana.
3. Su cumpleaños es mañana.
4. Roberto está en la tienda de ropa.
5. Roberto va a comprar un regalo.
6. Va a comprar un regalo para Clarita.
7. Sí, la familia de Clarita va a dar una fiesta.
8. Sí, van a invitar a sus amigos a la fiesta.

Ejercicio 5 *(page 149)*
1. Los calcetines son blancos.
2. La blusa es amarilla.
3. La corbata es verde.
4. El suéter es azul.
5. La falda es anaranjada.
6. La camisa es blanca.

Ejercicio 1 *(page 150)*
1. Sí, Clarita va a cumplir quince años.
2. Sí, sus padres van a dar una fiesta.
3. Sí, van a invitar a sus amigos.
4. Sí, van a comer durante la fiesta.
5. Sí, voy a ir a la fiesta.
6. Sí, voy a comprar un regalo para Clarita.
7. Sí, voy a comprar una blusa.
8. Sí, voy a ir a la tienda con Roberto.
9. Sí, vamos a mirar la ropa en el escaparate.

Ejercicio 2 *(page 150)*
1. Voy a preparar una merienda.
2. Voy a tomar la merienda con mis amigos.
3. Luego vamos a mirar la televisión.
4. Vamos a ver una película en la televisión.
5. Luego, Pablo va a ir a casa.
6. Él va a estudiar.
7. Carmen y yo vamos a ir a la tienda.
8. Vamos a comprar un regalo para Clarita.
9. Sus padres van a dar una fiesta.
10. Nosotros vamos a asistir a la fiesta.

Ejercicio 3 *(page 151)*
1. Sí, miro el escaparate.
2. Sí, miro al empleado.
3. Sí, escucho el disco.
4. Sí, escucho a la profesora.
5. Sí, veo la camisa.
6. Sí, veo al muchacho.
7. Sí, recibo un regalo.
8. Sí, recibo a mis amigos.

Ejercicio 4 *(page 151)*
1. la televisión
2. los discos
3. a la profesora
4. al muchacho
5. español
6. un regalo

Ejercicio *(page 153)*
1. Enrique va a una tienda de ropa.
2. Enrique va a comprar una camisa.
3. Va a comprar una camisa de mangas cortas.
4. Enrique necesita la talla 38.
5. No, él no compra la camisa a rayas azules.
6. Sí, él compra la camisa sin rayas.
7. No, no necesita nada más.
8. La camisa es quinientos pesos.

Ejercicio *(page 155)*
1. Clarita Gómez Guzmán tiene (cumple) quince años.
2. Sus padres van a dar una fiesta.
3. Los abuelos, los tíos, los primos y los padrinos llegan a la fiesta.
4. Los padres invitan a todos los parientes a la fiesta.
5. No, la fiesta no es solamente para los jóvenes. (Es para toda la familia.)
6. Todos los invitados tienen regalos para Clarita.
7. Clarita recibe discos, libros, blusas, una falda, *blue jeans* y *T-shirts*.
8. Los padrinos dan un regalo especial.
9. Clarita recibe un collar de perlas de sus padrinos.
10. Clarita agradece (mucho) a sus padrinos, a sus parientes y a sus amigos.

Actividad 3 *(page 156)*
un par de zapatos
¿De tacones bajos o de tacones altos?
De tacones bajos
número
son los zapatos que están
número
los zapatos que están

Actividad 4 *(page 156)*
Sí, a veces hay una fiesta especial en honor del cumpleaños de una muchacha.
Por lo general la muchacha tiene dieciséis años.
Sí, sus amigos van a la fiesta.
No, todos sus parientes no van a la fiesta también.
La fiesta es para los jóvenes.
No, sus padrinos no van a la fiesta.
No, la muchacha no recibe un regalo especial de sus padrinos.

Ejercicio 1 *(page 161)*
1. Sí, los dos equipos están en el campo de fútbol.

2. El segundo tiempo empieza.
3. Hay dos equipos en el campo.
4. Sí, un jugador tiene el balón.
5. Sí, lanza el balón con el pie.
6. No, el portero no para (no puede parar) el balón.
7. Sí, el jugador mete un gol.
8. Sí, marca un tanto.
9. Perú gana.
10. Argentina pierde.

Ejercicio 2 *(page 161)*
1. ¿Cuántos equipos hay en el campo?
2. ¿Cómo es un equipo?
3. ¿Quiénes juegan al fútbol?
4. ¿Qué lanza un jugador?
5. ¿Dónde está el portero?

Ejercicio 3 *(page 161)*
1. tablero   4. lanza, mete
2. portero   5. marca
3. vuelven   6. pierde

Ejercicio 1 *(page 162)*
1. Sí, empezamos a jugar.
2. Sí, empezamos a las dos.
3. Sí, queremos meter un gol.
4. Sí, queremos ganar el partido.
5. Sí, perdemos a veces.
6. Preferimos jugar en el parque.
7. Preferimos jugar con un equipo bueno.

Ejercicio 2 *(page 162)*
1. Sí, el segundo tiempo empieza.
2. Sí, los jugadores empiezan a jugar.
3. Sí, los dos equipos prefieren ganar.
4. Sí, quieren marcar muchos tantos.
5. Sí, González quiere meter un gol.
6. Sí, el portero quiere parar el balón.
7. Sí, el equipo de González pierde.

Ejercicio 3 *(page 163)*
1. Prefiero jugar al . . . .
2. Prefiero . . . .
3. Sí, siempre quiero marcar muchos tantos.
4. Sí, quiero ganar.
5. Sí, pierdo a veces.

Ejercicio 4 *(page 163)*
quiere, quiero, prefieres, prefieres, quieres, pierde, quieres, pierdo
quiero, quiere, empiezo, empieza, empiezas, quiero

Ejercicio 5 *(page 163)*
1. preferimos tocar la guitarra, prefiere cantar
2. preferimos comer, prefiere mirar la televisión
3. preferimos escuchar discos, prefiere escribir tarjetas

Ejercicio 6 *(page 163)*
Nosotros queremos ir a la carnicería porque preferimos comprar la carne allí y no en el supermercado. Nuestro amigo prefiere comprar todo en el supermercado. Él cree que nosotros perdemos mucho tiempo porque vamos de una tienda a otra.

Ejercicio 7 *(page 164)*
1. Sí, jugamos al fútbol.
2. Sí, podemos jugar en el patio de la escuela.
3. Sí, volvemos a casa después del partido.
4. Sí, dormimos después de un partido de fútbol.

Ejercicio 8 *(page 164)*
1. Sí, juego al fútbol en la clase de educación física.
2. Sí, la clase juega en el gimnasio.
3. Sí, podemos jugar en el patio de la escuela.
4. Sí, después del partido de fútbol, volvemos a la escuela.

Ejercicio 9 *(page 165)*
juego, Juegas   vuelve
juego, puedo   vuelve, quiero
puedes   jugamos
puedo, vuelve   puede

Ejercicio *(page 167)*
1. Las muchachas van a jugar al fútbol.
2. Van a jugar ahora.
3. Sí, Carmen quiere jugar.
4. No, Elena no puede jugar.
5. Ella juega muy bien.
6. Elena no puede jugar porque ya tiene once jugadoras.
7. Sí, puede jugar mañana si quiere.

Ejercicio *(page 169)*
1. b   5. a
2. c   6. a
3. b   7. b
4. a   8. a

Actividad 1 *(page 170)*
Sí (No), (no) soy muy aficionado(a) a los deportes.
Sí (No), (no) soy muy aficionado(a) al fútbol.
Estudio en la Escuela . . . .
Sí (No), el fútbol (no) es popular en mi escuela.
Sí (No), mi escuela (no) tiene un equipo.
Sí (No), el equipo (no) es bueno.
Sí (No), (no) ganan muchos partidos.
Hay once jugadores en el equipo.
Sí (No), (no) juego con el equipo.
Sí (No), (no) juego a otro deporte. Juego al . . . .

Ejercicio 1 *(page 174)*
1. Tomás habla con Clarita.
2. Clarita está muy bien.
3. Clarita quiere jugar al fútbol.
4. Su hermano está en casa.
5. No, él no puede jugar también.
6. No puede jugar porque tiene que estudiar.
   (Mañana tiene examen.)

Ejercicio 2 *(page 175)*
Empieza, tiene, podemos, quiero, pierde, puede,
   queremos, tenemos, tiene

Ejercicio 3 *(page 175)*
1. Soy de . . . .
2. Ahora estoy en la escuela (en la clase de
   español).
3. Mi casa está en . . . .
4. Mis padres son de . . . .
5. Estoy . . . hoy.
6. Soy . . . .

Ejercicio 4 *(page 175)*
es, es, es, está, está, está, está, está, es, es

Ejercicio *(page 177)*
1. Teresa vive en Guanajuato, México.
2. Hay un ruido en la calle.
3. Un ruido despierta a Teresa.
4. El ruido despierta a Teresa a las seis de la
   mañana.
5. Ella va a la ventana.
6. En la calle ella ve a un grupo de amigos.
7. Hoy es el cumpleaños de Teresa.
8. Sus amigos cantan y tocan la guitarra porque
   le dan una serenata en honor de su
   cumpleaños.

Ejercicio *(page 181)*
1. c
2. a
3. b
4. b
5. c
6. c
7. c
8. c
9. a
10. a

McGRAW-HILL

Spanish

saludos

first part

Conrad J. Schmitt
Protase E. Woodford
Randall G. Marshall

Webster Division
McGraw-Hill Book Company

NEW YORK · ST. LOUIS · SAN FRANCISCO · ATLANTA
AUCKLAND · BOGOTÁ · DALLAS · HAMBURG · JOHANNESBURG · LONDON
MADRID · MEXICO · MONTREAL · NEW DELHI · PANAMA · PARIS
SÃO PAULO · SINGAPORE · SYDNEY · TOKYO · TORONTO

credits

EDITOR • *Teresa Chimienti*
DESIGN SUPERVISOR • *James Darby*
PRODUCTION SUPERVISOR • *Salvador Gonzales*
ILLUSTRATORS • *Olivia Cole* • *Tom Eaton*
  • *Conrad Hack* • *Laura Hartman*
  • *Ray Skibinski* • *Joel Snyder*
  • *Joe Veno*
PHOTO EDITOR • *Alan Forman*
PHOTO RESEARCH • *Ellen Horan*
LAYOUT AND DESIGN • *Function thru Form, Inc.*
COVER DESIGN • *Group Four, Inc.*
CARTOGRAPHER • *David Lindroth*

This book was set in 10/12 point Century Schoolbook
by Monotype Composition Co., Inc.

Color separation was done by Beaumont Graphics, Ltd.

Library of Congress Cataloging in Publication Data

Schmitt, Conrad J.
  McGraw-Hill Spanish—Saludos: first part

  Includes index.
  1. Spanish language—Text-books for foreign speakers
—English. 2. Spanish language—Grammar—1950–
I. Woodford, Protase E. II. Marshall, Randall G.
III. Title.
PC4112.S3594 1986   468.2'421   84-17130
ISBN 0-07-056241-5

ISBN 0-07-056241-5

  3 4 5 6 7 8 9 10 DOCDOC 94 93 92 91 90 89 88 87

acknowledgments

The authors wish to express their appreciation to the many foreign language teachers throughout the United States who have shared with us their thoughts and experiences. We express our particular gratitude to those teachers listed below who have carefully reviewed samples of the original manuscript and have willingly given of their time to offer their comments, suggestions, and recommendations. With the aid of the information supplied to us by these educators we have attempted to produce a text that is contemporary, communicative, authentic, and useful to a wide variety of students from all geographic areas.

Hampton P. Abney
Newark Academy
Livingston, New Jersey

Gloria B. Alarcón
Highland High School
Highland, Illinois

Rhonda Barnebee
Eastside High School
Taylors, South Carolina

Pat Bayot
Fairport Int. Magnet School
Dayton, Ohio

Rose Marie Bennett
MacArthur High School
San Antonio, Texas

Mary W. Brown
Lake Taylor High School
Norfolk, Virginia

J. Patricio Concha
Overbrook High School
Philadelphia, Pennsylvania

Susan Creutz
Rancocas Valley High School
Mount Holly, New Jersey 08060

Leonora Damiano
Vailsburg High School
Newark, New Jersey

Robert D. Decker
Long Beach Unified School District
Long Beach, California

Emelda L. Estell
Bureau of Foreign Languages
Chicago, Illinois

Laura Garvey
Southern Senior High School
Harwood, Maryland

Frances H. Gordon
Falling Creek Middle School
Richmond, Virginia

Gail B. Heffner
Walnut Ridge High School
Columbus, Ohio

Mary M. Hellen
Carlisle Area School District
Carlisle, Pennsylvania

Carmen E. Iglesias
Belmont High School
Dayton, Ohio

Shirley Israel
Carman High School
Flint, Michigan

Susan C. Johnston
J. L. Mann High School
Greenville, South Carolina

Rock F. Kelly
Vista High School
Vista, California

Mary Ann Kosut
Providence Middle School
Richmond, Virginia

Argelia Krohn
Roosevelt High School
San Antonio, Texas

Virginia Luft
Orange High School
Cleveland, Ohio

Ruth Miller
Teaneck Public Schools
Teaneck, New Jersey

Mary Jean Mohn
Gresham High School
Gresham, Oregon

Janice A. Nease
Sissonville High School
Charleston, West Virginia

John P. Nionakis
Hingham Public Schools
Hingham, Massachussets

John O'Donnell
W. E. Groves High School
Birmingham, Michigan

Eugene J. Paciarelli
Dulaney Senior High School
Timonium, Maryland

Jayne Lolita Ray
Addison Junior High School
Roanoke, Virginia

Calvin R. Rossi
Irvine High School
Irvine, California

Maria Sciancalepore
Essex Junction Educational Center
Essex Junction, Vermont

Daniel J. Sheridan
Swartz Creek High School
Swartz Creek, Michigan

Eugene C. Sneary, Ph.D
Wade Hampton High School
Greenville, South Carolina

Julia B. Suid
Woodward High School
Cincinnati, Ohio

Judith Speiller
Cherry Hill West High School
Cherry Hill, New Jersey

Rebecca Stracener
Edison Public Schools
Edison, New Jersey

George Weinrauch
Morris Hill High School
Rockaway, New Jersey

The authors would also like to thank the following persons and organizations for permission to include the following photographs:

2:(tl) Robert Frerck/Woodfin Camp; **2:**(tr) Peter Menzel; **2:**(b) F. Lisa Beede/DPI; **3:**(l) Lisa Limer; **3:**(r) Lisa Limer; **3:**(b) Peter Menzel; **4:** Chip and Rosa Maria Peterson; **5:** Bob Capece/MGH; **6:**(l) Bob Capece/MGH; **6:**(r) Bob Capece/MGH; **8:** Peter Menzel; **11:** Harry Gruyaert/Magnum; **12:** Peter Menzel; **13:**(l) Manuel Rodriguez; **13:**(m) Porterfield-Chickering/Photo Researchers; **14:**(l) Tom and Michelle Grimm/Intl. Stock Photo; **14:**(r) Peter Menzel; **15:**(tl) Catherine Ursillo/Photo Researchers; **15:**(tr) Alan Riding/Monkmeyer Press Photo; **15:**(bl) Len Speier; **15:**(br) Serraillier/Photo Researchers; **16 & 22:**(l) Owen Franken; **17 & 22:**(r) Beryl Goldberg; **21:** Cary Wolinsky/Stock Boston; **23:**(t) Len Speier; **23:**(b) Peter Menzel; **26**(r), **31**(r), **42:**(r); Bill Wrenn/Intl. Stock Photo; **26:**(l) & **42:**(l): Chip and Rosa Peterson; **29:**(t) Carl Frank/Photo Researchers; **29:**(b) Ken Lax; **31:**(l) Mark Mittelman/Taurus Photo; **32:**Terry McKoy/Taurus Photo; **33:** Chip and Rosa Peterson; **36:** Beryl Goldberg; **37:** Stan Pantovic/Photo Researchers; **40:**(t) Beryl Goldberg; **40:**(b) Chip and Rosa Peterson; **43:** Beryl Goldberg; **46:** Bob Capece/MGH; **49:** Porterfield/Chickering/Photo Researchers; **50:**(t) Peter Menzel; **50:**(b) Peter Menzel; **51:**(bl) Bob Capece; **51:**(br) Bob Capece; **56:** Beryl Goldberg; **58:**Peter Menzel; **61:**(l) Lisa Limer; **61:**(r) Chip and Rosa Peterson; **62:** Beryl Goldberg; **63:**(l) Dick Walker/Taurus Photos; **63:**(r) Ulf Sjostedt/FPG; **72:** Chip and Rosa Peterson; **75:**(l) Roger Clark/Photo Researchers; **75:**(r) Lisa Limer; **90:**(l) Bernard Pierre Wolff/Photo Researchers; **76:** Chip and Rosa Peterson; **90:**(m) Russ Kinne/Photo Researchers; **90:**(tr) Peter Menzel; **90:**(r) Cary Wolinski/Stock Boston; **91:** Chip and Rosa Peterson; **94:**(l) Bendick Associates/Monkmeyer Press Photos; **94:**(r) Lisa Limer; **95:** Nancy J. Pierce/Photo Researchers; **96:**(t) Peter Menzel; **96:**(b) F. Lisa Beebe/DPI; **99:** Peter Menzel; **103:**(t & b) Beryl Goldberg; **103:**(m) Beryl Goldberg; **104:**(l) Enrique Shore/Woodfin Camp & Assoc.; **104:**(r) Owen Franken/Stock Boston; **105:** White/Pite/Intl. Stock Photo; **107:**(t) Beryl Goldberg; **107:**(b) William A. Graham/Photo Researchers; **113:**(l) Chris Brolon/Stock Boston; **113:**(r) Kal Muller/Woodfin Camp and Assoc.; **114:**(m) Margaret Mc Carthy/Peter Arnold Inc.; **114–115:**(b) Robert Frerck/Woodfin Camp; **115:**(tl) Chris Brown/Stock Boston; **115:**(tr) Peter Menzel; **117:**(tl) Giles Peress/Magnum Photos; **117:**(tr) Giansanti/Sygma; **117:**(m) Chip and Rosa Peterson; **127:**(t) Robert Frerck/Woodfin Camp; **127:**(m) Stephanie Maze/Woodfin Camp; **128:**Scott Thode/Intl. Stock Photo; **140:**(tl) Anita Douthat/Photo Researchers; **140:**(tm) Lenore Weber/Taurus Photos; **140:**(tr) Peter Menzel; **140:**(bl) Beryl Goldberg; **140:**(bl) Beryl

Preface

¡Bienvenidos! *Welcome!* You have selected one of the most interesting studies available anywhere in any school—a foreign language.

This will be a most unique study because it focuses not only on written language but also on spoken language. This is a communications course; therefore, *all* means of communication are a part of your study of Spanish. Even gestures and body language play a significant role.

The "mystery" of things foreign is about to be revealed to you. Foreign sounds, foreign symbols, foreign customs, and foreign life-styles are all a part of your foreign language experience. This experience can become one of the most exciting, appealing, and long-lasting of your life.

Spanish is the second language of the United States. It has become a part of our daily lives through place names **(Florida, Santa Fé)**, food names **(taco, tortilla)**, common expressions **(pronto, adiós)**, peoples' names **(Martínez, López)**, names of songs **(«Vaya con Dios», «Que será, será»)**, names of dances **(tango, rumba)**, and even names of animals **(armadillo)**, cars **(Córdoba)**, and clothing **(sombrero)**.

In addition to the many Spanish speakers who live within the United States, there are about 250,000,000 Spanish speakers throughout the world.

You have selected a language that reflects international importance and a varied cultural heritage which has united the old and the new worlds. It is a language that, in its vocabulary, reminds us of the many civilizations it has survived and which have enriched the idiom.

Many other reasons can be given for encouraging you to learn a foreign language, but the most important reason of all is that a foreign language can open doors for you that you didn't know existed. One of these could be a career using the language itself. The study of a foreign language may help you to enjoy life even more. You will gain a greater understanding of another culture; you will be able to communicate with the people coming from this culture; and you will be able to read the many newspapers, magazines, and books written in the language. Many new facets will be added to your life which would not have been available to you before.

¡Saludos! *Greetings!* Welcome to a new study, a new language, a new life-style!

Carry with you our hopes for your complete success in this endeavor and experience which could change your outlook on life from this moment on.

about the authors

Conrad J. Schmitt

Mr. Schmitt was Editor-in-Chief of Foreign language, ESL, and bilingual publishing with McGraw-Hill Book Company. Prior to joining McGraw-Hill, Mr. Schmitt taught languages at all levels of instruction, from elementary school through college. He has taught Spanish at Montclair State College, Upper Montclair, New Jersey; French at Upsala College, East Orange, New Jersey; and Methods of Teaching a Foreign Language at the Graduate School of Education, Rutgers University, New Brunswick, New Jersey. He also served as Coordinator or Foreign Languages for the Hackensack, New Jersey, Public Schools. Mr. Schmitt is the author of *Schaum's Outline of Spanish Grammar, Schaum's Outline of Spanish Vocabulary, Español: Comencemos, Español: Sigamos,* and the *Let's Speak Spanish* and *A Cada Paso* series. He is also coauthor of *Español: A Descubrirlo, Español: A Sentirlo, La Fuente Hispana, Le Français: Commençons, Le Français: Ccntinuons, McGraw-Hill French Rencontres* and *McGraw-Hill French Connaissances,* and *Schaum's Outline of Italian Grammar.* Mr. Schmitt has traveled extensively throughout Spain, México, the Caribbean, Central America, and South America.

Protase E. Woodford

Mr. Woodford is Director of the Foreign Language Department, Test Development, Schools and Higher Education Programs Division with Educational Testing Service, Princeton, New Jersey. He has taught Spanish at all academic levels. He has also served as department chairperson in New Jersey high schools and has worked extensively with Latin American and Asian ministries of education in the areas of tests and measurements and has served as a consultant to numerous state and federal government agencies. He has taught Spanish at Newark State College, Union, New Jersey, and methods at the University of Texas. Mr. Woodford has traveled extensively throughout Spain, the Caribbean, Central America, South America, Europe, and Asia. He is coauthor of *Español: A Descubrirlo, Español: A Sentirlo, Español: Lengua y Letras, La Fuente Hispana,* and *Bridges* to *English.* He is also the author of *Spanish Language, Hispanic Culture.*

Randall G. Marshall

Mr. Marshall is a Consultant in Foreign Language Publishing with the Webster Division, McGraw-Hill Book Company and is an experienced foreign language instructor at all academic levels. He was formerly Consultant in Modern Foreign Languages with the New Jersey State Department of Education. Mr. Marshall has served as methods and demonstration teacher at Iona College, New Rochelle, New York; at Rutgers University; and at the University of Colorado. He has traveled extensively throughout Spain, Mexico, the Caribbean, and South America. He is coauthor of *Español: A Descubrirlo, Español: A Sentirlo,* and *La Fuente Hispana.*

Contents

Lección 1 ¿Quién es?

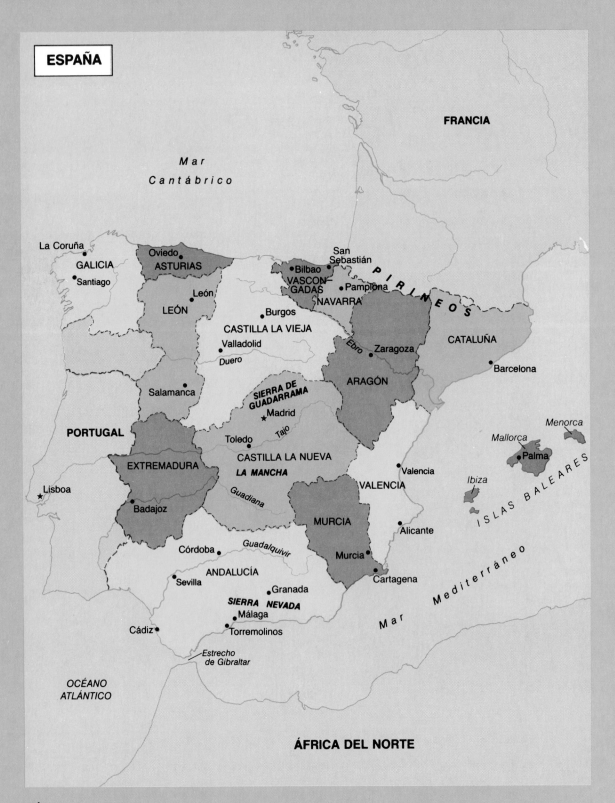

ESPAÑA

FRANCIA

Mar Cantábrico

La Coruña
GALICIA
• Santiago

Oviedo •
ASTURIAS

San Sebastián
• Bilbao
VASCON-
GADAS
NAVARRA
• Pamplona

P I R I N E O S

León •
LEÓN

• Burgos

CASTILLA LA VIEJA

• Valladolid

Duero

Ebro
Zaragoza •
CATALUÑA

ARAGÓN

• Barcelona

Salamanca •

SIERRA DE
GUADARRAMA

★ Madrid

Tajo

PORTUGAL

Toledo •

CASTILLA LA NUEVA

Menorca
Mallorca
• Palma

EXTREMADURA

LA MANCHA

Lisboa ★

VALENCIA

• Valencia

Ibiza

I S L A S   B A L E A R E S

• Badajoz

Guadiana

MURCIA

• Alicante

Córdoba •

Guadalquivir

Murcia •

• Cartagena

ANDALUCÍA

Sevilla •

• Granada

SIERRA NEVADA

Cádiz •

• Málaga

M a r   M e d i t e r r á n e o

• Torremolinos

Estrecho
de Gibraltar

OCÉANO
ATLÁNTICO

ÁFRICA DEL NORTE

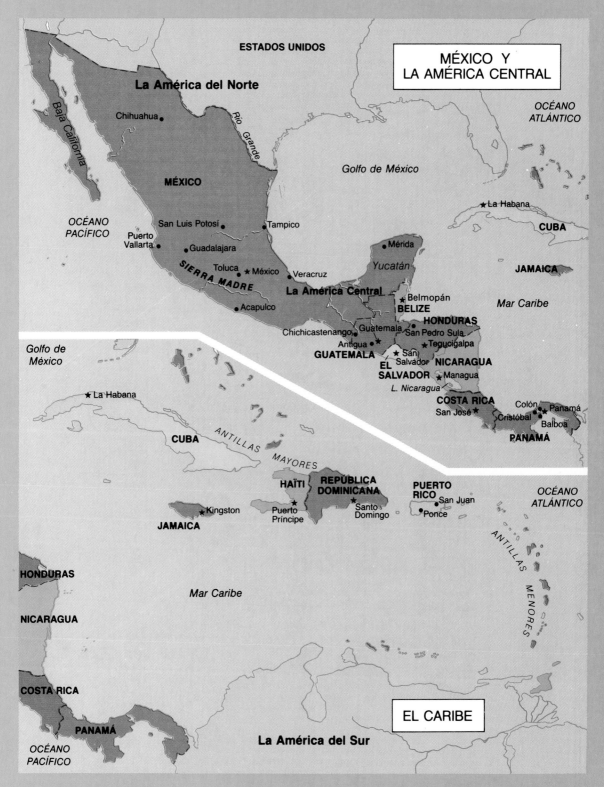

ESTADOS UNIDOS

La América del Norte

MÉXICO Y
LA AMÉRICA CENTRAL

OCÉANO
ATLÁNTICO

Baja California

Chihuahua •

Río Grande

Golfo de México

MÉXICO

★ La Habana

OCÉANO
PACÍFICO

San Luis Potosí •

• Tampico

CUBA

Puerto
Vallarta •

• Guadalajara

• Mérida

JAMAICA

SIERRA MADRE

Toluca • ★ México

Yucatán

Mar Caribe

• Veracruz

La América Central

• Belmopán

• Acapulco

BELIZE

Chichicastenango •

• Guatemala

HONDURAS

San Pedro Sula •

Antigua •

Tegucigalpa •

GUATEMALA

★ San
Salvador

NICARAGUA

EL
SALVADOR

★ Managua

L. Nicaragua

COSTA RICA

Colón •

• Panamá

San José ★

Cristóbal •

• Balboa

PANAMÁ

Golfo de
México

★ La Habana

ANTILLAS

CUBA

MAYORES

HAÏTI

REPÚBLICA
DOMINICANA

PUERTO
RICO

OCÉANO
ATLÁNTICO

• San Juan

★ Kingston

Puerto
Príncipe

Santo
Domingo

• Ponce

JAMAICA

ANTILLAS

HONDURAS

Mar Caribe

MENORES

NICARAGUA

COSTA RICA

PANAMÁ

EL CARIBE

OCÉANO
PACÍFICO

La América del Sur

Mar Caribe

La América
Central

Barranquilla
Maracaibo
★ Caracas

VENEZUELA

Orinoco

Medellín

Magdalena

Cali
★ Bogotá

COLOMBIA

GUAYANAS

CORDILLERA

★ Quito

ECUADOR

Guayaquil

Iquitos

DE

Amazonas

Manaus

Amazonas

Belém

Fortaleza

PERÚ

Marañón

Ucayali

LOS

Madeira

Tapajós

SELVAS

Xingú

Recife

Callao ★ Lima

ANDES

Cuzco

BRASIL

São Francisco

Salvador

L. Titicaca

★ La Paz

BOLIVIA

Sucre

**MATO
GROSSO**

★ Brasilia

**OCÉANO
PACÍFICO**

Paraguay

GRAN

CHACO

PARAGUAY

Paraná

São Paulo

Río de Janeiro

Asunción

DE

Tucumán

LOS

Uruguay

Pôrto Alegre

**OCÉANO
ATLÁNTICO**

Córdoba

ANDES

Valparaíso
Viña del Mar
Santiago ★

Rosario

P
A
M
P
A
S

URUGUAY

★ Montevideo

Buenos
Aires

Río de la Plata

CHILE

CORDILLERA

ARGENTINA

Valdivia

San Carlos
Puerto Montt de Bariloche

Islas Malvinas

Tierra
del Fuego

LA AMÉRICA DEL SUR

McGRAW-HILL

Spanish

saludos

first part

Conrad J. Schmitt
Protase E. Woodford
Randall G. Marshall

Lección PRELIMINAR A Los saludos

Actividad 1

Say *hi* in Spanish to your friends seated near you. Use their Spanish names when you address them.

> Hola, Sara.

Pablo Emilio Calderón

> Hola, Pablo.

Sara María Morales

Assign each student in class a Spanish name. Have each student greet his/her neighbor using **hola** and the student's Spanish name.

Hola, Carlos.   (Tape Activity 1)
Hola, Anita.
¿Qué tal?
Muy bien. ¿Y tú?
Así, así.

Have each student ask his/her neighbor ¿**Qué tal?** As neighbor responds, have him/her point to original student when asking ¿**Y tú?**

Actividad 2

These exercises can be done with students working in pairs or with the entire class.

Say *hi* in Spanish to a friend in your class. Use his/her Spanish name.

Actividad 3

Ask several friends in your class how things are going. Have each friend answer you.

Actividad 4

Get together with a friend and make up a conversation. Say *hi* to each other, ask how things are going, and respond to one another on whether things are going well or so-so. Some students may present their conversation to the class.

𝒩ota

In Spanish-speaking countries, people tend to be more formal than in the United States. Among friends, the informal greeting **Hola** is used frequently. However, when young people greet adults, they would use **Buenos días** in the morning, **Buenas tardes** in the afternoon, and **Buenas noches** in the evening. They would also use the person's title—**señor, señora,** or **señorita.** The title is used with or without the person's family name.

Actividad 5

Say *hello* to each of your teachers using his/her name and the appropriate greeting for the time of day—morning, afternoon, or evening.

Actividad 6

Which greeting is being used in each photograph: **Hola** or **Buenos días**?

3

PRELIMINAR **B** Las despedidas

(Tape Activity 1)

Hola, Paco.
Hola, Tadeo. ¿Qué tal, hombre?
Muy bien, ¿y tú?
Muy bien.
Adiós, amigo.
Adiós. Hasta luego.

Nota

In English we use several expressions when we take leave of a person. We may use the more formal *Good-bye* or we may say things such as *So long!* or *I'll be seeing you*. These same types of options exist in Spanish.

Formal (Tape Activity 2)
¡Adiós!
Informal
¡Hasta luego!
¡Hasta la vista!
¡Hasta pronto!

Actividad 1

Say *hi* in Spanish to several of your friends.

4

Actividad 2

Ask a friend in class how things are going. Have him/her answer you.

Actividad 3

Say *good-bye* in Spanish to a friend.

Actividad 4

Say *so long* to a friend.

More-able students can present a complete conversation to the class—from greeting to farewell.

Actividad 5

Look at the photograph. Notice the hand gesture. Do you think the people are saying **Buenos días** or **Adiós?**

Note that as they say **Adiós,** the movement of the hand is toward them. Why? As Spanish speakers say *good-bye,* their gesture indicates that they want their friends to return.

Actividad 6

Practice this new hand gesture as you say *good-bye* to a friend.

C LOS NÚMEROS

PRELIMINAR C

(Tape Activity 1)

1	**uno**	11	**once**	21	**veintiuno**
2	**dos**	12	**doce**	22	**veintidós**
3	**tres**	13	**trece**	23	**veintitrés**
4	**cuatro**	14	**catorce**	24	**veinticuatro**
5	**cinco**	15	**quince**	25	**veinticinco**
6	**seis**	16	**dieciséis**	26	**veintiséis**
7	**siete**	17	**diecisiete**	27	**veintisiete**
8	**ocho**	18	**dieciocho**	28	**veintiocho**
9	**nueve**	19	**diecinueve**	29	**veintinueve**
10	**diez**	20	**veinte**	30	**treinta**

31 **treinta y uno**   32 **treinta y dos**

40	**cuarenta**	80	**ochenta**
50	**cincuenta**	90	**noventa**
60	**sesenta**	100	**ciento**
70	**setenta**		

102 **ciento dos**   103 **ciento tres**

Write random numbers on the board and call on students to give the number in Spanish.

Nota

Note that the numbers 16 through 29 are usually written in Spanish as one word. Beginning with **treinta,** they are written as two words and separated by **y.**

Actividad 1   ¿Cuál es el número en español?

Say each number in Spanish; then write each number.

15	76	82
21	37	12
115	73	66

Actividad 2

Here's a batch of test papers. Say what grades the students received in Spanish.

𝒩ota ____

When giving a telephone number, Spanish speakers will frequently break the number as follows.

734-25-60   **siete, tres, cuatro; veinticinco, sesenta**

Actividad 3

Give your telephone number in Spanish.

Actividad 4

Here are some numbers from the **Guía telefónica de San Juan.** Give the numbers in dark type.

DE LALAMA, P. –Pelicano, 35	....	**471 4963**
LAMA, A. –Pº Gral M Campos, 13	.....	**446 9875**
DE LAMA, F.		
Nicaragua (Alfonso XIII), 23	....	**741 5688**
RODRIGUEZ DE LAMA, F.		
Nicaragua (Alfonso XIII), 25	....	**741 5689**
RODRIGUEZ DE LAMA, F. –Mercería		
Cde Peñalver, 43	....	**402 3379**
RODRIGUEZ LAMA, R.		
Av. M. de Lemos, 143	....	**739 1646**
RODRIGUEZ DE LAMA, S. –V. Vega, 10	..	**222 7060**
LAMA, V. –Pozohalcón, 15	......	**785 9249**
LAMA, V. –Pensión E. San Miguel, 17	..	**248 5158**
LAMAS, F. –Arzobispo Morcillo, s/n	....	**733 6892**
LAMAS, F. –Arzobispo Morcillo, 1	....	**215 6101**
LAMAS, F. –Los Yebenes, Bl. 4	......	**717 1234**
LAMAS, M. –A. Nervo, 3	....	**251 3843**
LAMEIRO, J.		
Col. Cdad. Angeles, Bl. 247	....	**217 9123**
RODRIGUEZ LAMEIRO, J. –Lavandería		
Donados, 1	....	**241 1115**
RODRIGUEZ LAMELA, C. –Restaurante		
Ctra. Sto. Cristo, s/n	....	**736 0946**
RODRIGUEZ LAMELAS, N.		
Col. Cdad. Angeles, Bl. 49	....	**217 0696**

200	**doscientos**	900	**novecientos**	The higher numbers can be reinforced throughout the year.
300	**trescientos**	1000	**mil**	
400	**cuatrocientos**	1985	**mil novecientos ochenta y cinco**	
500	**quinientos**	1492	**mil cuatrocientos noventa y dos**	
600	**seiscientos**	1808	**mil ochocientos ocho**	
700	**setecientos**	1776	**mil setecientos setenta y seis**	
800	**ochocientos**			

Actividad 5

Give the following years in Spanish:
- the year you were born.
- the year you started school.
- the year you will graduate from high school.

Actividad 6

Here are some bills in pesos. How much does the person have to pay?

Lección **D** **LA CORTESÍA**

pRELiMiNAR

Perdón, señor. Una limonada, por favor.
¿Una limonada? Sí, señorita.
¿Cuánto es, por favor?
Diez pesos.
Gracias, señorita.
De nada.

(Tape Activity 1)

*Nota*____

Expressions of politeness exist in all languages. In English some frequently used expressions are *please, thank you,* and *you're welcome.*

The Spanish equivalents for these expressions are:

por favor
gracias
de nada
no hay de qué

Actividad 1

Have a friend in your class hand you a piece of paper. Thank your friend and have him/her answer you.

Actividad 2

Order the following Mexican foods. Be sure to be polite and add **por favor** to your request.

un taco

una enchilada

una tostada

un burrito

Actividad 3 El menú en un restaurante

¿Cuánto es una enchilada?
¿Cuánto es una tostada?
¿Cuánto es un taco?
¿Cuánto es un burrito?

Menú

enchilada..... 48 pesos
tostada ...... 25 pesos
taco.......... 59 pesos
burrito....... 22 pesos

Actividad 4

What do you say in Spanish when:

- you ask someone for something?
- someone gives you something?
- someone says *thank you*?

Lección PRELIMINAR E LAS fechas

(Tape Activity 1)

lunes martes miércoles jueves viernes sábado domingo

enero febrero marzo abril mayo

junio julio agosto septiembre octubre noviembre diciembre

el 25 de septiembre de 1984

Hoy es martes, el veinticinco de septiembre de mil novecientos ochenta y cuatro.

el 10 de octubre de 1985

Hoy es jueves, el diez de octubre de mil novecientos ochenta y cinco.

(Tape Activity 2)

el 1 de mayo de 1986

Hoy es jueves, el primero de mayo de mil novecientos ochenta y seis.

Nota

Note that the numbers that we have already learned are called *cardinal numbers*. The cardinal numbers are used to give the day of the month. The only exception is the first of the month when the ordinal number is used.

el primero de enero
el primero de julio

Actividad 1   ¿Cuál es la fecha de hoy?

Give today's date in Spanish. Include the day, month, and year.

Actividad 2

See how much Spanish you can already read. Give the dates in Spanish of these famous events.

1. el descubrimiento de América   *(October 12, 1492)*
2. la independencia de México   *(September 16, 1821)*
3. la independencia de los Estados Unidos   *(July 4, 1776)*

Nota

In English we write the date on the top of a letter as follows: month, day, year.

> *September 25, 1986*

In Spanish the date would be written in this way: day, month, year.

> *el 25 de septiembre de 1986*

Very often in both Spanish and English only numbers are used to convey the date. September 25, 1986 would be 9/25/86. Note that in Spanish, however, the day comes before the month. **El 25 de septiembre de 1986** would be 25/9/86.

Actividad 3

Give the following dates in Spanish, according to the Spanish system.

1. *25/6/85*
2. *6/8/84*
3. *8/6/86*
4. *12/11/87*
5. *2/3/88*

Actividad 4

The seventh of July is the day of San Fermín. On this day in the town of Pamplona in northern Spain, there is much celebration. Bulls run through the streets to the bullring. During the festivities there is a song that people sing. Sing along with the cassette.

SAN FERMÍN

Uno de enero, dos de febrero,
Tres de marzo, cuatro de abril,
Cinco de mayo, seis de junio,
Siete de julio, ¡San Fermín!

Lección PRELIMINAR F LA HORA

(Tape Activity 1)

Es la una.

Son las dos.

Son las cinco.

Es la una
y diez.

Son las siete
y cinco.

Son las seis
menos diez.

Son las once
y cuarto.

Son las nueve
y media.

Son las diez
menos cuarto.

Actividad 1 ¿Qué hora es?

Give the time in Spanish according to each clock illustrated below.

1.

2.

3.

4.

5.

6.

Son las seis de la mañana. **Son las dos de la tarde.** **Son las diez de la noche.**

Actividad 2

Los Ángeles   Chicago   Nueva York   San Juan   Madrid

Son las seis de la mañana en Los Ángeles.

- ¿Qué hora es en Chicago?
- ¿Qué hora es en Nueva York?
- ¿Qué hora es en San Juan?
- ¿Qué hora es en Madrid?

 *Nota*

To express in Spanish at what time something is happening, the word **a** is used.

> **A la una**
> **A las dos**
> **A las tres y cuarto**
> **A las cinco y media**

Actividad 3

Read this busy school schedule of classes.

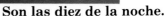

Hora	Asignatura	Profesor(a)
8:10 – 9:00	álgebra	
9:00 – 9:50	historia	
9:50 – 10:40	español	
10:40 – 11:30	biología	
11:30 – 12:20		
12:20 – 1:10	educación física	
1:10 – 2:00	música	
2:00 – 2:50	inglés	

Horario de Clases

- ¿A qué hora es la clase de álgebra?
- ¿A qué hora es la clase de historia?
- ¿A qué hora es la clase de español?
- ¿A qué hora es la clase de biología?
- ¿A qué hora es la clase de educación física?
- ¿A qué hora es la clase de música?
- ¿A qué hora es la clase de inglés?

G El tiempo

PRELiMiNAR

En el verano:
Hace mucho calor.
Hace buen tiempo.
Hace sol.

(Tape Activity 1)

En el invierno:
Hace frío.
Hace mal tiempo.
Hace viento.
Nieva.

En la primavera:
Hace buen tiempo.
No hace mucho calor.
No hace mucho frío.
Llueve a veces.

En el otoño:
Hace fresco.
Hay nubes.

Actividad 1

¿Qué tiempo hace hoy?

Actividad 2

Hoy es el veintiocho de diciembre.

¿Qué tiempo hace en Nueva York?

¿Qué tiempo hace en Buenos Aires, Argentina?

Actividad 3

Hoy es el cinco de julio.

¿Qué tiempo hace en Nueva York?

¿Qué tiempo hace en Buenos Aires?

Actividad 4

- ¿Qué tiempo hace en el verano?
- ¿Qué tiempo hace en el invierno?
- ¿Qué tiempo hace en la primavera?
- ¿Qué tiempo hace en el otoño?

- ¿Cuándo hace calor, en el verano o en el invierno?
- ¿Cuándo hace frío, en el invierno o en el verano?

Actividad 5

See how much you can already read in Spanish.

Cuando es el invierno en Nueva York, no es el invierno en Buenos Aires, Argentina. Es el verano en Buenos Aires. Cuando es el invierno en Buenos Aires, es el verano en Nueva York. Cuando hace frío en Nueva York, hace calor en Buenos Aires. Y cuando hace calor en Nueva York, hace frío en Buenos Aires.

Do you know why this is true?

1 ¿QUIÉN ES?

In this lesson only nouns and adjectives ending in –o and –a are presented to assist students in grasping the first important concept of agreement: –o, –o; –a, –a.

Vocabulario

(Tape Activity 1)

una muchacha   **una alumna**   **un colegio**

Have students repeat words.

Have students repeat and read.

(Tape Activity 2)

Es Lupita.
Lupita es una muchacha **mexicana.**
Ella es alumna.
Es alumna **en** un colegio mexicano.

¿Cómo es?

baja   **alta**   **morena**   **rubia**   **tonta**   **lista**

(Tape Activity 3)

Expansion: Students can make up original sentences using these adjectives.

Ejercicio 1   Una muchacha mexicana

Contesten. *(Answer.)*   (Tape Activity 4)

1. ¿Es mexicana Lupita?
2. ¿Es ella alumna?
3. ¿Es ella alumna en un colegio mexicano?

4. ¿Es baja o alta?
5. ¿Es morena o rubia?
6. ¿Es ella una muchacha lista o tonta?

Ejercicio 2   ¿Quién es mexicana?

Contesten con el nombre de la persona. *(Answer with the person's name.)*

Emphasize ¿**quién?** as you ask these questions.

1. ¿Quién es mexicana?
2. ¿Quién es alumna en un colegio mexicano?   (Workbook, Exercise A)

3. ¿Quién es alta?
4. ¿Quién es rubia?
5. ¿Quién es lista?

2) Students can read and answer.
3) Students can write answers at home and go over them the next day in class.

16

Options for exercises:
1) Go over exercises orally with books closed.

un muchacho

un alumno

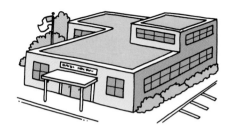

una escuela   (Tape Activity 5)

Es Roberto.
Roberto **no** es mexicano.
Es un muchacho **americano.**
Él es alumno **también.**
Es alumno en una escuela **secundaria.**

(Tape Activity 6)

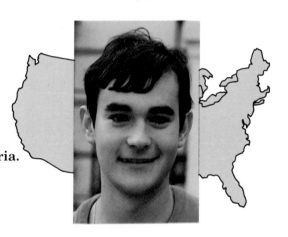

¿Cómo es?

moreno

rubio

bajo   **alto**
(Tape Activities 7, 8)

tonto   **listo**

Ejercicio 3   Un muchacho americano
Contesten. *(Answer.)*

(Tape Activity 9)

1. ¿Es Roberto un muchacho americano?
2. ¿Es él alumno?
3. ¿Es alumno en una escuela secundaria?

4. ¿Es Roberto alto o bajo?
5. ¿Es moreno o rubio?
6. ¿Es él listo o tonto?

A complete vocabulary list is provided in the Teacher's Resource Kit.

Ejercicio 4   ¿Cómo es Roberto?
Contesten. *(Answer.)*

1. ¿Cómo es Roberto? ¿Es alto o bajo?
2. ¿Cómo es Roberto? ¿Es moreno o rubio?
3. ¿Cómo es Roberto? ¿Es listo o tonto?

Expansion: Students can make up questions using **¿cómo?** and the name of a student in class.
Another student can answer
the question.

(Workbook, Exercises B–G)
(Quiz 1)   *Observation:* Ask students what sound they hear when they talk about a boy in Spanish. What sound do they hear when they talk about a girl?

Estructura

Los artículos definidos—*el, la*

The name of a person, place, or thing is called a *noun*. Every Spanish noun has a gender, either masculine or feminine. Almost all nouns that end in **-o** are masculine and almost all nouns that end in **-a** are feminine. A definite article (*the* in English) very often comes before a noun. Study the following examples:

masculine	*feminine*
el muchacho	**la muchacha**
el alumno	**la alumna**
el colegio	**la escuela**

Note that the definite article **el** accompanies a masculine noun. The definite article **la** accompanies a feminine noun.

Ejercicio 1 El muchacho americano y la muchacha mexicana
Completen con *el* o *la*. *(Complete with **el** or **la**.)*

Options:
1) Go over exercise in class.
2) Have students write exercise at home.
3) Correct exercise in class.

1. _____ muchacho es americano.
2. _____ muchacho no es mexicano.
3. _____ muchacho americano es Roberto.
4. _____ muchacha mexicana es Lupita.
5. _____ muchacho es moreno y _____ muchacha es rubia.
6. _____ muchacho es alumno en _____ escuela Thomas Jefferson.
7. _____ muchacha es alumna en _____ Colegio Hidalgo.
8. _____ alumno es listo.
9. _____ alumna también es muy lista.

(Workbook, Exercise H)
(Quiz 2)

Expansion:
One student reads entire exercise. A very-able student retells all the information in the story in his/her own words.

Los artículos indefinidos—*un, una*

The word *a (an)* is called an *indefinite article* in English. In Spanish the indefinite article **una** accompanies a feminine noun and the indefinite article **un** accompanies a masculine noun. Observe the following:

Roberto es un muchacho.	*Robert is a boy.*
Lupita es una muchacha.	*Lupita is a girl.*

Ejercicio 2 Un muchacho y una muchacha
Completen con *un* o *una*. *(Complete with **un** or **una**.)*

1. Roberto es _____ muchacho.
2. Lupita es _____ muchacha.
3. Roberto es _____ muchacho americano y
   Lupita es _____ muchacha mexicana.
4. Roberto es _____ alumno muy listo.

5. Él es alumno en _____ escuela secundaria americana.
6. Lupita es _____ alumna muy lista también.
7. Ella es alumna en _____ colegio mexicano.

(Workbook, Exercise I)
(Quiz 3)

La concordancia de los adjetivos—formas singulares

A word that describes a noun is called an *adjective* in English. Study the following sentences. The underlined words are adjectives.

La muchacha es rubia. **El muchacho es rubio.**
La alumna es lista. **El alumno es listo.**

A Spanish adjective must agree with the noun it describes, or modifies.

Note that in Spanish many masculine adjectives end in **-o** and many feminine adjectives end in **-a**.

Ejercicio 3 Lupita y Roberto
Contesten. *(Answer.)*

It is suggested that you first do Exercise 3 orally with books closed.

1. ¿Es Lupita mexicana o americana?
2. Y Roberto, ¿es él americano o mexicano?
3. ¿Es Lupita baja o alta?
4. Y Roberto, ¿es alto o bajo?
5. ¿Es Lupita morena o rubia?
6. ¿Es Roberto moreno o rubio?
7. ¿Es Lupita alumna en un colegio mexicano o en una escuela secundaria americana?
8. ¿Es Roberto alumno en un colegio mexicano o en una escuela secundaria americana?

Ejercicio 4 ¿Cómo es Lupita? ¿Cómo es Roberto?
Completen. *(Complete.)*

1. Lupita es _____. **mexicano**
2. Roberto es _____. **americano**
3. Lupita es _____. **listo**
4. Ella es _____. **rubio**
5. Roberto también es _____. **listo**
6. Él no es _____. Él es _____. **rubio, moreno**
7. Lupita es _____ y Roberto también es _____. **alto, alto**

(Workbook, Exercises J–L)
(Tape Activities 10–11)
(Quiz 4)

Nota _____

Note that in Spanish we use an upside-down question mark at the beginning of a sentence to introduce a question in addition to the question mark at the end of the sentence.

¿Es él alto o bajo? *Is he tall or short?*
¿Quién es mexicano? *Who is Mexican?*

19

Pronunciación

La vocal a

When you speak Spanish, it is extremely important to pronounce the vowels very carefully. The vowel sounds in Spanish are very concise, short, and clear. Unlike English vowels, Spanish vowels do not change sounds. The *a* in English has several different pronunciations, but the **a** in Spanish has only one sound.

The vowel **a** is pronounced like *ah* in English. It is similar to the *a* in *father*, but it is somewhat clearer and more concise.

a   (Tape Activity 12)

A̲na̲
a̲ma̲
a̲la̲
a̲sa
a̲sí

Trabalenguas y dictado

La muchacha es mexicana.
Ella es alumna.
La alumna es alta y rubia.

(Tape Activity 13)

Expresiones útiles

Very often when English speakers receive a piece of news that they would prefer not to hear, they sometimes say *Oh, gosh!* Spanish speakers will frequently say **¡Ay de mí!**

A commonly used English expression is *What luck!* In English the tone of the voice often indicates whether we mean good luck or bad luck. The same is true of the Spanish expression **¡Qué suerte!**

el novio   **la novia**

conversación

¿Quién es ella?

Manuel	¿Quién es la muchacha?
Julio	¿Quién? ¿La rubia?
Manuel	No, no. La rubia, no. La morena.
Julio	La morena. Es Isabel. ¡Pero, cuidado! Es la novia de Pablo.
Manuel	¡Ay de mí! ¡Qué suerte!

¿Quién es él?

Juana	¿Quién es el muchacho?
Conchita	¿Quién? ¿El moreno alto?
Juana	No, él no. El rubio.
Conchita	¡Ay! ¡El rubio!
Juana	Sí, él. ¿Quién es?
Conchita	Es Carlos. ¡Pero, cuidado! Es el novio de Lupita.
Juana	¡Ay de mí! ¡Qué suerte!

Lectura cultural

Options for **Lectura:**
1) Have class repeat each sentence after you.
2) After each paragraph, ask questions.
3) Call on individuals to read.
4) Assign **Lectura** and Exercise to be done at home.

Lupita y Roberto

Lupita es una muchacha mexicana. Ella es alumna en el Colegio Hidalgo. Lupita es una muchacha muy lista. Ella es rubia y alta.

Roberto es un muchacho americano. Él es moreno. Él es muy alto. Él es alumno en una escuela secundaria americana.

Ejercicio   Escojan la respuesta apropiada. *(Choose the correct answer.)*

1. Lupita es _____.
   a. una muchacha
   b. un muchacho
   c. americana

2. Ella es _____.
   a. rubia
   b. morena
   c. americana

3. Ella es alumna en _____.
   a. una escuela secundaria americana
   b. un colegio mexicano
   c. una escuela americana en México

4. Roberto es _____.
   a. mexicano
   b. bajo
   c. americano

5. Él es _____.
   a. rubio
   b. moreno
   c. bajo

6. Él es _____.
   a. bajo
   b. alumno
   c. rubio

Expansion:
These multiple choice exercises can elicit a great deal of free conversation.
Example:
1) ¡Ay de mí! Lupita no es un muchacho.
Roberto es un muchacho.
Lupita es una muchacha.
Lupita no es americana.
Roberto es americano.
Lupita es mexicana.

Actividades

(optional)

1 Here is Gloria Salinas. She is a Mexican student from Mexico City. Say all you can about her in Spanish.

2 Here is Peter Clark. He is an American student from Miami. Say all you can about him in Spanish.

3 Look again at the photograph of Gloria. Based on everything you know about her, complete this conversation.

¿Quién es la muchacha?

_____

¿Es ella americana?

No, _____. Es _____.

¿Cómo es Gloria?

Ella _____.

¿Es ella alumna?

Sí, _____.

Options: Students can look at the photographs and make up as many questions about each photograph as they can. Other members of the class can answer their questions.

These activities can be done orally, can be written, or both.

A puzzle appears in the Workbook.

Revista

Es Enrique Torres.
Él es de Santo Domingo.
Es dominicano.
Es bastante guapo, ¿no?

Es Isabel Casas. Isabel es
cubana. Ella es alumna en
una escuela secundaria de
Miami. Ella es bonita, ¿no?

Es Dwight Sullivan. Dwight es americano. Él es alumno en una escuela secundaria de Atlanta. Dwight es un alumno muy listo, ¿no?

Es Maripaz García-Bravo. Maripaz es de España. Ella es alumna en un colegio de Madrid. ¿Es una alumna lista Maripaz?

Harriet Williams es una muchacha americana. Ella es alumna en una escuela secundaria de Nueva York. Ella es una alumna muy lista, ¿no?

2 ¿Cómo eres tú?

Most students know the meaning of **amigo**. Ask them if they know any other Spanish words.

Bogotá

una amiga

un amigo

vocabulario

(Tape Activity 1)

(Tape Activity 2)

¡Hola, todos!
Yo soy Marisa Jiménez.
Soy **colombiana.**
Yo soy **de** Bogotá.
Yo soy una amiga de Elena Ochoa.

Expansion: Students can use **amigo(a)** in original sentences using the names of classmates.
_____ **es el(la) amigo(a) de** _____.

guapa   **fea**   **divertida**   **aburrida**

Nota
(Tape Activity 3)

As you continue your study of Spanish, you will be amazed at how many Spanish words you already know or can guess the meanings of. Do you have any trouble understanding these words?

Have students pronounce carefully. They will probably anglicize the pronunciation of cognates.

fantástico   **inteligente**
serio   **interesante**
sincero   **popular**

Words such as those above that look alike and mean the same thing in both languages are called *cognates*. Be very careful, however. Although they look alike and have the same meaning, they are pronounced very differently in each language.

There are also many words that really do not have a precise meaning when one attempts to translate them from one language into another. Such a word is **simpático(a).** This word has no translatable definition in English. It means *nice, pleasant, warm, friendly* all wrapped up in one word.   (Tape Activity 4)
(Quiz 1)

Expansion: Explain to students that many words do not have a precise meaning in English either. What does "nice" mean in the following sentences? "It's a nice day. He/she is nice. It's a nice house. That's a nice job. That's a nice idea."

26

Ejercicio 1 Marisa Jiménez
Contesten. *(Answer.)*

1. ¿Es colombiana Marisa Jiménez?
2. ¿Es ella de Bogotá?
3. ¿Es ella una amiga de Elena Ochoa?
4. ¿Cómo es Elena?
5. ¿Es guapa también?
6. ¿Es ella una persona divertida?

Options:
1) Do orally with books closed.
2) Read and have students answer.
3) Have students write answers at home.

(Tape Activity 5)
(Workbook, Exercise A)

Ejercicio 2 Soy yo.
Completen. *(Complete each sentence about yourself.)*

¡Hola, amigos!
Yo soy _____. *(name)*
Yo soy _____. *(nationality)*
Yo soy de _____. *(place)*
Yo soy _____. *(student)*

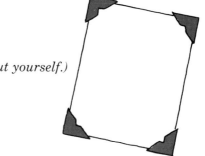

Ejercicio 3 ¿De dónde es?
Contesten. *(Answer.)*

Expansion:
After student tells about himself/herself, have student give the same information about someone else.

(Workbook, Exercise B)

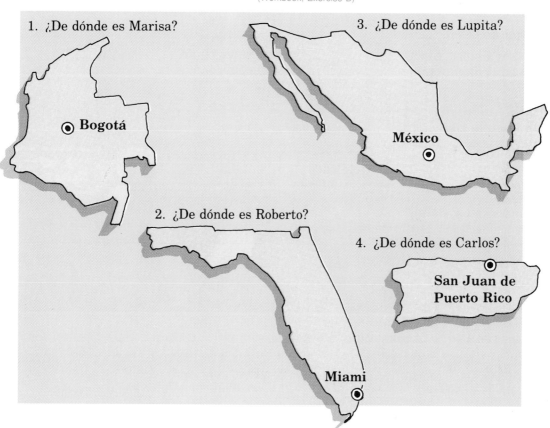

1. ¿De dónde es Marisa?

⊙ **Bogotá**

3. ¿De dónde es Lupita?

México
⊙

2. ¿De dónde es Roberto?

4. ¿De dónde es Carlos?

⊙
San Juan de Puerto Rico

Miami
⊙

εstructura

El presente del verbo *ser*—formas singulares

The verb *to be* in Spanish is **ser.** Note the singular forms of the verb **ser.**

Infinitive	ser
yo	soy
tú	eres
él, ella	es

Note that the **yo** form is used when you talk about yourself—*I*. **Tú** is used to address a friend—*you*. The **él** or **ella** form is used when you talk about someone.

Since each form of the verb changes in Spanish, the subjects **yo, tú, él, ella** can be omitted. In English, however, the subject pronouns, *I, you, he, she* are always used. Note the following.

(Yo) Soy Juan.   **(Ella) Es Marisa.**

In order to make a sentence negative *(not)* in Spanish, you merely put the Spanish word **no** before the verb.

Yo soy americano(a).   **Marisa es rubia.**
No soy colombiano(a).   **No es morena.**

Ejercicio 1: The purpose of this mini-conversation is to permit students to hear, use, and see the forms of the verb **ser** in context before they have to use them on their own. Students can 1) read it, 2) go over it orally, 3) present it

Ejercicio 1 ¿Quién eres? to class, 4) work in pairs.
Practiquen la conversación. *(Practice the conversation.)*

— ¿Quién eres?
— ¿Yo?
— Sí, tú.
— Yo soy Federico. Federico Darío.
— ¿Eres americano, Federico?
— No, no soy americano. Soy colombiano.
— Tú eres americano, ¿verdad?
— Sí, soy americano. Soy de Chicago.

Ejercicio 2: *Expansion:* Have one or more students answer all the questions. In so doing, they will give a unified description of themselves.

Ejercicio 2 ¿Qué soy y cómo soy yo?
Contesten con *soy.* *(Answer with soy.)*

1. ¿Eres americano(a) o cubano(a)?
2. ¿Eres rubio(a) o moreno(a)?
3. ¿Eres alto(a) o bajo(a)?

4. ¿Eres divertido(a) o aburrido(a)?
5. ¿Eres alumno(a) en una escuela americana o en un colegio mexicano?

28

Ejercicio 3 Lo que no soy.

Contesten con *no soy*. *(Answer with **no soy**.)*

1. ¿Eres colombiano(a)?
2. ¿Eres de Bogotá?
3. ¿Eres alumno(a) en un colegio colombiano?
4. ¿Eres amigo(a) de Cervantes?

Ejercicio 4 ¡Hola, Enrique! ¿Eres . . . ?

Here is a photo of Enrique Figueroa. He is from Cali, Colombia. Ask him if he is:

1. colombiano   Enrique, ¿eres colombiano?
2. rubio
3. alumno
4. de Cali
5. listo

(Workbook, Exercise C)

Expansion:
Have students ask
Enrique any questions
they like.

(Workbook, Exercise D)

Ejercicio 5 ¡Hola, Isabel! ¿Eres . . . ?

Here is a photograph of Isabel Salazar. She is from San Juan. Ask her if she is:

1. de Puerto Rico
2. alumna
3. lista
4. una amiga de Enrique Figueroa

Expansion game:
Have one student take the role of **Isabel**. Another is an
interviewer. Have interviewer ask Isabel any question possible.
Isabel answers as if she were on the radio.
(Tape Activities 6, 7)

Ejercicio 6 La amiga de Marisa

Completen con *ser*. *(Complete with **ser**.)*

This is a test exercise that makes students use all singular forms.

1. Yo _____ Marisa Jiménez.
2. Yo _____ de Bogotá, Colombia.
3. ¿_____ tú colombiano(a)?
4. ¿No? ¿De dónde _____ tú?
5. Yo _____ amiga de Elena Ochoa.
6. Ella también _____ de Bogotá.
7. Ella _____ muy simpática.
8. Tú _____ simpático(a) también, ¿no?
9. Elena _____ una amiga muy sincera.

(Tape Activity 8)
(Quiz 2)

La concordancia de los adjetivos que terminan en *-e* o en consonante

Many adjectives in Spanish end in either **-e** or a consonant. Note that adjectives that end in **-e** or a consonant have the same form for the masculine and feminine.

un alumno inteligente	**un muchacho popular**
una alumna inteligente	**una muchacha popular**

Ejercicio 7 Lupita y Carlos
Completen. *(Complete.)*

1. Lupita es una muchacha _____. **mexicano**
2. Lupita es una muchacha _____. **inteligente**
3. Ella es una muchacha _____. **popular**
4. Carlos Gutiérrez no es _____. **mexicano**
5. Él es _____. **colombiano**
6. Carlos es un alumno muy _____. **inteligente**
7. Él es también muy _____. **divertido**
8. Es un muchacho _____. **popular**

(Quiz 3)

Expansion:
Have students give a description of different members of the class.

Posesión con *de*

In English the possessive is expressed by *'s (Linda's friend)*. In Spanish the preposition **de** is used.

el amigo de Carmen　　　　　　　　　**la amiga de Pepe**

Ejercicio 8 ¿De quién es?
Completen con las palabras apropiadas. *(Complete with the correct words.)*

1. _____ amigo _____ Carmen es inteligente, sincero y divertido.
2. _____ escuela _____ Roberto no es una escuela primaria. Es una escuela secundaria.
3. _____ amiga _____ Marisa es de Cali.
4. _____ colegio _____ Marisa no es una escuela pública. Es una escuela privada.

(Workbook, Exercises E–G)

Expansion:
Have students tell whom they are friends of.

Pronunciación　　　　　　　**La vocal *e***

The Spanish vowel **e** is pronounced somewhat like the *a* in the English word *mate,* but the sound is shorter, clearer, and more concise in Spanish.

e
Elena
peso
de
enero
ella

(Tape Activity 9)

Trabalenguas y dictado

Elena es amiga de Felipe.
Ella es inteligente.
Eva es interesante y sincera.

(Tape Activity 10)

Expresiones útiles

Very often Spanish speakers will add the expressions **¿no?, ¿verdad?,** or **¿no es verdad?** after they make a statement in order to receive confirmation of what they have just said. If the person answering agrees, he or she will respond **sí.**

A common expression used among friends to get someone's attention and have the person listen is **¡oye!**

conversación

(Tape Activity 11)

¿Quién eres?

David   ¡Hola! Tú eres Marisa Jiménez, ¿no?

Marisa   Sí, soy Marisa Jiménez. Y tú eres David, ¿verdad?

David   Sí, soy David Andrews.

Marisa   Tú eres el amigo americano de Elena Ochoa, ¿no?

David   Sí, ella es muy simpática.

Marisa   Es verdad. Es una persona muy sincera y también muy divertida.

Ejercicio 1   ¿Verdadero o falso?   *(True or false?)*

1. Marisa Jiménez es americana.   (Tape Activity 12)
2. David Andrews es colombiano.
3. David es un amigo de Marisa Jiménez.
4. David es un amigo de Elena Ochoa.
5. Marisa Jiménez es una amiga de Elena Ochoa también.

Ejercicio 2   Describan a Elena Ochoa.   *(Describe Elena Ochoa.)*

(Workbook, Exercise H)

A puzzle appears in the Workbook.

Actividades

(Tape Activities—**Segunda parte** 1–2)
(Workbook—**Más Vocabulario y Cultura**)

1 (optional)

You just received this photo from your new pen pal in Mexico. Write him a letter in Spanish. Tell him who you are, your nationality, where you are from, where you are a student, and give a brief description of yourself.

Querido amigo,
yo soy . . .

2 Read the cartoon.

3

Change the preceding conversation based on this cartoon.

4

Make a list of characteristics that you look for in a friend.

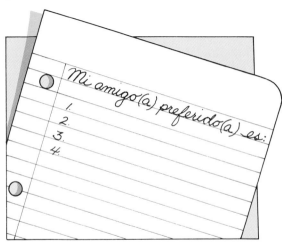

5

Look at the photograph of this girl. Ask her as many questions about herself as you can.

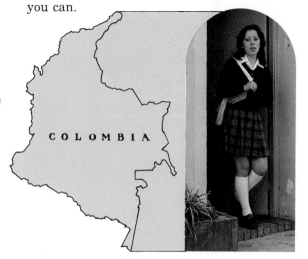

Revista

¡Hola, todos!
Soy Alba Fernández.
Soy alumna en el
Instituto Joaquín Turina
en Madrid.
¿Soy una alumna seria?

Yo soy María
Bustamante.
Soy colombiana.
Pero yo no soy de
Bogotá, la capital.
¿De dónde soy?

¡Hola!
Soy Jaime Pacheco.
Soy alumno en una escuela técnica de
la Ciudad de México.
¿Eres tú alumno(a) en una escuela
técnica?

¡Hola!
¿Quién soy?
Soy Guadalupe Méndez.
Soy de la Ciudad de México.
¿Qué opinas?
¿Soy divertida o aburrida?

¡Hola, amigos!
Yo soy Catalina Llanos.
Soy chilena.
¿Soy morena o rubia?
Y tú, ¿eres morena(o) como yo?
¿O eres rubia(o)?

3 NUEVOS AMIGOS

los hermanos   **los amigos**

(Tape Activity 1)

vocabulario

(Tape Activity 2)

Son Tadeo y Alfonso.
Los dos muchachos son amigos.
Ellos no son hermanos.

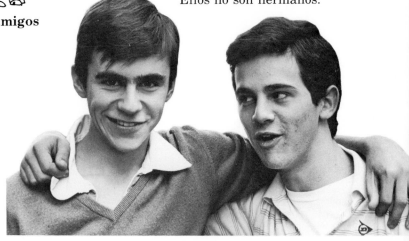

Ellos son **muy aficionados**
a **los deportes.**

(Tape Activity 3)

pequeño   **grande**

fuerte

 **débil**

atlético

A vocabulary list is provided in the Teacher's Resource Kit.

Ejercicio 1   Tadeo y Alfonso
Contesten.   *(Answer.)*

(Tape Activity 4)

1. ¿Son amigos Tadeo y Alfonso?
2. ¿Son hermanos?
3. ¿Son ellos muy aficionados a los deportes?
4. ¿Son ellos pequeños o grandes?
5. ¿Son ellos fuertes o débiles?

(Tape Activity 5)
(Workbook, Exercises A–B)

Expansion: Give a complete description of **Tadeo** and **Alfonso.** Have students use all the adjectives they know.

Ejercicio 2 ¿Quiénes son atléticos y fuertes?

Contesten con los nombres de los muchachos. *(Answer with the boys' names.)*

1. ¿Quiénes son amigos?
2. ¿Quiénes son muy aficionados a los deportes?
3. ¿Quiénes son muy atléticos?
4. ¿Quiénes son fuertes?

Expresiones útiles

You have already learned that Spanish speakers will frequently add **¿no?,** **¿verdad?,** or **¿no es verdad?** to a statement in order to get confirmation of what they have just said.

If the person answering does not agree, he or she will say **no.**

In order to request clarification of the disagreement and to find out what the other person thinks, Spanish speakers will frequently ask **¿Entonces?**

The person answering will often say **Pues,** and then give his or her response. For example:

—**Son rubios, ¿verdad?**
—**No, no son rubios.**
—**Entonces, ¿qué son?**
—**Pues, son morenos.**

Ejercicio 3 ¿No? ¿Entonces? (Tape Activity 6)

Contesten según el modelo. *(Answer according to the model.)*

Son rubios, ¿verdad?
No.
¿Entonces?
Pues, son morenos.

In addition to having students prepare a very natural, flowing conversation, this exercise gives practice with antonyms.

1. Son bajos, ¿verdad?
2. Son débiles, ¿verdad?
3. Son divertidos, ¿verdad?
4. Son morenos, ¿verdad?

Observation: What sound do we add in Spanish when we talk about more than one person?

Ejercicio 4 ¿Cómo son las amigas?

Contesten. *(Answer.)*

1. Las dos muchachas, ¿son hermanas o amigas?
2. ¿Son ellas aficionadas a los deportes?
3. ¿Son ellas altas o bajas?
4. ¿Son ellas fuertes o débiles?
5. ¿Son atléticas?

(Tape Activity 7)
(Quiz 1)
(Workbook, Exercises C–D)

Exercise 4 can be written as a guided composition.

37

Estructura

Los sustantivos y los artículos—formas plurales

Look at the following words. The words in the first column are in the singular. The words in the second column are in the plural.

el muchacho	los muchachos
el colegio	los colegios
la muchacha	las muchachas
la escuela	las escuelas

Many Spanish nouns form their plural by merely adding an **-s** to the singular form.

The plural form of the definite article **el** is **los.** The plural of the definite article **la** is **las.**

Note that the noun **deporte** ends in **-e** and takes the definite article **el. Deporte** is a masculine noun. There is no way to determine the gender (masculine or feminine) of nouns ending in **-e.** Some are masculine and some are feminine. You will have to learn each one individually. Nouns that end in **-e** also add an **-s** to form their plural.

el deporte	los deportes

Expansion:
After students do the exercise, have them tell a story about **Luis** in their own words.

Ejercicio 1 Los hermanos de Luis

Completen. *(Complete.)* (Tape Activities 8–9)

1. _____ dos hermanos de Luis son rubios.
2. _____ dos hermanas de Luis no son rubias.
3. _____ dos hermanas de Luis son morenas.
4. _____ amigos de Luis son muy aficionados a _____ deportes.
5. _____ amigos de Luis son muy atléticos.

(Quiz 2)

Los pronombres—formas singulares y plurales

A pronoun is a word that replaces a noun.

Roberto *(noun)*
el muchacho *(noun)*
él *(pronoun)*

Lupita *(noun)*
la muchacha *(noun)*
ella *(pronoun)*

Tadeo y Alfonso *(nouns)*
los muchachos *(noun)*
ellos *(pronoun)*

Marisa y Elena *(nouns)*
las muchachas *(noun)*
ellas *(pronoun)*

When you speak about more than one person, the form of the verb **ser** that is used is **(ellos/ellas) son.**

> **Los dos muchachos son amigos.**
> **Ellos no son hermanos.**

> **Las dos muchachas son amigas.**
> **Ellas no son hermanas.**

Ejercicio 2   Amigos y amigas

Completen con *ellos, ellas, los, las* y *ser.* *(Complete with *ellos, ellas, los, las,* and ser.)* This exercise is quite challenging. Students must determine whether to use an article, pronoun, or verb form.

María y Elena son amigas. _____ dos muchachas son colombianas. _____ son alumnas en un colegio colombiano. Las dos amigas _____ muy aficionadas a _____ deportes. _____ son muy fuertes.

Tadeo y Alfonso son amigos también. Pero _____ no son colombianos. Ellos _____ mexicanos. _____ dos muchachos son alumnos en un colegio mexicano. _____ también son muy aficionados a _____ deportes. _____ dos amigos son fuertes y atléticos. Y ellos _____ inteligentes también.

(Workbook, Exercise E)
(Quiz 3)

La concordancia de los adjetivos—formas plurales

Study the following sentences. The sentences in the first column are in the singular. The sentences in the second column are in the plural.

El muchacho es americano.	**Los muchachos son americanos.**
El muchacho es atlético.	**Los muchachos son atléticos.**
La muchacha es mexicana.	**Las muchachas son mexicanas.**
La muchacha es atlética.	**Las muchachas son atléticas.**
El muchacho fuerte es muy atlético.	**Los muchachos fuertes son muy atléticos.**
La muchacha fuerte es muy atlética.	**Las muchachas fuertes son muy atléticas.**

To form the plural of many Spanish adjectives, an **-s** is added to its masculine or feminine singular form.

> **atlético   atléticos**
> **atlética   atléticas**

Adjectives that end in **-e** have only one form in the singular. To form the plural you merely add an **-s.**

> **fuerte   fuertes**

Note, however, that adjectives that end in a consonant add **-es** to form the plural.

El muchacho es popular.	**Los muchachos son populares.**
La muchacha es popular.	**Las muchachas son populares.**

39

Ejercicio 3 ¿Cómo son los dos muchachos?
Contesten. *(Answer.)*

1. ¿Son rubios los dos muchachos?
2. ¿Son ellos americanos?
3. ¿Son atléticos los dos amigos?
4. ¿Son fuertes o débiles?
5. ¿Son populares los dos muchachos?

Ejercicio 4 Y las dos muchachas, ¿cómo son?
Contesten. *(Answer.)*

1. ¿Son morenas las dos muchachas?
2. ¿Son ellas americanas?
3. ¿Son atléticas las dos amigas?
4. ¿Son fuertes o débiles?
5. ¿Son populares las dos muchachas?

Ejercicio 5 Dos amigos colombianos y dos amigas mexicanas
Completen. *(Complete.)*

1. Las dos amigas son _____. **mexicano**
2. Ellas son muy _____ a los deportes. **aficionado**
3. Las dos muchachas son _____ y ellas son _____ también.
   inteligente, simpático
4. Ellas son muy _____. **atlético**
5. Ellas no son _____. Son _____. **débil, fuerte**
6. Tadeo y Alonso no son _____. **mexicano**
7. Ellos son _____. **colombiano**
8. Los dos muchachos son también muy _____ a los deportes. **aficionado**
9. Ellos son _____. No son _____. **fuerte, débil**
10. Ellos son _____, _____ y _____. **inteligente, divertido, atlético**
11. Los dos muchachos son _____. **fantástico**
12. Y ellos son muy _____. **popular**

Ejercicio 6 ¿Cómo son ellos?

Describan a los dos muchachos. *(Describe the two boys.)*

1. ¿Son atléticos?
2. ¿Son fuertes o débiles?
3. ¿Son aficionados a los deportes?
4. ¿Son simpáticos?
5. ¿Son altos o bajos?
6. ¿Qué más son?

Students can now use many –o, –e, and consonant adjectives.

Ejercicio 7 ¿Cómo son ellas?

Describan a las dos muchachas. *(Describe the two girls.)*

1. ¿Son atléticas?
2. ¿Son fuertes o débiles?
3. ¿Son aficionadas a los deportes?
4. ¿Son simpáticas?
5. ¿Son altas o bajas?
6. ¿Qué más son?

(Workbook, Exercises F–I)
(Quiz 4)

Pronunciación

La vocal *i*

The Spanish vowel **i** is pronounced like the *ee* in the English word *bee* or *see*, but the sound is somewhat shorter and more concise in Spanish than in English.

i

(Tape Activities 12–13)

Inés
Isabel
italiano
amigo
sí

Trabalenguas y dictado

Inés es atlética.
Isabel es italiana.
Sí, Rita es inteligente y divertida.

41

Lectura cultural

☆ Bogotá

Call on students to read aloud. Either ask them or have them make up questions about what was just read.

Marisa y Elena

Marisa y Elena son dos muchachas colombianas. Ellas son de Bogotá, la capital de Colombia. Ellas son alumnas en un colegio en Bogotá. Las dos amigas son muy inteligentes. ¿Son ellas pequeñas? No, ellas no son pequeñas. Entonces, ¿cómo son? Ellas son altas. Ellas son muy atléticas. Las dos muchachas son muy aficionadas a los deportes. Y además,* son muchachas sinceras y simpáticas. Ellas son muy populares.

Ejercicio   Corrijan las frases falsas. *(Correct the false statements.)*

1. Marisa y Elena son americanas.
2. Ellas son de Cali, la capital de Colombia.
3. Las dos muchachas son alumnas en una escuela secundaria en Miami.
4. Ellas son pequeñas.
5. Ellas son muy aficionadas a la música.

---

*   **además**   *moreover, besides*

Actividades

1 (optional)

Rewrite the story from the **Lectura cultural.** Change **Marisa y Elena** to **Diego y Federico.** Make all other necessary changes.

Diego

Federico

2 Tell all you can about the people in the illustration below.

43

Son Luis y Rafael.
Ellos son de San José, Costa Rica.
¿Son ellos alumnos?

Son Rosita y Alfonso.
Ellos son de la Ciudad de
México. ¿Qué opinas? ¿Son
ellos amigos o novios?

Teresa y Rosario son alumnas
de Madrid. ¿Qué opinas? ¿Son
ellas hermanas o amigas?

44

En el patio de una escuela pública, La Ciudad de México

Es Alberto Juan Torena. Él es de Los Ángeles. Alberto es de origen cubano. ¿Es él fuerte o débil?

Los muchachos son de Barcelona, España. ¿Son ellos atléticos?

Somos de México

You may wish to call two of the more-able students
to the front of the class to read the sentences.
Have them point to themselves as they say **nosotros**
and to other class members as they say **Uds.**

vocabulario

¡Hola, amigos!
Nosotros somos americanos.
¿Qué son **Uds.?**
¿Son Uds. americanos también?
Nosotros somos alumnos de **español.**

Ask students if they know the meaning of the English
words "facile" or "facilitate."

El español es **bastante fácil.**
No es **difícil.**

(Tape Activity 1)

Ejercicio 1   Los alumnos de español
Contesten. *(Answer.)*

1. ¿Son americanos los alumnos?
2. ¿Son ellos alumnos de español?
3. ¿Es fácil o difícil el español?

(Tape Activity 2)

Ejercicio 2   Él, ella y yo
Completen. *(Complete about yourself and a friend.)*

Yo soy _____. *(your name).*
Yo soy un(a) amigo(a) de _____. *(your friend's name)*
Nosotros somos alumnos en la Escuela _____. *(school name)*
Nosotros somos alumnos de _____. *(subject)*
Para nosotros el español no es difícil. Es _____. *(rather easy)*
Pero nosotros somos _____. *(rather smart)*

εstructura

El presente del verbo *ser*—formas plurales

We have already learned the singular forms of the verb **ser.**

Infinitive	ser
yo	soy
tú	eres
él, ella, Ud.	es

Now note the plural forms of the verb **ser.**

nosotros, nosotras	somos
ellos, ellas, Uds.	son

When you speak about yourself, you use the **yo** form of the verb—**soy.** When you speak about yourself and someone else (*we*, in English), you use the **nosotros(as)** form of the verb—**somos.**

To speak about another person, you use the **él** or **ella** (*he* or *she*) form of the verb—**es.** To speak about more than one person, you use the **ellos** or **ellas** *(they)* form of the verb—**son.**

When speaking to one friend (*you*, in English), you use the **tú** form—**eres.** Note that when you speak to or address more than one friend, you must use the **Uds.** form of the verb—**son. Uds.** is a common abbreviation for **Ustedes.**

Ejercicio 1   ¿Qué son Uds.?
Practiquen la conversación.   *(Practice the conversation.)*

— ¿Son Uds. americanos?
— Sí, somos americanos.
— ¿Son Uds. alumnos?
— Sí, somos alumnos.
— ¿En qué escuela son Uds. alumnos?
— Somos alumnos en la Escuela _____.

Students can practice the mini-conversation from their seats working in groups of four.

Ejercicio 2   Somos alumnos americanos.
Contesten con *somos*. *(Answer with **somos**.)*

1. ¿Son Uds. alumnos?
2. ¿Son Uds. americanos?
3. ¿Son Uds. alumnos de español?
4. ¿Son Uds. muy listos?
5. ¿Son Uds. muy aficionados a los deportes?

Options for exercises:
1) Go over exercises orally with books closed.
2) Have students read the exercises and respond.
3) Assign the exercises to be written at home.

(Tape Activities 3–5)

Ejercicio 3   ¿Son Uds. alumnos también?
Formen Uds. preguntas según el modelo. *(Form questions according to the model.)*

Pablo y Sandra / americanos
Pablo y Sandra, ¿son Uds. americanos?

1. Pablo y Sandra / americanos
2. Pablo y Sandra / alumnos
3. Pablo y Sandra / alumnos de español
4. Pablo y Sandra / amigos de José
5. Pablo y Sandra / aficionados a los deportes

Additional exercises for oral practice can be found in the Teacher's Resource Kit.

(Tape Activity 6)

Ejercicio 4   ¿Son Uds. . . . ? Somos . . . .
Choose several friends in your class. Ask them questions about themselves, using the following words. Then have them answer you.

americanos o cubanos
María y José, ¿son Uds. americanos o cubanos?
Somos americanos.

1. americanos o cubanos
2. bajos o altos
3. hermanos o amigos
4. morenos o rubios
5. listos o tontos
6. guapos o feos
7. divertidos o aburridos
8. fuertes o débiles

(Workbook, Exercises A–C)

Ejercicio 5   Juan García y yo
Completen con la forma apropiada del verbo *ser*. *(Complete with the appropriate form of the verb **ser**.)*

This exercise will have students use all forms of the verb **ser**.

1. Yo _____ amigo(a) de Juan García.
2. Él _____ un muchacho muy simpático.
3. Tú _____ simpático(a) también, ¿no?
4. Nosotros _____ alumnos en una escuela secundaria.
5. Nosotros _____ muy aficionados a los deportes.
6. ¿_____ Uds. aficionados a los deportes también?
7. Nosotros _____ de San Juan.
8. ¿De dónde _____ Uds.?
9. ¿_____ Uds. alumnos de español?
10. ¿Cómo _____ el español? ¿_____ fácil o difícil?
11. Los alumnos de español _____ muy inteligentes, ¿no?

Pronunciación

Las vocales *o, u*

The sound of the Spanish vowel **o** is similar to the *o* sound in the English words *hope* and *most,* but the sound is clearer, shorter, and more concise in Spanish.

o

o
no
son
oso
Paco

Trabalenguas y dictado

Somos amigos.
Nosotros somos alumnos.
¿Son Uds. americanos?

The sound of the Spanish vowel **u** is similar to the *u* sound in the English word *flu* or the *oo* in the English words *moon; moo, moo* (the sound a cow makes), but again in Spanish the sound is shorter and more concise.

u

uno
una   (Tape Activity 9)
cubano
muchacho
alumno

Trabalenguas y dictado

Ud. es un alumno.   (Tape Activity 10)
Lupita es una muchacha.
En junio y julio hace mucho calor.

Una vista panorámica de Guadalajara, México

49

Lectura cultural

Una tarjeta postal

Guadalajara, México

Queridos amigos,
    Yo soy Marta Aguilar. Soy mexicana y soy de Guadalajara. Yo soy alumna en un colegio privado en Guadalajara. Soy una amiga de Carmen Salinas. Carmen es una amiga fantástica. Ella es simpática y generosa. Es también muy inteligente. Y además, es divertida.
    Carmen y yo somos muy aficionadas a los deportes. Somos bastante atléticas. ¿Son Uds. muy aficionados a los deportes también? ¿De dónde son Uds.? ¿Son Uds. alumnos de español?
                Con cariño,
                Marta Aguilar

Students can read the postcard at home and write the answers to the questions below.

(Tape Activity 11)

Ejercicio Contesten. *(Answer.)*

1. ¿De quién es la tarjeta postal?
2. ¿De qué nacionalidad es Marta?
3. ¿De dónde es ella?
4. ¿Dónde es ella alumna?
5. ¿Quién es la amiga de Marta?
6. ¿Cómo es Carmen?
7. ¿Son ellas muy aficionadas a los deportes?
8. ¿Cómo son las dos muchachas?

A Final Test appears in the Test Package.

Actividades

(optional)

Write a postcard to Marta. Tell her all you can about yourself and one of your best friends. You can tell her your nationality, where you are from, and where you are students. You can also give her a description of yourself.

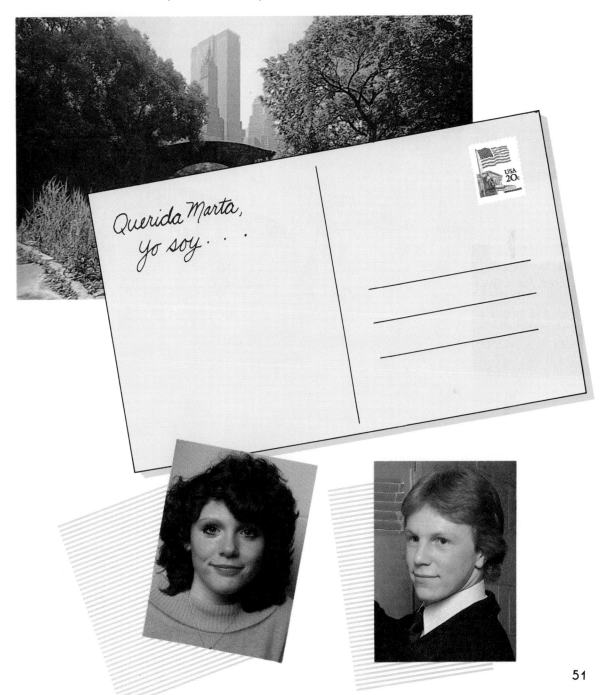

Querida Marta,
Yo soy . . .

Revista

¡Hola, todos!
Nosotros somos amigos dominicanos.
¿Qué son Uds.?
¿Son Uds. dominicanos también?

¡Hola, amigos!
Nosotras somos de Lima, Perú. Somos alumnas de inglés. ¿Son Uds. alumnos de español?

¡Hola! Somos Anita Echeverría y Victoria Pretti. Nosotras somos de Buenos Aires. ¿Somos argentinas o chilenas?

Somos alumnos
en la clase de la
señora Castillo. Ella
es profesora en un
colegio en Granada,
España. En la
fotografía, ¿quién es
la señora Castillo?

En un parque de Oaxaca,
México. ¿De qué
nacionalidad son los
muchachos?

Repaso

¡Hola, todos! Yo soy Marisa Jiménez. Soy colombiana. Yo soy de Bogotá. Yo soy una amiga de Carlos Gutiérrez. Carlos es colombiano también. Pero él no es de Bogotá. Él es de Cali. Carlos es muy simpático. Es un amigo muy sincero. Carlos y yo somos muy atléticos. Somos muy aficionados a los deportes. Carlos es alumno en un colegio en Cali. ¿Y yo? Yo también soy alumna. Soy alumna en un colegio en Bogotá.

Ejercicio 1   Contesten. *(Answer.)*

1. ¿De dónde es Marisa Jiménez?
2. ¿Quién es un amigo de Marisa?
3. ¿De dónde es él?
4. ¿Cómo es Carlos?
5. ¿Son atléticos Carlos y Marisa?
6. ¿Quiénes son muy aficionados a los deportes?
7. ¿Dónde es alumno Carlos?
8. ¿Y Marisa? ¿Dónde es ella alumna?

El verbo *ser*

Review the following forms of the verb **ser**—*to be.*

Infinitive	ser
yo	soy
tú	eres
él, ella, Ud.	es
nosotros, -as	somos
(vosotros, -as)	(sois)
ellos, ellas, Uds.	son

Ejercicio 2   Completen. *(Complete.)*

1. Marisa Jiménez _____ de Bogotá.
2. Carlos Gutiérrez _____ de Colombia también. Pero él no _____ de Bogotá. Él _____ de Cali.
3. ¿_____ tú colombiano(a)?
4. ¿No? ¿Tú no _____ colombiano(a)?
5. Entonces, ¿de qué nacionalidad _____ (tú)?
6. Yo _____ americano(a).
7. Yo _____ de _____.
8. Yo _____ amigo(a) de _____.
9. Nosotros _____ muy inteligentes.
10. Y nosotros _____ muy atléticos también.
11. ¿_____ Uds. muy aficionados a los deportes?
12. ¿_____ Uds. alumnos en una escuela secundaria?
13. Sí, nosotros _____ alumnos en la Escuela _____.
14. Marisa y Carlos _____ alumnos también. Ellos _____ alumnos en un colegio colombiano.

Los artículos y los sustantivos

Many Spanish nouns end in **-o** or **-a**. Most nouns that end in **-o** are masculine. Most nouns that end in **-a** are feminine. The definite article **el** *(the)* accompanies masculine nouns, and the definite article **la** accompanies feminine nouns. The indefinite article **un** *(a, an)* accompanies masculine nouns, and the indefinite article **una** accompanies feminine nouns.

el muchacho	**la muchacha**	**un muchacho**	**una muchacha**
el colegio	**la escuela**	**un colegio**	**una escuela**

To form the plural of **-o** and **-a** nouns, an **-s** is added. In the plural, **el** becomes **los** and **la** becomes **las.**

los muchachos	**las muchachas**
los colegios	**las escuelas**

Ejercicio 3   Completen. *(Complete.)*

— ¿Quién es _____ muchacho?
— ¿Quién? ¿_____ rubio?
— Sí, él.
— Él es Roberto Salas.
— ¿Y _____ muchacha? ¿Quién es ella?
— ¿Quién? ¿_____ morena?
— Sí, ella.
— Pues, es Elena Salas. Ella es _____ hermana de Roberto. Elena es _____ novia de Jaime Iglesias y Roberto es _____ novio de Teresa Unamuno. Es interesante. _____ dos muchachos son rubios y _____ dos muchachas son morenas. Ellos son alumnos en _____ Colegio Hidalgo.

La concordancia de los adjetivos

Adjectives must agree with the noun they describe or modify. Adjectives that end in **-o** have four forms.

el muchacho alto	**los muchachos altos**
la muchacha alta	**las muchachas altas**

Adjectives that end in **-e** or a consonant have two forms.

el muchacho fuerte	**los muchachos fuertes**
la muchacha fuerte	**las muchachas fuertes**
el muchacho popular	**los muchachos populares**
la muchacha popular	**las muchachas populares**

Ejercicio 4   Completen con los adjetivos apropiados. *(Complete with any appropriate adjectives.)*

Roberto y Elena son hermanos. Roberto es _____ y Elena es _____. Los dos hermanos son muy _____. Roberto es _____ y Elena es _____ también. Los dos son muy _____.

A student Self-test, with answers for self-correction, appears in the Workbook.
Two Unit Tests (one written, one oral) appear in the Test Package.

55

5 En la escuela

As you present vocabulary with the overhead transparencies, you may wish to intersperse questions about each sentence:
¿Quién es la profesora?
¿Qué es la Sra. Mariscal?
¿Qué enseña ella?
¿Con quiénes habla?
¿Cómo habla?

vocabulario

En **la clase de español:**

La profesora **canta.**

La señora Mariscal es **la profesora** de español.
Ella **enseña** español.
Ella **habla con** los alumnos.   (Tape Activity 1)
Ella habla **muy bien.**

(Tape Activity 2)

Un alumno **toca la guitarra.**

Carlos **estudia mucho.**

Rosita **toma apuntes** en **un cuaderno.**

Carlos **saca buenas notas.**
No saca **malas** notas.

56   (Tape Activity 3)

Nota

Once again you will see how many Spanish words you already know. Here are some of the subjects you may be studying in school. Note how similar these words are to their English equivalents. Do you remember what we call these words?

Las asignaturas

matemáticas
álgebra
geometría
trigonometría
cálculo
ciencias
biología
química
física

geografía
historia

inglés
español
francés
latín
italiano

educación cívica
educación física
arte
ciencias domésticas
música

Ejercicio 1   En la clase de español

(Tape Activity 4)

Contesten. *(Answer.)*

1. ¿Enseña español la señora Mariscal?
2. ¿Habla ella con los alumnos?
3. ¿Habla español en la clase de español?
4. ¿Estudia mucho Carlos?
5. ¿Toma apuntes Rosita?
6. ¿Canta la profesora?
7. ¿Toca la guitarra un alumno?
8. ¿Saca Carlos buenas o malas notas?

Ejercicio 2   ¿Quién? ¿Qué? ¿Dónde?

Note that the new interrogative word for this lesson is **¿qué?**

Contesten. *(Answer.)*

1. **La señora Mariscal enseña español en la Escuela Thomas Jefferson.**
   ¿Quién enseña español?
   ¿Qué enseña la señora Mariscal?
   ¿Dónde enseña ella español?

   Variation:
   Write key sentence on board. Have students make up as many original questions as possible.

2. **Rosita toma apuntes en la clase de español.**
   ¿Quién toma apuntes?
   ¿Qué toma Rosita?
   ¿Dónde toma ella apuntes?

Ejercicio 3   En la clase de la señora Mariscal

Contesten según el dibujo.
(Answer according to the drawing.)

1. ¿Con quiénes habla la profesora de español?
2. ¿Qué toma Rosita?
3. ¿Dónde canta la profesora?
4. ¿Quién toca la guitarra?
5. ¿Qué saca Carlos?

Variations: 1) Have students answer first with a complete sentence. 2) Have students answer with only the word or expression that responds to the specific interrogative word.
(Workbook, Exercises A–C) (Quiz 1)

57

Estructura

El presente de los verbos regulares en -ar—formas singulares

All verbs or action words in Spanish belong to a family or conjugation. The first-conjugation verbs are referred to as the **-ar** verbs because the infinitive (**hablar** *to speak;* **cantar** *to sing*) ends in **-ar**. Note that Spanish verbs change endings according to the subject. Study the following.

Write the verbs on the board and underline the endings for additional visual reinforcement.

Infinitive	hablar	cantar	estudiar	Endings
Stem	habl-	cant-	estudi-	
yo	hablo	canto	estudio	**-o**
tú	hablas	cantas	estudias	**-as**
él, ella, Ud.	habla	canta	estudia	**-a**

Since the ending changes in Spanish for each subject pronoun (**yo, tú, él, ella, Ud.**), the subject pronoun can be omitted.

(Yo) Hablo inglés.
(Yo) Estudio español en la escuela.

Remember that to make a sentence negative *(not)*, you merely put the word **no** before the verb in Spanish.

No hablo francés.

Ejercicio 1   ¿Estudias español?

Practiquen la conversación. *(Practice the conversation.)*

This mini-conversation permits students to use and see all singular verb forms in a natural context.

— Oye, Enrique. Tú hablas español, ¿no?
— Sí, amigo. Hablo bastante bien.
— ¿Estudias español en la escuela?
— Sí, estudio con la señora Mariscal.
— ¿Sacas buenas notas?
— Sí, saco buenas notas. El español es muy fácil y además yo soy muy inteligente.

(Tape Activity 5)

Ejercicio 2 ¿Hablas mucho en la clase de español?

Contesten con la forma *yo*. (*Answer with the **yo** form.*) (Tape Activity 6)

1. ¿Estudias español?
2. ¿Hablas español?
3. ¿Hablas bien?
4. ¿Hablas español con el (la) profesor(a) de español?

5. En la clase de español, ¿tomas apuntes?
6. ¿Cantas?
7. ¿Tocas la guitarra?
8. ¿Sacas buenas o malas notas en español?

Expansion: Call on a student to speak about his/her activities in Spanish class in his/her own words.

Ejercicio 3 ¿Qué más estudias?

Contesten. (*Answer.*)

1. ¿Estudias matemáticas?
2. ¿Sacas buenas notas en matemáticas?
3. ¿Estudias ciencias?
4. ¿Sacas buenas notas en ciencias?
5. ¿Estudias historia?

6. ¿Sacas buenas notas en historia?
7. ¿Estudias inglés?
8. ¿Sacas buenas notas en inglés?
9. ¿En qué asignaturas sacas buenas notas?
10. ¿En qué asignaturas sacas malas notas?

(Workbook, Exercise E)

Ejercicio 4 ¿Y tú?

Formen una pregunta con *tú*. (*Make up a question with **tú**.*)

En la clase de español:

3.

1.

2.

4.

(Tape Activity 7)

Ejercicio 5 ¿Quién habla, canta, estudia . . . ?

Escojan la respuesta apropiada. (*Choose the correct answer.*)

1. Yo _____ muy bien el español.
   a. habla   b. hablo   c. hablas

2. ¿_____ tú en la clase de español?
   a. Canto   b. Canta   c. Cantas

3. Rosita _____ mucho.
   a. estudia   b. estudias   c. estudio

4. Ella _____ muchos apuntes.
   a. tomo   b. tomas   c. toma

5. Yo _____ muy buenas notas en español.
   a. saco   b. saca   c. sacas

Variation:
Have students change subject to fit each verb form given.

59

Ejercicio 6 Yo estudio español.

Completen. *(Complete.)*

Hola, amigos. Yo soy _____. Yo soy alumno(a) en la Escuela _____. En la escuela yo _____ (estudiar) español. Yo _____ (hablar) mucho con el (la) profesor(a) de español. Él (Ella) _____ (enseñar) muy bien. Es una persona muy simpático(a). Él (Ella) _____ (enseñar) y yo _____ (tomar) apuntes en un cuaderno. A veces él (ella) _____ (cantar). Yo _____ (cantar) también pero no _____ (cantar) muy bien. El (La) profesor(a) no _____ (tocar) la guitarra. José es un alumno en la clase de español. Él _____ (tocar) la guitarra. La clase de español es muy divertida. Yo _____ (estudiar) mucho en la clase de español y _____ (sacar) muy buenas notas.

Tú también eres alumno(a) de español, ¿no? ¿Dónde _____ (estudiar) español? En la clase de español, ¿_____ (cantar)? ¿_____ (Hablar) mucho con el (la) profesor(a) de español? ¿_____ (Sacar) buenas o malas notas en español?

Expansion: 1) Have one or more students retell the story in their own words. 2) Have students make up questions about the story. 3) Have students make up true/false statements. 4) Have students correct false statements.

Tú y Ud.

(Workbook Exercise F) (Tape Activities 8–9) (Quiz 2)

In Spanish there are several ways to say *you*. When you are speaking to a friend, a relative, or a person of the same age, you would use **tú.**

¡Oye, amigo! ¿Estudias español?
Catalina, ¿tocas la guitarra?

You may wish to draw stick figures of a child and an adult on board. Point to child each time you use **tú** and to adult each time you use **Ud.**

When speaking to an adult or a person you do not know very well, it would be impolite to use **tú.** It is necessary to use the **usted** form of the verb. The **usted** form is called the formal or polite form of address. The **tú** form is called the informal (friendly) form of address. **Usted** is commonly abbreviated **Ud.** Note that the subject **Ud.** takes the same ending as the **él** or **ella** form of the verb.

Señor, ¿habla Ud. español?
Señora, ¿enseña Ud.?
Señorita, ¿canta Ud.?

Ejercicio 7 Señor, señora, señorita, ¿ . . . ?

Get the following information from your teacher by asking him or her in Spanish if:

1. he / she speaks French
2. he / she sings in class
3. he / she plays the guitar
4. he / she teaches history

Ejercicio 8 ¿Tú o Ud.?

*Look at the illustrations. Ask each person what he / she is doing. Use **tú** or **Ud.** as appropriate.*

1.
2.
3.
4.
5.

(Workbook, Exercise G) (Tape Activities 10–11) (Quiz 3)

Pronunciación　　　Las consonantes *f, l, m*

The pronunciations of the consonants **f, l,** and **m** are quite similar in both Spanish and English.

(Tape Activities 12–13)

fa	**fe**	**fi**	**fo**	**fu**
famoso	feo	física	foto	futuro
fácil	fecha	fino		
	Felipe			

la	**le**	**li**	**lo**	**lu**
la	Elena	Lolita	Lola	lunes
latín				Lupita

ma	**me**	**mi**	**mo**	**mu**
mala	mexicano	amigo	momento	muchacha
toma		amiga	monumento	mucho
matemáticas			tomo	

Trabalenguas y dictado

La amiga de Lolita es Lupita.
El monumento de Felipe es famoso.
La muchacha mexicana toma matemáticas.

Expresiones útiles

In Spanish there are several expressions that mean *Of course!* in English. They are:

¡Cómo no!
¡Por supuesto!
¡Claro!
¡Claro que sí!

Un colegio, Perú

Alumnos de una escuela secundaria, Madrid

conversación

¡Oye, Roberto!

Antonio   Oye, Roberto. Tú hablas español, ¿no?

Roberto   Claro que hablo español.

Antonio   Pero no eres español, ¿verdad?

Roberto   No, no. Estudio español en la escuela.

Antonio   Hablas muy bien.

Roberto   Pues, gracias. Eres muy simpático.

Antonio   No, hombre. Es verdad. Hablas muy bien.

Options:
1) Go over conversation orally in class.
2) Listen to cassette.
3) Have students work on conversation in pairs.
4) Have students read conversation.

Ejercicio Contesten. *(Answer.)*

1. ¿Con quién habla Roberto?
2. ¿Habla Roberto español?
3. Y Antonio, ¿habla español también?
4. ¿Es español Roberto?
5. ¿Dónde estudia español?
6. ¿Habla muy bien?

(Workbook, Exercise H)
(Tape Activities 14–15)

62

Lectura cultural

Un americano y una argentina

Roberto es un muchacho americano. Él estudia en una escuela secundaria americana. Él es un alumno muy listo y saca muy buenas notas. Roberto toma cinco cursos: inglés, español, historia, álgebra y biología.

Maripaz es una muchacha argentina. Ella estudia en un colegio en Buenos Aires. El colegio de Maripaz no es una escuela pública. Es una escuela privada. Como Roberto, Maripaz es una alumna muy lista. Ella también saca muy buenas notas. Maripaz no toma cinco cursos. Ella toma nueve cursos: español, inglés, latín, historia, matemáticas, química, biología, geografía y educación cívica. ¿Cómo es posible? Pues, en muchas escuelas de España y de Latinoamérica todas las clases no son diarias° y los alumnos toman muchos cursos en un semestre.

Ejercicio Escojan. *(Choose.)*

1. Roberto es _____.
   a. un muchacho argentino
   b. alumno en una escuela secundaria americana
   c. un alumno muy malo

2. Roberto saca _____.
   a. muy buenas notas
   b. cinco cursos
   c. malas notas

3. Maripaz es de _____.
   a. Bogotá
   b. Chicago
   c. Buenos Aires

4. Ella estudia en _____.
   a. una escuela secundaria pública
   b. un colegio privado
   c. una escuela americana en Buenos Aires

5. Maripaz toma _____.
   a. nueve cursos
   b. cinco cursos
   c. muy buenas notas

°**diarias** *daily*

Actividades

(optional)

1 Fill in your school schedule in Spanish.

ESCUELA SECUNDARIA								
Horario de Clases para el _____ semestre de 19____								
HORA	ASIGNATURA	LUN	MAR	MIER	JUE	VIER	SAB	PROFESOR(A)	AULA

2 Tell which is your favorite subject in school. **Mi asignatura favorita es . . . .** You can include the name of your teacher, whether the class is fun or serious, whether the subject is hard or easy, and what grades you get in this subject.

Mi asignatura favorita es...

3 Get together with a classmate and make up a conversation about your school. Some of the information you may want to get can include the answers to the following questions.

¿En qué escuela estudia ella/él?

¿Estudia mucho o no?

¿Qué cursos toma?

¿En qué cursos saca buenas notas?

¿En qué cursos saca malas notas?

¿Qué cursos son fáciles?

¿Qué cursos son difíciles?

¿Qué clases son divertidas?

¿Qué clases son muy aburridas?

Tell what each student in the illustration below is doing.

Revista

La señora Ramírez enseña historia en una escuela secundaria en la Ciudad de México. ¿Es una escuela para muchachas solamente o es una escuela para muchachos y muchachas?

Los muchachos son alumnos en un colegio en Cartagena, Colombia. Ellos toman apuntes y usan una calculadora. ¿Qué asignatura estudian?

Es la clase de la señora Irizarry. Ella enseña en una escuela superior en San Juan, Puerto Rico. ¿Es una clase divertida o aburrida?

Es una clase de inglés en el Instituto Joaquín Turina en Madrid. Para los alumnos madrileños, ¿es fácil o difícil el inglés?

HORARIO ESCOLAR

Nombre: *Luis Jaime Cisneros* Año *1986*

Horas	Lunes	Martes	Miércoles	Jueves	Viernes
7-8	Dibujo	Música	Matemáticas	Geografía	Mat.
8-9	Literatura	Geografía	Inglés	Biología	Civismo
9-10	Educación Física	Arte y Dibujo	Biología	Talleres	Oratoria
10-11	Civismo	Literatura	Química	Inglés	Geografía
11-12	////	////	////	Período de estudio	E
12-1	Biología	Mat.	Dibujo	Período de estudio	Dibujo
2-3	Química	Inglés	Período de estudio Educación	Física	Física
3-4	Período de estudio	Física	Física	Arte	Ciencias

Cuadernos y Sobres "PATRIA" los mejores

Es el horario de un colegio peruano. ¿De quién es el horario? ¿Cuántas asignaturas toma él? ¿Son diarias todas las clases?

MINISTERIO DE EDUCACION
TARJETA DE INFORMACION
EDUCACION SECUNDARIA

SECRETARIA DE ED...
DIRECCION GENERAL DE EDUCACION...

DEPARTAMENTO DE ESCUELAS SECUNDARIAS *DIURNAS EN EL DISTRITO FEDERAL (MEXICO)*
ESCUELA SECUNDARIA ES *1-10 "FRANCISCO I. MADERO"*
ALUMNO(A) *ALBERTO LÓPEZ HOYOS*
GRADO *3º* GRUPO *A* PERIODO ESCOLAR 19 *85* 19 *86* TURNO *MATUTINO*
ASESOR DEL GRUPO *JOSÉ, CALAVERA I.*

INFORME DE INASISTENCIAS Y DE EVALUACIONES DEL APRENDIZAJE

ASIGNATURAS:	INASISTENCIAS					EVALUACIONES DEL APRENDIZAJE				
	PERIODOS				TOTAL	PERIODOS				CALIF FINAL
	1	2	3	4		1	2	3	4	
ESPANOL	1	1	0	1	3	8	8	9	8	8
MATEMATICAS	0	0	1	0	1	5	6	6	5	6
LENG. EXT. (INGLES)	2	0	0	1	3	8	8	8	9	8
BIOLOGIA	1	1	0	0	2	7	6	7	5	7
FISICA	0	2	1	1	4	6	5	6	6	6
QUIMICA	0	0	0	1	1	6	5	6	5	6
HISTORIA	2	1	0	0	3	8	7	8	8	8
GEOGRAFIA	3	0	1	0	4	7	7	7	7	7
EDUC. CIVICA	0	1	0	0	1	7	8	8	8	8
EDUC. FISICA	0	0	1	0	1	9	10	9	9	9
EDUC. ARTISTICA.	2	1	0	0	3	10	9	10	10	10
EDUC. TEC. ABREV. ( )	0	0	3	1	4	10	10	9	10	10

LA ESCALA DE CALIFICACIONES ES:
10 Excelente, 9 Muy Bien, 8 Bien, 7 Regular, 6 Suficiente, 5 No Suficiente

La tarjeta de información
Alberto estudia en una escuela secundaria en la Ciudad de México.
- ¿Cuál es una nota muy alta?
- ¿Cuál es una nota muy baja?
- ¿En qué asignaturas saca buenas notas Alberto?
- ¿En qué asignaturas saca malas notas Alberto?

6 LOS PASATIEMPOS

Vocabulary can be presented with the overhead transparencies.

vocabulario

Después de las clases: (Tape Activity 1)

Los jóvenes llegan a casa.

Miran la televisión.

Preparan una merienda.

Escuchan discos.

Hablan **por teléfono.**

Trabajan en **una tienda.**

la sala

la cocina

Ejercicio 1 Después de las clases ...
Contesten. *(Answer.)*

(Tape Activities 2–3)
(Workbook, Exercises A–B)

1. ¿Adónde llegan los alumnos?
2. ¿Dónde preparan una merienda?
3. ¿Dónde miran la televisión?
4. ¿Dónde hablan por teléfono?
5. ¿Dónde escuchan discos?
6. ¿Dónde trabajan?

Ejercicio 2 ¿Qué, quiénes y dónde?
Completen con la palabra interrogativa apropiada.
(Complete with the appropriate question word.)

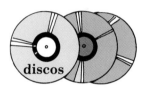

1. ¿———— escuchan los amigos?

en la cocina

2. ¿———— preparan ellos una merienda?

los amigos

3. ¿———— hablan por teléfono?

la televisión

4. ¿———— miran ellos en la sala?

en una tienda

5. ¿———— trabajan los jóvenes?

(Tape Activity 4)
(Workbook, Exercise C)
(Quiz 1)

Estructura

El presente de los verbos regulares en -ar—formas plurales

In the preceding lesson we learned the singular forms of regular **-ar,** or first-conjugation, verbs. Observe now the plural forms of the **-ar** verbs.

Infinitive	hablar	mirar	trabajar	Endings
Stem	habl-	mir-	trabaj-	
nosotros, nosotras	hablamos	miramos	trabajamos	**-amos**
ellos, ellas, Uds.	hablan	miran	trabajan	**-an**

Note that in all areas of the Spanish-speaking world, except in some parts of Spain, there is no difference between formal and informal address in the plural. Whenever you are speaking to more than one person, you would use the **ustedes (Uds.)** form of the verb. In Spain, the **vosotros (vosotras)** form of the verb is used when speaking to two or more friends, relatives, or people of the same age. Learn to recognize these forms.

vosotros, vosotras	habláis	miráis	trabajáis	**-áis**

We have now learned all forms of the present tense of regular **-ar,** or first-conjugation, verbs. Review the following.

Infinitive	hablar	mirar	trabajar	Endings
Stem	habl-	mir-	trabaj-	
yo	hablo	miro	trabajo	**-o**
tú	hablas	miras	trabajas	**-as**
él, ella, Ud.	habla	mira	trabaja	**-a**
nosotros, -as	hablamos	miramos	trabajamos	**-amos**
(vosotros, -as)	(habláis)	(miráis)	(trabajáis)	**(-áis)**
ellos, ellas, Uds.	hablan	miran	trabajan	**-an**

Ejercicio 1 Después de las clases, ellos . . .
Contesten. *(Answer.)*

1. ¿Preparan una merienda los amigos?
2. ¿Toman la merienda en la cocina?
3. Después, ¿miran la televisión en la sala?
4. ¿Escuchan discos?
5. ¿Hablan por teléfono?

(Tape Activity 5)
(Workbook, Exercise D)
Options:
1) Exercises can be done orally in class.
2) They can be read by students.
3) They can be assigned for homework.

Ejercicio 2 Después de las clases, nosotros . . . (Tape Activity 6)
Contesten con la forma de *nosotros*. *(Answer with the **nosotros** form.)*

1. ¿Estudian Uds. español?
2. ¿Estudian Uds. mucho?
3. ¿Sacan Uds. buenas notas?
4. ¿Hablan Uds. mucho en la clase de español?
5. Después de las clases, ¿preparan Uds. una merienda?
6. ¿Toman Uds. la merienda en un café o en casa?
7. A veces, ¿miran Uds. la televisión?
8. ¿Escuchan Uds. discos?
9. ¿Escuchan Uds. discos de rock, de jazz o de música clásica?
10. ¿Hablan Uds. mucho por teléfono?
11. Con los amigos, ¿hablan Uds. inglés o español?

Expansion:
Have students retell their daily activities in their own words. This can be done orally or can be written.

Ejercicio 3 ¿Qué . . . Uds.?
Formen preguntas con la forma de *Uds*. *(Make up questions with **Uds.**)*

1.

2.

3.

4.

Ejercicio 4 Trabajamos mucho.

Exercises 4 and 5 make students use all verb forms at random.

Contesten. *(Answer.)*

1. ¿Estudias español?
2. ¿Hablas español con la profesora de español?
3. La profesora, ¿habla ella inglés también?
4. ¿Trabajas mucho en la clase de español?
5. ¿Sacas buenas o malas notas?
6. En la clase de español, ¿cantan Uds.?
7. Después de las clases, ¿toman los amigos una merienda?
8. ¿Escuchan Uds. discos también?
9. ¿Miran Uds. la televisión?
10. ¿Quién trabaja después de las clases?
11. ¿Estudian Uds. en casa?

Ejercicio 5 Un muchacho en un colegio de Madrid

Completen. *(Complete.)*

Emilio es un muchacho español. Él _____ (estudiar) en un colegio de Madrid, la capital de España. Emilio es un muchacho muy listo. Él _____ (trabajar) mucho en la escuela. Él _____ (estudiar) inglés. En la clase de inglés los alumnos _____ (hablar) mucho. A veces ellos _____ (cantar) también.

Yo _____ (estudiar) español en una escuela secundaria en los Estados Unidos. Yo también _____ (trabajar) mucho y _____ (sacar) muy buenas notas en español. En la clase nosotros _____ (hablar) mucho con el profesor. A veces, nosotros _____ (cantar) y _____ (tocar) la guitarra.

Después de las clases, los amigos _____ (tomar) una merienda. A veces nosotros _____ (mirar) la televisión. Cuando no _____ (mirar) la televisión, nosotros _____ (escuchar) discos o _____ (hablar) por teléfono.

Ejercicio 6 ¿Quién trabaja después de las clases?

Escojan la respuesta correcta. *(Choose the correct answer.)*

1. Después de las clases, José y yo (nosotros) _____ en una tienda.
   a. trabajan
   b. trabajo
   c. trabajamos

2. A veces yo _____ español con los clientes.
   a. hablo
   b. hablas
   c. hablan

3. En la tienda muchos clientes _____ español.
   a. hablamos
   b. hablan
   c. habla

4. Nosotros _____ español en la escuela.
   a. estudias
   b. estudiamos
   c. estudian

5. Yo _____ muy buenas notas en español.
   a. saco
   b. saca
   c. sacamos

(Quiz 2)

Pronunciación   ## Las consonantes *n, p*

The consonants **n** and **p** are pronounced very similarly in both Spanish and English. However, the **p** is not followed by any puff of air from your breath as it often is in English. Round your lips as you make the **p** sound in Spanish.

(Tape Activities 10–11)

na	**ne**	**ni**	**no**	**nu**
una	gasolinera	Anita	nota	monumento
alumna			alumno	
termina			uno	

pa	**pe**	**pi**	**po**	**pu**
papá	peso	pipa	popular	popular
prepara	Pepe		postal	apuntes
país	Pedro			

Trabalenguas y dictado

El papá de Pepe es popular.
La alumna en la cocina es Anita.
El alumno termina en un momento.

conversación

Your teacher is asking you and your friend what you do and where you go after school. Answer her/his questions by completing the following conversation.

Después de las clases...

¿Quiénes hablan?

Profesor(a) Después de las clases, ¿toman Uds. una merienda?
Uds. _____

Profesor(a) Luego, ¿escuchan Uds. discos o miran Uds. la televisión?
Uds. _____

Profesor(a) A veces, ¿hablan Uds. por teléfono?
Uds. _____

Profesor(a) ¿Con quiénes hablan?
Uds. _____

Profesor(a) ¿Trabajan Uds. después de las clases o no?
Uds. _____

74 *Variation and Expansion:* Permit students to make up any original questions they can think of. They can call on other classmates to answer their questions.

Lectura cultural

Additional cultural information to the teacher is provided in the
Teacher's Resource Kit.

¿Quiénes trabajan después de las clases?

En los Estados Unidos muchos alumnos de las escuelas secundarias trabajan
después de las clases. Trabajan, por ejemplo, en una tienda o en una gasolinera.
    Muchos jóvenes trabajan en los países hispánicos también. Pero los jóvenes
que trabajan no son alumnos. Son jóvenes que terminan con la educación después
de la primaria y trabajan todo el día. En muchos colegios las clases no terminan
hasta las cuatro o las cinco de la tarde. Los sábados las clases terminan al
mediodía. Los alumnos de las escuelas secundarias trabajan mucho—pero no
trabajan en una tienda o en una gasolinera. Ellos trabajan muy duro durante el
día en la escuela.

(Tape Activities 12–14)
(Workbook, Exercise G)

---

por ejemplo *for example*   **gasolinera** *gas station*   **jóvenes** *young people*   **países**
countries   **terminan** *end, finish*   **primaria** *elementary school*   **todo el día** *all day*
hasta *until*   **al mediodía** *at noon*   **duro** *hard*

75

Ejercicio **Completen.** *(Complete.)*

1. En los Estados Unidos muchos alumnos trabajan después de _____ _____.
2. Ellos trabajan en una gasolinera o en _____ _____.
3. Los alumnos no trabajan después de las clases en los países _____.
4. Los jóvenes que trabajan en los países hispánicos son jóvenes que terminan con la educación después de la _____.
5. Ellos no trabajan después de las clases. Trabajan _____ _____ _____.
6. En muchos colegios hispánicos las clases no terminan hasta las _____ o las _____ de la tarde.
7. Los alumnos en los países hispánicos trabajan muy duro en _____ _____.

Los alumnos estudian mucho en clase, Madrid

Actividades

1 (optional)

Interview several friends in your class about their after-school activities. Begin with **Después de las clases . . . .** Use the following verbs in your questions.

preparar   tomar   trabajar

hablar

mirar   escuchar

estudiar

3 Role play. Pretend you are also involved in the activities in **Actividad 2.** Tell what you and your friends are doing together.

2 Look at the illustration and tell all you can about it.

Revista

Después de las clases las muchachas toman un refresco en la Ciudad de México. ¿Qué toman? ¿Una coca o un jugo de frutas?

Las clases terminan a las cuatro de la tarde en este colegio en Lima.

Los amigos de Luis visitan una tienda de discos en Buenos Aires. ¿Escuchan los discos o sólo miran los discos?

Los juegos «video» son muy populares con los jóvenes en España. ¿Son populares aquí también?

Carmen, una joven mexicana, habla por teléfono. ¿Habla ella de casa o de una cabina telefónica?

Programas de televisión en Madrid ¿Qué cadena (canal) presenta los programas?

EL PAIS, martes 5 de abril de 1

PROGRAMAS DE TELE

MARTES

Primera cadena

13.45 Carta de ajuste.
14.00 Programación de cobertura r
      gional.
14.55 Conexión con la programac
      nacional.
15.00 Telediario.
15.35 España, sin ir más lejos.
16.05 Q.E.D. Atrapar a un fantas
17.00 Un mundo para ellos.
18.00 Barrio Sésamo. La caseta
18.30 3, 2, 1... Contacto.
18.55 El libro gordo de Petet
19.00 Micky y Donald.
19.30 El paraíso de los anim
      comediante de la este
20.00 Encuentros en libe
      mía: La carrera fata
      la carrera de armar
      os Unidos y la L
      conó

Marta es alumna en un colegio en la Ciudad de México. Después de las clases, ella estudia. ¿Dónde estudia? ¿En casa o en la escuela?

7 DE COMPRAS

(Tape Activity 1)

el pan

la panadería

la caja

el dinero

el panadero

Él **está** en la panadería.
Necesita pan.
Compra pan

(Tape Activity 2)

Juanito **va de compras.**
Va de compras por la mañana.

Paga en la caja.
Da el dinero **al** panadero.

All exercises in the vocabulary section can be done orally, can be written, or both.

Ejercicio 1   ¿Quién va de compras?   (Tape Activity 3)
Contesten. *(Answer.)*

1. ¿Va Juanito de compras?
2. ¿Va de compras por la mañana?
3. ¿Está él en la panadería?

4. ¿Compra pan en la panadería?
5. ¿Paga en la caja?
6. ¿Da el dinero al panadero?

Ejercicio 2   Juanito va a la panadería.
Completen. *(Complete.)*

Juanito va de compras por _____
_____. Él está en la _____ donde compra
pan. Él paga en la _____. Da el _____ al
panadero.

(Workbook, Exercises A–C)

¿Adónde va la señora y qué compra?

la lechería

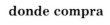

leche.

carne.

la carnicería

La señora va a

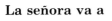

donde compra

pescado.

la pescadería

frutas y legumbres.

la frutería

pasteles.

la pastelería

el mercado   el supermercado   el empleado

Ejercicio 3   ¿Qué compra la señora Ochoa?
La señora Ochoa va de compras. ¿Qué compra ella?

1. Ella compra _____.

2. Ella compra _____.

3. Ella _____.

4. _____.

5. _____.

Ejercicio 4   ¿Adónde va ella?
La señora Ochoa va de compras. ¿Adónde va ella?

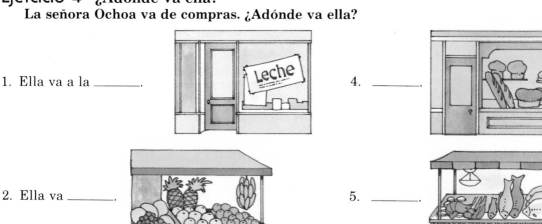

1. Ella va a la _____.

2. Ella va _____.

3. Ella _____.

4. _____.

5. _____.

Ejercicio 5   ¿Qué necesita la señora?
Sigan el modelo. *(Follow the model.)*

La señora necesita pan.
¿Ah, sí? ¿Adónde va ella?
Pues, ella va a la panadería.

1. La señora necesita leche.
2. La señora necesita pescado.

3. La señora necesita frutas.
4. La señora necesita pasteles.

Estructura

El presente de los verbos *ir, dar, estar*

The verbs **ir, dar,** and **estar** are considered irregular verbs in Spanish, since they do not conform to the pattern of other regular verbs. Note, however, that in the present tense, these verbs have the same endings as other regular **-ar,** or first-conjugation, verbs. The only exception is the **yo** form of the verb. Note the forms of these verbs in the present tense. Pay particular attention to the **yo** form.

Infinitive	ir	dar	estar
yo	**voy**	**doy**	**estoy**
tú	vas	das	estás
él, ella, Ud.	va	da	está
nosotros, -as	vamos	damos	estamos
(vosotros, -as)	(vais)	(dais)	(estáis)
ellos, ellas, Uds.	van	dan	están

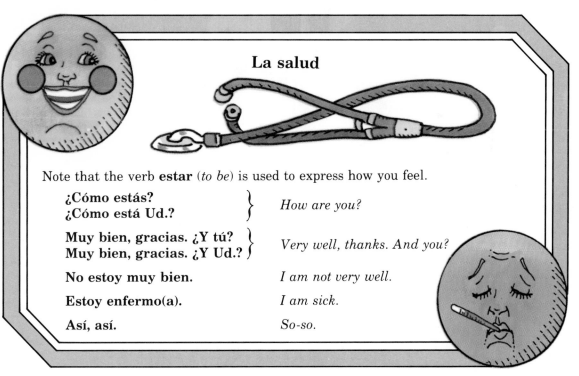

La salud

Note that the verb **estar** (*to be*) is used to express how you feel.

¿Cómo estás? **¿Cómo está Ud.?**	*How are you?*
Muy bien, gracias. ¿Y tú? **Muy bien, gracias. ¿Y Ud.?**	*Very well, thanks. And you?*
No estoy muy bien.	*I am not very well.*
Estoy enfermo(a).	*I am sick.*
Así, así.	*So-so.*

A complete study of the differences between **ser** and **estar** is presented in Lesson 10.

Ejercicio 1 Yo voy a la escuela. ¿Y tú?

(Tape Activity 6)

Contesten con *voy, doy* o *estoy.* *(Answer with **voy, doy,** or **estoy.**)*

1. ¿Vas a la escuela?
2. ¿Vas a la escuela por la mañana?
3. ¿Estás en la escuela ahora?
4. ¿Estás en la clase de español?
5. ¿Das el cuaderno a la profesora?
6. A veces, ¿vas de compras?

7. ¿Vas de compras después de las clases?
8. ¿Vas al supermercado?
9. ¿Estás en el supermercado ahora?
10. En el supermercado, ¿das el dinero al empleado en la caja?

Please refer to the Culture Information booklet in the Teacher's Resource Kit for an explanation concerning the redundant **le.**

Ejercicio 2 No estoy enfermo(a).
Contesten. *(Answer.)*

1. ¿Estás bien?
2. ¿Estás enfermo(a)?
3. ¿Cómo estás?

(Workbook, Exercises E–F)

Ejercicio 3 ¿Quién va con quién?
Contesten según el dibujo. *(Answer according to the illustration.)*

1. ¿Va Juan a la tienda?
2. ¿Va a la tienda con Teresa?

3. ¿Está Juan en la tienda ahora?
4. ¿Está Teresa también?
5. ¿Están ellos en la panadería?

6. ¿Están ellos en la caja?
7. ¿Dan ellos el dinero al empleado?

Ejercicio 4 Por la mañana, vamos a la escuela.
Contesten con *nosotros.* *(Answer with the **nosotros** form.)*

1. ¿Van Uds. a la escuela por la mañana?
2. ¿A qué escuela van Uds.?
3. ¿Están Uds. en la escuela ahora?
4. ¿En qué clase están Uds.?
5. ¿Están Uds. con la profesora de español?

6. Después de las clases, ¿van Uds. a veces a un café?
7. Y a veces, ¿van Uds. de compras?
8. ¿Van Uds. a un supermercado?
9. ¿A qué supermercado van Uds.?

Ejercicio 5 ¿Adónde vas tú?

Sigan el modelo. *(Follow the model.)*

Yo voy a la clase de español.
Perdón. ¿Adónde vas?

1. Yo voy a la clase de biología.
2. Yo voy a la clase de álgebra.
3. Yo voy a la clase de historia.
4. Yo voy a la clase de inglés.

Ejercicio 6 ¿Adónde va Ud.?

Pregúntenle al (a la) profesor(a). *(Ask your teacher.)*

1. if he / she goes to school in the morning
2. if he / she is in school now
3. if he / she gives good grades
4. if he / she goes shopping after school

(Tape Activity 7)

Note that many –ar verbs are used in the conversation below to reinforce the grammatical point from the two previous lessons.

Ejercicio 7 La señora Ochoa va de compras.

Completen. *(Complete.)*

Por la mañana, la señora Ochoa _____ (ir) de compras. A veces ella _____
(ir) con una amiga. Hoy la señora Ochoa necesita leche. Ella pregunta a su amiga:
  —¿Por qué no _____ (ir) (nosotras) a la lechería?   (Tape Activities 8–9)
  —No. Yo no necesito leche. Yo no _____ (ir) a la lechería. Tú _____ (ir) a la
lechería y yo _____ (ir) a la carnicería. Yo necesito carne.
  —Pero yo también necesito carne. Yo también _____ (ir) a la carnicería.
  Las dos señoras _____ (estar) en la carnicería. Hoy la carne _____ (estar)
muy buena.
  Habla el carnicero: Point out to students that it is customary in Spanish-speaking countries to exchange greetings
                               and niceties before getting down to business matters.
  —Buenos días, señoras. ¿Cómo _____ (estar) Uds. hoy?
  —(Nosotras) _____ (estar) bien. ¿Y cómo _____ (estar) Ud., señor Molina?
  —Yo _____ (estar) muy bien, gracias. ¿Y qué necesitan las señoras hoy?   ← This use of the third person
  Las dos señoras compran la carne que necesitan. El señor Molina _____ (dar)   is commonly used when
                                                                                  one wishes to be
la carne a las señoras. Las señoras pagan en la caja. Ellas _____ (dar) el dinero a   extremely polite.
la empleada que trabaja en la caja.

(Workbook, Exercises G–H)
(Quiz 2)

La contracción *al*

The preposition **a** means *to*. Study the following.

Yo voy al mercado.
Yo voy a la escuela.

Note that the definite article **el** contracts (combines) with the preposition **a** to
form one word—**al.**

a + el = al

There is no contraction with **la, los,** or **las.**

85

Ejercicio 8 ¿Adónde vas?

Contesten. *(Answer.)*

1. ¿Vas a la escuela por la mañana?
2. ¿Vas a la clase de español?
3. ¿Va Marisol al colegio por la mañana?

4. A veces, ¿vas al supermercado?
5. ¿Va Marisol al mercado?

Ejercicio 9 ¿Adónde van?

Completen según el dibujo. *(Complete according to the illustration.)*

1. Yo voy _____.

3. Vamos _____.

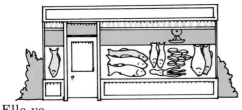

2. Ella va _____.

(Workbook, Exercise I)

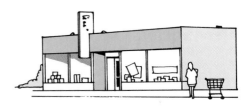

4. Ellos van _____.

La contracción *del*

The preposition **de** means *of* or *from* in English. Remember that **de** is also used to express the possessive in Spanish (*'s* or *s'* in English). For example:

el libro de Juan   *John's book*
la hermana de María   *Mary's sister*

When **de** is followed by the definite article **el,** it is contracted or combined to form one word—**del.**

> **de + el = del**

Note that with the definite articles **la, los,** and **las,** there is no contraction. Study the following.

> **Elena es de la Argentina.**
> **Ella es del continente sudamericano.**

Ejercicio 10 La amiga del muchacho

Contesten. *(Answer.)*

1. ¿Es argentina la amiga del muchacho?
2. ¿Es ella de la Argentina?
3. ¿Es ella del continente sudamericano?

4. ¿Son ellos amigos de los hermanos de Lupita?

La expresión impersonal *hay*

The impersonal expression **hay** means *there is* or *there are.*

Hay un empleado en la tienda.
Hay muchos clientes en la tienda.

Ejercicio 11 ¿Qué hay?

Completen según el dibujo. *(Complete according to the illustration.)*

1. ¿Qué hay en la sala?

2. ¿Qué hay en la frutería?

(Workbook, Exercise J)

3. ¿Qué hay en la tienda?

4. ¿Qué hay en el cuaderno?

5. ¿Qué hay en la cocina?

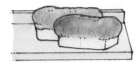

(Tape Activities 10–11)

Pronunciación

La consonante *t*

The **t** in Spanish is pronounced with the tip of the tongue pressed against the upper teeth. Like the Spanish **p,** it is not followed by any puff of air from your breath. The Spanish **t** is extremely clear.

ta	te	ti	to	tu
taco	Teresa	tienda	toma	tú
fruta	televisión	tiempo	tomate	estudia
necesita	teléfono	latín	Juanito	
está	frutería		cuanto	
lata	apuntes		alimento	
canta	bastante		tostada	

Students will probably need a great deal of practice with the **t** sound.

Trabalenguas y dictado

Teresa necesita alimentos en lata.
Juanito toma apuntes.
Tú estudias latín.
Las frutas en la frutería no están en lata.
¿Cuánto tiempo necesita Teresa en la tienda?

Expresiones útiles

A very useful expression to know is *How much does* _____ *cost?* Usually when shopping for fresh food products, a Spanish speaker will ask:

¿A cuánto está la lechuga?

¿A cuánto están las chuletas de cerdo?

When you shop for merchandise, you would use the expressions **¿Cuánto cuesta?** or **¿Cuánto es?**

¿Cuánto cuesta el disco?
¿Cuánto es el disco?

¿Cuánto cuestan los discos?
¿Cuánto son los discos?

When you are shopping, a clerk or merchant may ask you if you would like something else. He or she will ask:

¿Algo más?

If you want something else, you will, of course, tell the clerk what you want. If you want nothing else, you respond:

No, nada más, gracias.

To express the idea *How . . . !,* the expression **¡Qué . . . !** is used in Spanish.

¡Ay, qué bonito!	*Oh, how pretty!*
¡Ay, qué caro!	*Oh, how expensive!*

En el mercado
el precio

50 pesos el kilo

90 pesos la caja

(las) habichuelas

(las) fresas

En el supermercado

una botella de agua mineral

el jabón en polvo

el papel higiénico

los alimentos enlatados (en lata)

The expressions **jabón en polvo** and **polvo de jabón** are both used.

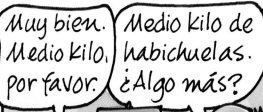

Ejercicio   Contesten. (Answer.)

1. ¿Cómo está Pedro hoy?
2. ¿Adónde va él?
3. ¿A cuánto están las habichuelas hoy?
4. ¿Cuántas habichuelas compra Pedro?
5. ¿Compra algo más en el mercado?

(Workbook, Exercise K)

Lectura cultural

¿A la tienda o al supermercado?

    ¿Hay supermercados en los países hispánicos? Claro que hay supermercados. Pero en España y en muchos países de Latinoamérica la gente[*] no va mucho a los supermercados. No compran todo[*] en la misma[*] tienda. Van de una tienda a otra.[*] En la carnicería compran carne. En la lechería compran leche.

    La gente va de compras casi todos los días.[*] ¿Por qué[*] van de una tienda a otra? ¿Y por qué van de compras casi todos los días? Pues, la calidad[*] de los productos en las tiendas especializadas es excelente. Todo está muy fresco.[*] Y los precios no son muy altos.

    Entonces, ¿qué compra la gente en los supermercados? En los supermercados compran, por ejemplo, alimentos enlatados, botellas de agua mineral, rollos de papel higiénico o cajas de jabón en polvo.

Ejercicio Contesten. *(Answer.)*

1. ¿Hay supermercados en los países hispánicos?
2. ¿Va la gente mucho a los supermercados?
3. ¿Compran todo en la misma tienda?
4. ¿Van de una tienda a otra?
5. ¿Qué compran en la carnicería?
6. ¿Qué compran en la lechería?
7. ¿Van de compras casi todos los días?
8. ¿Es buena la calidad de los productos en las tiendas pequeñas?
9. ¿Cómo está todo?
10. ¿Cómo son los precios?
11. ¿Qué compra la gente en los supermercados?

(Workbook, Exercises L–M)

---

[*]**gente** *people*　[*]**todo** *everything*　[*]**misma** *same*　[*]**otra** *another*　[*]**casi todos los días** *almost every day*　[*]**Por qué** *Why*　[*]**calidad** *quality*　[*]**fresco** *fresh*

Actividades

1 (optional)

Here is señora Ochoa's shopping list for the day. Tell what stores she will have to go to today.

leche
pescado
habichuelas
pan
carne
pasteles
papel higiénico
legumbres
fresas
polvo de jabón

2 Practice the following conversation with a classmate. Then change the conversation using the illustrations given.

— ¿Adónde vas, Inés?
— Voy de compras.
— ¿Qué necesitas?
— **Leche.**
— Ah, ¿tú vas a la lechería?
— Sí.

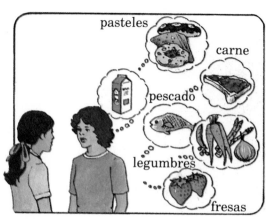

pasteles
carne
pescado
legumbres
fresas

3 Indicate whether the shopping customs described are basically those of the United States or those of the Hispanic countries.

- Vamos de compras casi todos los días.
- Compramos casi todo en la misma tienda.
- Vamos de una tienda a otra.
- Compramos casi todo en el supermercado.
- Vamos de compras uno o dos días a la semana.
- Vamos de compras en muchas tiendas pequeñas especializadas.

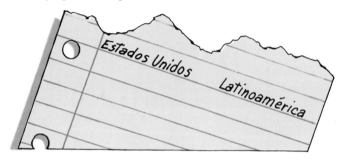

Estados Unidos

Latinoamérica

4 Describe all that you see in the photograph.

91

Revista

Noticiero

AURRERA

OCTUBRE 1983

la compra de los que saben comprar.

«La Aurrera» es un supermercado de Madrid. ¿En qué secciones hay ofertas especiales? ¿Cuál es el día de la fruta? ¿Cuántas pesetas cuesta un rollo de papel higiénico en el supermercado Aurrera?

Octubre mes de los alimentos frescos.

Ofertas muy especiales en nuestras secciones de charcutería, cremería, congelados, frutería, pescadería y carnicería.

Limpieza.

Detergente **COLON** barril 5 kilos	**629** p.
4 rollos papel higiénico **SCOTTEX**	**95** p.
MISTOL VAJILLAS, 1 litro	**65** p.

Todos los jueves día de la fruta.

Ofertas de ...

Cuando la señora Ochoa va de compras ella no compra *pounds* ni *ounces*. Ella compra kilos o gramos. En un kilo hay 2,2 *pounds* o libras. Hay cien gramos en un kilo. Hoy, ¿a cuánto está el kilo de berenjenas en el mercado en Santiago de Chile?

El señor Rivera está de compras en un supermercado de Cali, Colombia. ¿Dónde paga él?

92

Cuando un(a) argentino(a) va de compras, él o ella paga con pesos.
- ¿Con qué paga un español?
- ¿Y un guatemalteco?
- ¿Y un ecuatoriano?
- ¿Y un venezolano?
- ¿Y un peruano?

Varios mercados y tiendas

Una frutería, Barcelona

Un mercado, Guanajuato, México

Una carnicería, México

Una pastelería, Salamanca, España

8 Con la familia

La familia
Vázquez **vive** en

una casa particular.

un apartamento.

La familia **come** en el **comedor**.

(la) sopa   (las) papas   (la) ensalada   (el) helado

el desayuno   el almuerzo   la cena

Después de **la comida:**
Ellos **ven una película** en la televisión.

Ejercicio 1   La familia Vázquez
Contesten. *(Answer.)*

1. ¿Vive la familia Vázquez en un apartamento?
2. ¿Come la familia en casa?
3. ¿Comen ellos en el comedor?
4. Después de la comida, ¿ven ellos una película?
5. ¿Ven la película en la televisión?
6. ¿Ven la película en la sala?

94

Ejercicio 2 Diego Jiménez, el comilón
Completen. *(Complete.)*

Aquí está Diego Jiménez. Él come
mucho. Es muy comilón. ¿Qué come?

1. Él come _____ .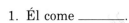

2. Él _____ .

3. _____ .

4. _____ .

5. _____ .

6. _____ .

7. _____ .

8. _____ .

En la escuela:
    Los jóvenes **escriben** mucho.

(Tape Activity 4)

(las) composiciones

(las) cartas

Ellos **leen** mucho también.

(los) libros   **(los) periódicos**   **(las) cartas**   **(las) revistas**

Ellos **aprenden** mucho.
Reciben muy buenas notas.

95

Ejercicio 3 Los alumnos aprenden mucho en la escuela. (Tape Activity 5)

Contesten. *(Answer.)*

1. En la escuela, ¿escriben mucho los jóvenes?
2. ¿Leen mucho también?

3. ¿Aprenden ellos mucho en la escuela?
4. ¿Reciben ellos buenas notas?

Ejercicio 4 Carmen Salazar escribe mucho.

Completen. *(Complete.)*

Aquí está Carmen Salazar. Ella escribe
mucho. ¿Qué escribe ella?

1. Ella escribe _____.

2. Ella _____.

3. _____.

4. _____.

Ejercicio 5 Francisco Velado lee mucho.

Contesten. *(Answer.)*

Aquí está Francisco Velado. Él lee
mucho. ¿Qué lee él?

1. Él lee _____.

3. _____.

2. Él _____.

4. _____.

Ejercicio 6 Contesten. *(Answer.)*

**Los jóvenes escriben muchas composiciones buenas
en la clase de español.**

1. ¿Quiénes escriben composiciones?
2. ¿Qué escriben los jóvenes?
3. ¿Cuántas composiciones escriben?

4. ¿Cómo son las composiciones?
5. ¿Dónde escriben las composiciones?

96   (Workbook, Exercises A–C)
      (Tape Activities 6–7)
      (Quiz 1)

Estructura

El presente de los verbos en *-er, -ir*

We have already learned that many Spanish verbs end in **-ar.** These verbs are referred to as first-conjugation verbs. Most regular Spanish verbs belong to the **-ar** group, or the first conjugation.

However, there are some very important Spanish verbs that end in **-er** and **-ir.** The **-er** verbs are referred to as second-conjugation verbs, and the **-ir** verbs are referred to as third-conjugation verbs. Note the forms of these verbs in the present tense. Pay particular attention to the endings.

-er verbs

Infinitive	comer	leer	Endings
Stem	com-	le-	
yo	como	leo	**-o**
tú	comes	lees	**-es**
él, ella, Ud.	come	lee	**-e**
nosotros, -as	comemos	leemos	**-emos**
(vosotros, -as)	(coméis)	(leéis)	**(-éis)**
ellos, ellas, Uds.	comen	leen	**-en**

Write verbs on board and underline endings for additional visual reinforcement.

-ir verbs

Infinitive	vivir	escribir	Endings
Stem	viv-	escrib-	
yo	vivo	escribo	**-o**
tú	vives	escribes	**-es**
él, ella, Ud.	vive	escribe	**-e**
nosotros, -as	vivimos	escribimos	**-imos**
(vosotros, -as)	(vivís)	(escribís)	**(-ís)**
ellos, ellas, Uds.	viven	escriben	**-en**

Note that the endings for the **-er** and **-ir** verbs are the same in all forms except **nosotros** (and **vosotros**).

nosotros	comemos	leemos	vivimos	escribimos
(vosotros)	(coméis)	(leéis)	(vivís)	(escribís)

Nota

We have already learned that many words in Spanish and English look very much alike. For this reason, it is extremely easy to guess their meanings. Do you remember that such words are called *cognates?*

To guess the meaning of certain cognates, we must stretch our imaginations. For example, let us take the verb **comprender.** Can you guess what it means? It looks somewhat similar to the English word *comprehend* and it means *to understand.* Another somewhat more difficult word is the verb **beber.** It is related to the English word *beverage* and it means *to drink.*

However, we must be very careful. There are also words called *false cognates.* A false cognate is a word that looks the same in the two languages but really has very different meanings in each language. A good example of this is the verb **asistir.** You probably think this word means *to assist,* but it more frequently means *to attend* rather than *to assist.* **Asistir** is an example of a false cognate.

Ejercicio 1   ¿A quién escribes la carta?
Practiquen la conversación. *(Practice the conversation.)*

— Oye, Enrique. ¿Qué escribes?
— Escribo una carta.
— Una carta. ¿A quién?
— A un amigo, Paco Machado.
— ¿Paco Machado? ¿Dónde vive él?
— Vive en Costa Rica. Él y yo somos buenos amigos.

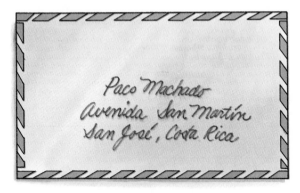

Ejercicio 2   Paco vive en Costa Rica.
Contesten según la conversación. *(Answer according to the conversation.)*

1. ¿Vive Paco Machado en Costa Rica?
2. ¿Vive Enrique en Costa Rica también?
3. ¿Escribe Enrique una carta?
4. ¿Escribe Enrique la carta o recibe la carta?

Expansion: Upon completion of each exercise, students can retell each brief story in their own words.

Ejercicio 3   Los alumnos aprenden mucho.
Contesten. *(Answer.)*

1. En la escuela, ¿aprenden mucho los alumnos?
2. ¿Aprenden español?
3. ¿Leen mucho en la clase de inglés?
4. ¿Escriben mucho también?
5. ¿Reciben buenas notas?

Ejercicio 4 Donde vivo yo

Preguntas personales. *(Answer the following personal questions.)*

1. ¿Dónde vives?
2. ¿Vives en un apartamento o en una casa particular?
3. En casa, ¿comes con la familia?
4. ¿Comes en el comedor o en la cocina?
5. Después de la cena, ¿lees el periódico?
6. ¿Lees el periódico en la sala?
7. A veces, ¿lees un libro?
8. A veces, ¿escribes una carta a un amigo o a una amiga?

A veces is new. Say **lunes, sí. Martes, no. Miércoles, sí. A veces.**

Ejercicio 5 ¡Oye! ¿Qué . . . ?

Formen preguntas según el modelo. *(Form questions according to the model.)*

Oye, Catalina. ¿Qué lees?

1.   2.   3.   4.

(Workbook, Exercise D)

Ejercicio 6 Nosotros vivimos en los Estados Unidos.

Contesten con *nosotros*. *(Answer with **nosotros**.)*

1. ¿Dónde viven Uds.?
2. ¿Viven Uds. en una casa particular?
3. ¿Viven Uds. en un apartamento?
4. ¿Escriben Uds. mucho en la clase de español?
5. Y en la clase de inglés, ¿escriben Uds. mucho?
6. ¿Reciben Uds. buenas notas en español?
7. ¿Aprenden Uds. mucho en la escuela?
8. ¿Leen Uds. muchos libros?
9. ¿Comen Uds. en la cafetería de la escuela?

(Workbook, Exercise E)

Ejercicio 7 ¿Y Uds. también?

Sigan el modelo. *(Follow the model.)*

Nosotros vivimos en los Estados Unidos.
Y Uds. también viven en los Estados Unidos, ¿no?

1. Vivimos en los Estados Unidos.
2. Recibimos el periódico todos los días.
3. Leemos el periódico todos los días.
4. Aprendemos mucho del periódico.

(Workbook, Exercise F)

Ejercicio 8 La familia Vázquez vive en Caracas.

Completen. *(Complete.)*

1. La familia Vázquez _____ en Caracas, la capital de Venezuela. **vivir**
2. Ellos _____ en un apartamento. **vivir**
3. ¿Dónde _____ Uds.? **vivir**
4. Nosotros _____ en _____. **vivir**
5. ¿_____ tú en un apartamento o en una casa particular? **Vivir**
6. Yo _____ en _____. **vivir**
7. La familia Vázquez _____ en casa. **comer**
8. ¿Dónde _____ Uds.? **comer**
9. Nosotros _____ en casa también, pero a veces _____ en un restaurante.
   comer, comer
10. Diego y Carmen Vázquez _____ a un colegio en Caracas. **asistir**
11. Uds. no _____ a un colegio, ¿verdad? **asistir**
12. No, nosotros _____ a una escuela secundaria. **asistir**
13. Diego y Carmen Vázquez _____, _____ y _____ mucho en el colegio.
    escribir, leer, aprender
14. Y yo también _____, _____ y _____ mucho en la escuela. **escribir, leer,
    aprender**

(Tape Activities 8–11)

Expansion: More-able students can write a story about the Vázquez family.

El verbo *ver*

The verb **ver** functions the same as a regular **-er** verb. Note, however, that in the **tú**, **él**, and **ellos** forms, there is only one syllable.

Infinitive	ver
yo	veo
tú	ves
él, ella, Ud.	ve
nosotros, -as	vemos
(vosotros, -as)	(veis)
ellos, ellas, Uds.	ven

Ejercicio 9 ¿Qué ve?

Completen con el verbo *ver*. *(Complete with the correct form of the verb **ver**.)*

1. Muchas veces yo _____ una película en la televisión.
2. Yo _____ las películas con la familia.
3. Las películas que nosotros _____ son muy interesantes.
4. ¿_____ tú muchas películas en la televisión también?
5. ¿_____ Uds. películas también en la escuela?

(Workbook, Exercise G)
      (Quiz 2)

Nota

You will come across many Spanish nouns that end in **-dad** or **-tad.** The **-dad** or **-tad** endings in Spanish almost always correspond to the *-ty* ending in English. Most words that end in **-dad** or **-tad** are cognates. See if you can guess the meaning of the following words.

la universidad	**la capacidad**
la generalidad	**la responsabilidad**
la oportunidad	**la popularidad**

Note that all Spanish nouns that end in **-dad** or **-tad** are feminine and take the definite article **la.** To form the plural, an **-es** is added.

Ejercicio 10 *Give the Spanish equivalent for each of the following.*

1. facility
2. mentality
3. universality
4. entity

Ejercicio 11 *Write the plural of the following words.*

1. la universidad
2. la responsabilidad
3. la oportunidad
4. la capacidad

(Tape Activities 12–13)

Pronunciación   La consonante *d*

The pronunciation of the consonant **d** in Spanish varies according to its position in the word. When a word begins with **d** (initial position) or follows the consonants **l** or **n,** the tongue gently strikes the back of the upper front teeth.

da	**de**	**di**	**do**	**du**
da	de	Diego	donde	duda
tienda	desayuno	disco	aprendo	duro
merienda	derecho	día	comprendo	
	aprende	dinero	segundo	
	comprende	difícil	cuando	

D is a very difficult sound for English speakers to make. Have students practice the tongue positions described.

When **d** appears within the word between vowels (medial position), the **d** almost sounds like the *th* in the English word *then.* To make the proper sound, the tongue strikes the lower part of the upper teeth, almost between the upper and lower teeth.

da	**de**	**di**	**do**	**du**
ensalada	Adela	periódico	helado	educación
comida	panadero	edificio	estado	
		adiós	todo	
			divertido	
			pescado	
			mercado	
			empleado	

101

When a word ends in **d** (final position), the **d** is either pronounced like a *th*, omitted completely, or given a very, very soft **d** sound.

ciudad
universidad
oportunidad

Trabalenguas y dictado

Diego da el dinero al empleado en la tienda.
¿Dónde está el disco de Donato?
La panadería está en un edificio en la avenida de los Estados Unidos.
El empleado vende pescado en el mercado.
Diego estudia en la universidad en la ciudad de Madrid.

Expresiones útiles

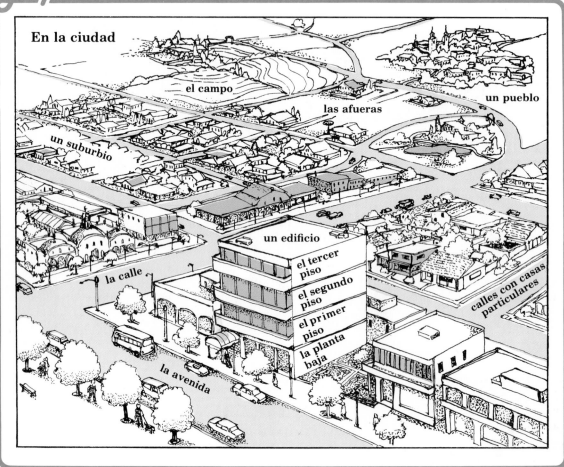

En la ciudad

el campo

las afueras

un pueblo

un suburbio

un edificio

la calle

el tercer piso
el segundo piso
el primer piso
la planta baja

calles con casas particulares

la avenida

conversación

¿Dónde vives?

Carlos   Oye, Cristina. Tú vives en Madrid, ¿no?

Cristina   Sí, vivo en Madrid. Soy madrileña.

Carlos   ¿Dónde vives en Madrid?

Cristina   Vivo en la Calle Velázquez, ciento treinta.

Carlos   ¿Viven Uds. en la planta baja?

Cristina   En la planta baja, no. Vivimos en el segundo piso, derecho.

(Tape Activities 14–15)

Ejercicio Contesten. *(Answer.)*

1. ¿Vive Cristina en Madrid?
2. ¿Es ella madrileña?
3. ¿En qué calle vive ella?
4. ¿Vive ella con la familia?
5. ¿Viven ellos en la planta baja?
6. ¿En qué piso viven?

(Workbook, Exercises H–I)

En las grandes ciudades

En los países hispánicos la mayoría° de la gente vive en las grandes ciudades. Por consiguiente, muchas familias viven en apartamentos. Es verdad que hay también suburbios con casas particulares en las afueras de las ciudades. Pero la mayoría de la gente vive en las ciudades; no vive en los suburbios.

En las ciudades de España, como Madrid y Barcelona, los edificios no son muy altos. Al contrario, en muchas ciudades de Latinoamérica, como Caracas y Bogotá, hay edificios muy altos como en las ciudades de los Estados Unidos.

Como° muchas familias viven en las ciudades, mucha gente va a casa al mediodía. Toman el almuerzo en casa. No toman el almuerzo en un restaurante o en un café. Por lo general el almuerzo es una comida bastante importante. Comen sopa, ensalada, carne y legumbres. La cena es una comida bastante ligera.° En muchos países hispánicos la familia cena a eso de° las ocho. En España no cenan hasta las nueve y media o las diez de la noche.

° **mayoría** *majority*   ° **Como** *Since*   ° **ligera** *light*   ° **a eso de** *at about*

Ejercicio   Escojan. *(Choose.)*

1. En los países hispánicos, la mayoría de la gente vive en _____.
   a. los suburbios
   b. apartamentos en las grandes ciudades
   c. casas particulares

2. Muchas familias viven en apartamentos porque _____.
   a. viven en las grandes ciudades
   b. viven en las afueras de las ciudades
   c. no hay suburbios

3. Los edificios son muy altos en _____.
   a. las ciudades de España
   b. muchas ciudades de Latinoamérica
   c. los suburbios

4. Muchas familias toman el almuerzo en _____.
   a. un restaurante
   b. una cafetería
   c. casa

5. _____ es una comida bastante importante para las familias hispánicas.
   a. El desayuno
   b. El almuerzo
   c. La cena

6. En muchos países las familias cenan _____.
   a. a eso de las diez
   b. al mediodía
   c. a eso de las ocho

Actividades

1 (optional) **Entrevista**

- ¿Vives en una ciudad, en un suburbio o en el campo?
- ¿Vives en un apartamento o en una casa particular?
- ¿En qué calle vives?
- ¿En qué ciudad o pueblo vives?
- ¿A qué hora tomas el almuerzo?
- ¿Al mediodía comes en casa o en la cafetería de la escuela?
- ¿Es el almuerzo una comida muy importante o es una comida ligera?
- ¿A qué hora cenas?
- ¿A qué hora cenan en muchos países de Latinoamérica?
- ¿A qué hora cenan en España?

2 Make a list of the things that you do after dinner.

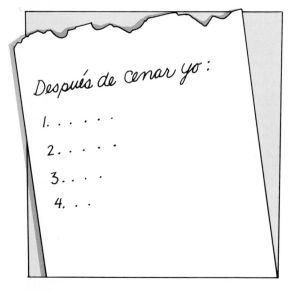

Después de cenar yo:

1. . . . . .
2. . . . . .
3. . . . .
4. . . .

3 Answer the following questions based on the illustrations.

- ¿Come la familia en el comedor o en la cocina?
- ¿Qué comen?
- Después de la comida, ¿van a la sala?
- ¿Leen el periódico?
- ¿Miran la televisión?
- ¿Ven una película en la televisión?

4 Speak about the photographs. Say all you can about them.

5 Have a contest with a classmate. In three minutes make up as many questions as you can about the preceding photographs. Whoever makes up the most questions is the winner.

6 Así soy yo.

Let's keep going. Pretend you are writing a letter to your pen pal in Latin America. Think of all you can say about yourself in Spanish. Tell your friend some things about your school life:

- what subjects you study
- who your teachers are
- what courses are fun
- what courses are easy or difficult
- in what subjects you get good or bad grades

Continue by telling your friend some of the things you do after school. Let him or her know:

- where you live
- some of the things you do at home after school
- some of the things you eat for dinner
- where you eat
- with whom you eat
- that you sometimes watch a movie on television but that you also study
- that you sometimes speak with a friend on the telephone
- what you talk about on the telephone
- who your telephone companion is
- what he or she is like

107

Revista

Apartamientos en Santiago de Chile

Apartamientos en Madrid, España

Una casa particular en la Ciudad de México

Una casa particular en Venezuela

EDIFICIO COCHABAMBA 13

PASEO DE LA HABANA

POTOSI

BELAUNDE

13

COCHABAMBA

(TIPE DE VERGARA)

A 20 MTS. DEL PASEO DE

1 DORM. 4.975.0

2 DORM. 5.875.0

CON SALONES DE 30 y 35 M

La familia Iriarte vive en la Ciudad de México. Ellos toman el almuerzo en casa. ¿Comen ellos en el comedor o en la cocina? ¿Es una comida ligera? ¿Qué comen ellos?

EL PAIS

Graciela Tejada lee el periódico «El País» en un quiosco de Madrid. ¿Hay muchas revistas en el quiosco también?

Repaso

La familia Ureña vive en un apartamento en la ciudad de Caracas. Caracas es la capital de Venezuela. Ellos viven en el cuarto piso de un edificio alto en la avenida Simón Bolívar.

Isabel y Rafael Ureña asisten a un colegio privado en la capital. Ellos toman muchos cursos. Son muy listos y sacan muy buenas notas. En el colegio ellos estudian inglés. Ellos aprenden mucho. Ellos hablan mucho en la clase de inglés. A veces cantan también. El profesor de inglés es el señor Brown. Él es de Chicago pero ahora vive en Caracas y enseña inglés en el colegio de Isabel y Rafael. El señor Brown es muy simpático. Isabel y Rafael son muy aficionados al inglés.

Después de las clases, Isabel y Rafael y otros amigos del colegio van a un café. En el café hablan y toman una limonada. Luego van a casa. En casa cenan con la familia. Después de la cena ellos estudian. Luego van a la sala donde miran la televisión.

Ejercicio 1   Corrijan las oraciones falsas. *(Correct the false statements.)*

1. La familia Ureña vive en una casa privada.
2. Ellos viven en Bogotá, la capital de Colombia.
3. Ellos viven en la planta baja de un edificio pequeño en la avenida San Martín.
4. Isabel y Rafael asisten a una escuela pública en las afueras de Caracas.
5. En la escuela ellos toman dos cursos y sacan muy malas notas.
6. Ellos estudian francés.
7. El profesor de inglés es de Caracas.
8. Después de las clases, Isabel y Rafael trabajan en una tienda.
9. Luego ellos van a un restaurante donde cenan con la familia.

El presente de los verbos regulares

Review the following forms of the present tense of regular **-ar, -er,** and **-ir** verbs.

Infinitive	hablar	comer	vivir
yo	hablo	como	vivo
tú	hablas	comes	vives
él, ella, Ud.	habla	come	vive
nosotros, -as	hablamos	comemos	vivimos
(vosotros, -as)	(habláis)	(coméis)	(vivís)
ellos, ellas, Uds.	hablan	comen	viven

Ejercicio 2 Contesten. *(Answer.)*

1. ¿Estudias español?
2. En la clase de español, ¿hablas? ¿Lees y escribes también?
3. A veces, ¿cantan Uds. en la clase de español?
4. ¿Toca el (la) profesor(a) la guitarra?
5. ¿Leen y escriben Uds. mucho en la clase de español?
6. Después de las clases, ¿trabajas?

Ejercicio 3 Completen. *(Complete.)*

1. Nosotros somos muy inteligentes. En la escuela nosotros _____ (tomar) muchos cursos. Nosotros _____ (aprender) mucho. _____ (Leer) muchos libros y _____ (escribir) muchas composiciones.
2. La señora Mariscal es la profesora de español. Ella _____ (enseñar) muy bien. A veces ella _____ (cantar) y _____ (tocar) la guitarra. Los alumnos de la señora Mariscal _____ (aprender) mucho. Muchos alumnos de la señora Mariscal _____ (recibir) muy buenas notas porque _____ (trabajar) mucho en la clase de la señora Mariscal. Ella es una profesora simpática.

Los verbos *ir, dar, estar*

Review the forms of the present tense of the verbs **ir, dar,** and **estar.** Remember to pay particular attention to the **yo** form.

Infinitive	ir	dar	estar
yo	**voy**	**doy**	**estoy**
tú	vas	das	estás
él, ella, Ud.	va	da	está
nosotros, -as	vamos	damos	estamos
(vosotros, -as)	(vais)	(dais)	(estáis)
ellos, ellas, Uds.	van	dan	están

Ejercicio 4 Completen. *(Complete.)*

Carlos ¡Hola, Roberto! ¿Cómo _____ (estar) hoy?

Roberto _____ (Estar) muy bien, gracias. ¿Y tú? ¿Cómo _____ (estar), hombre?

Carlos Yo también _____ (estar) muy bien. ¿Adónde _____ (ir) ahora?

Roberto Ahora yo _____ (ir) al café León. ¿Y tú? ¿Adónde _____ (ir)?

Carlos Yo _____ (ir) a casa.

A complete Unit Self-test is provided for the students in the Workbook.
Two Unit Tests, one written and one oral, appear in the Test Package.

Lectura cultural

opcional

un mercado al aire libre

un puesto

una canasta

El regateo° en un mercado

María Cortés es una muchacha mexicana. Cuando ella va de compras, ella va a un mercado grande al aire libre. En el mercado hay muchos puestos. Ella va de un puesto a otro. En uno compra carne. En otro compra legumbres.

En un puesto María ve una canasta bonita. Ella mira la canasta.

El empleado da un precio pero María paga otro. Es el regateo. En el mercado María siempre° regatea.° Pero cuando ella va a un supermercado moderno o a una tienda elegante, ella no regatea. Ella paga un precio fijo.°

° **regateo** *bargaining* ° **cara** *expensive* ° **siempre** *always* ° **regatea** *bargains*
° **fijo** *fixed*

112

Ejercicio 1 Escojan. *(Choose.)*

1. María Cortés es de _____.
   - a. México
   - b. Colombia
   - c. Costa Rica

2. Ella va a _____.
   - a. una tienda especializada
   - b. un supermercado
   - c. un mercado grande al aire libre

3. En el mercado hay _____.
   - a. muchas tiendas
   - b. muchos puestos
   - c. muchas pastelerías

4. En un puesto María ve _____.
   - a. un cuaderno
   - b. una canasta
   - c. una caja

5. María compra la canasta y paga _____.
   - a. cien pesos
   - b. trescientos pesos
   - c. doscientos pesos

6. María siempre regatea en _____.
   - a. el supermercado
   - b. la tienda
   - c. el mercado

Ejercicio 2 Preguntas personales *(Answer the following personal questions.)*

- A veces, ¿compras comida?
- ¿Vas a un mercado al aire libre o vas a un supermercado?
- ¿A qué supermercado vas? ¿Dónde está?
- ¿Hay muchos puestos distintos en el supermercado?
- En el supermercado, ¿regateas?
- ¿Pagas un precio fijo?
- ¿Regatean los mexicanos en un supermercado?
- ¿Regatean ellos en los mercados al aire libre?
- ¿Regateas tú a veces?

Un mercado en Madrid

El mercado «La Lagunilla», Ciudad de México

Lectura cultural

el parque

un lago

un barquito

Los amigos reman.

El señor vende refrescos.

Un domingo en el parque

En las ciudades de los países hispánicos hay muchos parques bonitos—el Retiro en Madrid, el Parque Palermo en Buenos Aires, el Bosque de Chapultepec en México.

Los parques en las ciudades hispánicas son muy populares. Mucha gente va a los parques los domingos. Pasan* toda la tarde en el parque. En el parque hay muchos puestos donde venden helados y otros refrescos. Los amigos toman una merienda, hablan, cantan, dan un paseo* o descansan.*

En el Bosque de Chapultepec y también en el Retiro y en el Parque Palermo hay un lago muy bonito. A veces la gente alquila* un barquito y rema en el lago.

---

*Pasan *They spend, pass (time)*   *dan un paseo *take a walk*   *descansan *rest*
*alquila *rent*

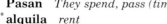

Ejercicio Contesten. *(Answer.)*

1. ¿Cuál es el parque famoso de Madrid?
2. ¿Cuál es el parque famoso de Buenos Aires?
3. ¿Cuál es el parque famoso de México?
4. ¿Cómo son los parques?
5. ¿Cuándo va mucha gente al parque?
6. ¿Qué venden en los puestos en el parque?
7. ¿Qué toman los amigos?
8. A veces, ¿dan un paseo en el parque?
9. ¿En qué parques hay un lago?
10. ¿Qué alquila la gente?
11. ¿Dónde reman?

Lectura cultural

las montañas

el techo

la paja

las piedras

el vestido

el maíz

las tortillas

el suelo

La vida en un pueblo indio

Elena Kunil es una muchacha india. Ella vive en un pueblo pequeño en las montañas de Guatemala, en Centroamérica. Ella vive en una casa de piedra con techo de paja. La familia de Elena no come en el comedor. En la casa no hay comedor. La familia come en el suelo delante de° la casa. Ellos no comen papas, carne y ensalada. Ellos comen habichuelas y tortillas de maíz.

Después de la comida, Elena no lee el periódico. No reciben periódicos en el pueblo donde vive. Y ella no ve una película en la televisión. No hay televisión en la casa de Elena.

La familia de Elena no habla mucho español. Ellos hablan una lengua° india. Elena no aprende el español en la escuela porque° ella no asiste a la escuela. La falta° de educación y la falta de nutrición son grandes problemas sociales en muchas regiones remotas de Latinoamérica.

Luego, ¿cómo es la vida° social de Elena? Pues, los domingos ella va al mercado con la familia. El mercado no está cerca de° la casa. Está lejos.° Ellos van al mercado a pie.° Ellos llevan° mucho al mercado. En las canastas que llevan hay productos que venden en el mercado. Con el dinero que reciben compran cosas que necesitan en casa.

En el mercado Elena habla con los amigos que viven en otros pueblos. Las muchachas que son de otros pueblos no llevan° el mismo vestido° que lleva Elena. Todas las señoras y todas las muchachas que viven en el mismo pueblo llevan el mismo vestido.

°**delante de** *in front of*　°**lengua** *language*　°**porque** *because*　°**falta** *lack*
°**vida** *life*　°**cerca de** *near*　°**lejos** *far*　°**a pie** *on foot*　°**llevan** *carry*
°**llevan** *wear*　°**vestido** *dress*

Ejercicio 1 *Look at these photographs and
tell all you can about a
young girl's life in a remote,
mountainous village of Guatemala,
Central America.*

Ejercicio 2 *Complete the following statements and make comparisons between your life and
the life of Elena Kunil.*

1. Elena Kunil vive en un pueblo remoto en las montañas de Guatemala, pero
   yo . . .
2. La familia de Elena come en el suelo delante de la casa, pero yo . . .
3. Elena come habichuelas y tortillas de maíz, pero yo . . .
4. Elena Kunil no lee el periódico porque no reciben periódicos en el pueblo donde
   vive, pero yo . . .
5. Elena Kunil no asiste a la escuela, pero yo . . .

Un árbol genealógico

(Tape Activity 1)

La familia Fuentes

el abuelo   la abuela   el abuelo   la abuela

el tío   la tía   el padre   la madre

el primo   la prima   los hijos

el hermano   la hermana

Es la familia Fuentes.
El señor y la señora Fuentes **tienen** dos **hijos**.
Tienen también un **perrito**.

Ejercicio 1 El señor y la señora Fuentes

Contesten. *(Answer.)*

1. ¿Tienen dos hijos el señor y la señora Fuentes?
2. ¿Tienen ellos un perrito también?
3. ¿Tienen primos Sarita y Pablo?
4. ¿Tienen ellos abuelos?
5. ¿Tiene un hermano Sarita?
6. ¿Tiene una hermana Pablo?

Ejercicio 2 La familia Fuentes

Lean el párrafo. *Read the paragraph. (The words in dark type are new. Can you guess their meanings by referring to the family tree?)*

El señor y la señora Fuentes son los padres de Pablo y Sarita. El señor Fuentes es **el marido** de la señora Fuentes y la señora Fuentes es **la esposa (la mujer)** del señor Fuentes. Los padres del señor Fuentes y los padres de la señora Fuentes son los abuelos de Pablo y Sarita. Pablo y Sarita son **los nietos** de sus abuelos. Los hermanos de los padres de Pablo y Sarita son sus tíos. Sarita y Pablo son **los sobrinos** de sus tíos. Los hijos de sus tíos son los primos de Sarita y Pablo.

You may wish to permit students to read the paragraph silently. Then have them read it orally. You can also ask questions in English such as, "You are the *what* of your aunts and uncles?" Have them respond with the appropriate Spanish word.

Note that the masculine plural form of a noun is used to include all members of that particular group.

el señor y la señora	→	los señores
el padre y la madre	→	los padres
el hijo y la hija	→	los hijos
el sobrino y la sobrina	→	los sobrinos

We have already learned about false cognates. The word **pariente** is another false cognate. It looks like the English word *parent*, but its real meaning in English is *relative*.

(Workbook, Exercises A–B)

Ejercicio 3 Los parientes

Completen el diccionario.
(Complete the dictionary.)

. . . el padre de su padre o de su madre
. . . la hermana de su padre
. . . el hermano de su madre
. . . los hijos de sus tíos
. . . los hijos de sus hermanos

(Quiz 1)

119

Estructura

El presente del verbo *tener*

The verb **tener** is a very useful and important verb. The verb **tener** is irregular. Study the following forms.

Infinitive	tener
yo	tengo
tú	tienes
él, ella, Ud.	tiene
nosotros, -as	tenemos
(vosotros, -as)	(tenéis)
ellos, ellas, Uds.	tienen

Note that the endings of the verb **tener** are the same as those of a regular **-er** verb. Note also that the **yo** form has a **g** and that the **e** in the stem changes to **ie** in the **tú, él,** and **ellos** forms.

La edad

Note that the verb **tener** is used to express age.

¿Cuántos años tienes?	*How old are you?*
Yo tengo dieciséis años.	*I'm 16 years old.*

Ejercicio 1 Los señores tienen dos hijos.
Contesten. *(Answer.)*

1. ¿Tienen los señores Fuentes dos hijos?
2. ¿Tiene Sarita un hermano?
3. ¿Tiene Pablo una hermana?
4. ¿Tienen ellos un perrito?

(Tape Activity 5)

Ejercicio 2 ¿Tienes una hermana?
Practiquen la conversación. *(Practice the conversation.)*

— Oye, Diego. ¿Tienes una hermana?
— Sí. Tengo una hermana.
— ¿Cuántos años tiene ella?
— Ella tiene catorce años.
— ¿Tienen Uds. un perrito?
— No, no tenemos un perrito. Tenemos un gato.

This conversation enables students to hear, see, and use all forms of the verb **tener** in a natural context.

120 *Expansion:* Have students change conversation based on their own families.

Ejercicio 3 ¿Cuántos hermanos tienes?
Preguntas personales *(Personal questions)*

1. ¿Tienes hermanos?
2. ¿Cuántos hermanos tienes?
3. ¿Tienes primos?
4. ¿Cuántos primos tienes?
5. ¿Tienes un perro o un gato?
6. ¿Cuántos años tienes?

Expansion:
Students can make up original questions using **cuántos** with other family members: **abuelos, tíos.**

Ejercicio 4 ¿Tienes . . . ? Sí, tengo . . . .

*Ask a friend questions using the **tú** form of the verb **tener** and the words below. Then have your friend answer your questions.*

1. un hermano
2. una hermana
3. un primo
4. una prima
5. un perro
6. un gato

Students can work in pairs to do this exercise.

Ejercicio 5 ¿Tiene Ud . . . ?

*Ask your teacher questions using the **Ud.** form of the verb **tener** and the words below.*

1. hijos
2. hermanos
3. primos
4. un perro o un gato

(Tape Activities 6–7)

Ejercicio 6 ¿Qué tienen Uds.?
Sigan el modelo. *(Follow the model.)*

Tenemos una casa en las afueras de Madrid.
¡Perdón! ¿Qué tienen Uds.?

1. Tenemos un apartamento en Madrid.
2. Tenemos una casa en las afueras.
3. Tenemos un perrito adorable.
4. Tenemos un gato divertido.

Ejercicio 7 Sí, tenemos . . . .
Contesten con *nosotros.* *(Answer with the **nosotros** form.)*

1. ¿Tienen Uds. una casa particular?
2. ¿Tienen Uds. un apartamento?
3. ¿Tienen Uds. un perro?
4. ¿Tienen Uds. un gato?
5. ¿Tienen Uds. una familia grande?

(Tape Activities 8–9)

Reminder: There are additional oral exercises for each structure point of each lesson in the Teacher's Resource Kit.

121

Ejercicio 8 La familia Flores

Enrique   Josefa

Completen con *tener*. *(Complete with **tener**.)*

Es la familia Flores. Ellos _____ un apartamento (piso) en Madrid. Ellos _____ una casa en la costa también.

En la familia Flores hay cuatro personas: la madre, el padre y los dos hijos. Enrique, el hijo, _____ una hermana. Josefa, la hija, _____ un hermano. Enrique _____ dieciséis años y Josefa _____ dieciocho.

¿Cuántos años _____ tú? ¿Y cuántos hermanos _____? ¿_____ Uds. un gato? ¿_____ Uds. un perro?

Yo soy Felipe. Yo _____ quince años. Yo _____ dos hermanos. Nosotros _____ un gato adorable, pero no _____ perro. (Workbook, Exercise C)
(Quiz 2)

La expresión *tener que*

Expansion: Have students compare their family with the Flores family.

The expression **tener que** means *to have to*. Note that **tener que** is followed by the infinitive, the form of the verb that ends in **-ar, -er,** or **-ir.** Observe the following.

> **Yo tengo que preparar la comida.**
> **Tenemos que comer.**
> **Y luego tenemos que ir al concierto.**

Ejercicio 9 ¡Ay! ¡Cómo tengo que trabajar!   (Tape Activity 10)
Preguntas personales

1. ¿Tienes que trabajar mucho en la clase de español?
2. ¿Tienes que hablar español en la clase de español?
3. ¿Tienes que estudiar mucho?
4. ¿Tienen Uds. que leer mucho?
5. ¿Tienen Uds. que aprender la gramática?
6. ¿Tienen Uds. que escribir muchas composiciones?

Ejercicio 10 Tenemos que aprender mucho.

The verb root is given so students will focus their attention on the importance of the correct infinitive ending.

Completen. *(Complete.)*

1. En la clase de español, nosotros _____ que habl____ mucho.
2. Todos los alumnos _____ que comprend____, habl____, le____ y escrib____.
3. A veces un(a) alumno(a) _____ que mir____ un dibujo y _____ que habl____ de lo que ve en el dibujo.   (Workbook, Exercises D–E) (Quiz 3)
4. Nosotros _____ que aprend____ mucho en la clase de español.

Expansion: Have students make up original sentences stating what they have to do now.

Los adjetivos posesivos

The possessive adjectives—*my, your, his, her, our, their*—are used to express possession or ownership. As with other adjectives, the possessive adjectives in Spanish must agree with the nouns they modify. Note that the adjectives **mi, tu,** and **su** have only two forms, singular and plural. Observe the following.

mi libro y mi carta	**mis libros y mis cartas**
tu libro y tu carta	**tus libros y tus cartas**
su libro y su carta	**sus libros y sus cartas**

The possessive adjective **su** also has only two forms. The adjective **su** can refer to many persons. For this reason, it has many meanings in English. It can mean *his, her, their,* or *your.*

el libro de Roberto	**su libro**
el libro de Susana	**su libro**
el libro de Ud.	**su libro**
el libro de Roberto y Susana	**su libro**
el libro de Uds.	**su libro**

Usually the meaning of the possessive adjective **su** is clear from its use in the sentence. If there should be any confusion, the preposition **de** plus a pronoun can be used.

el libro de Roberto	**el libro de él**
el libro de Susana	**el libro de ella**
el libro de Ud.	**el libro de Ud.**
el libro de Felipe y Roberto	**el libro de ellos**
el libro de Susana y María	**el libro de ellas**
el libro de Uds.	**el libro de Uds.**

Note that since the possessive adjective **nuestro** *(our)* ends in **-o**, it has four forms—**nuestro, nuestra, nuestros, nuestras**—the same as any other adjective that ends in **-o**.

nuestro apartamento	**nuestros apartamentos**
nuestra casa	**nuestras casas**

The possessive adjective **vuestro** corresponds to the subject pronoun **vosotros** and it is used in Spain when talking to two or more friends. Like **nuestro,** the adjective **vuestro** has four forms: **vuestro, vuestra, vuestros, vuestras.**

Ejercicio 11 Aquí está mi . . . .

(Tape Activity 11)

Contesten según el modelo. *(Answer according to the model.)*

¿Dónde está tu cuaderno?
Aquí está mi cuaderno.

1. ¿Dónde está tu amigo?
2. Y tu amiga, ¿dónde está?
3. ¿Dónde está tu libro?
4. ¿Dónde están tus amigos?
5. ¿Dónde están tus libros?

It is recommended that Exercises 11–16 be done orally first. Try to insist that students use proper intonation to reinforce the naturalness of the response.

123

Ejercicio 12 ¿Tienes tu . . . ?

(Tape Activity 12)

Sigan el modelo. *(Follow the model.)*

Tengo mi libro.
Ricardo, ¿tienes tu libro también?

1. Tengo mi cuaderno.
2. Tengo mi disco.
3. Tengo mi guitarra.

4. Tengo mis libros.
5. Tengo mis apuntes.
6. Tengo mis cartas.

(Tape Activity 13)

Ejercicio 13 ¿Y su hermano . . . ?

Sigan el modelo. *(Follow the model.)*

¿Está el hermano de Juanito?
Sí, sí. Su hermano está.

Exercises 13 and 14 separate masculine and feminine possessors. Students are sometimes confused as to whether the agreement is with the possessor or the thing possessed.

1. ¿Está el primo de Juanito?
2. ¿Está el amigo de Juanito?
3. ¿Está la hermana de Juanito?

4. ¿Está la amiga de Juanito?
5. ¿Están los primos de Juanito?
6. ¿Están los amigos de Juanito?

Ejercicio 14 ¿De quién? (Tape Activity 14)

Sigan el modelo. *(Follow the model.)*

Es el hermano de Susana.
Su hermano es muy simpático.

1. Es el amigo de Susana.
2. Es el primo de Susana.
3. Es la madre de Susana.

4. Es la hermana de Susana.
5. Son los hermanos de Susana.
6. Son los amigos de Susana.

Ejercicio 15 En nuestra clase de español (Tape Activity 15)

Contesten. *(Answer.)*

1. ¿Hablan Uds. con su profesor(a) de español?
2. ¿Leen Uds. su libro de español?
3. ¿Escriben Uds. en su cuaderno?

4. ¿Miran Uds. sus notas?
5. ¿Hablan Uds. con sus amigos en la clase de español?

Ejercicio 16 Los Ochoa y su familia

Contesten. *(Answer.)*

1. ¿Está el apartamento de la familia Ochoa en Madrid?
2. ¿Viven sus parientes en Madrid también?

3. A veces, ¿van ellos a la casa de sus parientes?
4. ¿Comen en su casa?
5. ¿Hablan ellos con sus parientes?

(Workbook, Exercises F–I)

Ejercicio 17   Mi familia

Completen con el adjetivo posesivo apropiado. *(Complete with the appropriate possessive adjective.)*

Yo tengo cuatro primos. _____ primos no viven en _____ casa. Yo vivo con _____ padres y ellos viven con _____ padres. _____ prima Adela tiene un hermano. _____ hermano es Carlos. Adela y Carlos son los hijos de _____ tía Isabel. _____ tía Isabel es la hermana de _____ padre. _____ marido es _____ tío Enrique. _____ otros dos primos son Paco y Tadeo. Ellos son los hijos de _____ tío Ricardo. _____ tío Ricardo es el hermano de _____ madre. _____ esposa es _____ tía Gertrudis. Ellos tienen un perro. _____ perro es Chispa. Nosotros no tenemos perro. Tenemos un gato. _____ gato es Estrella.

Oye, amigo. ¿Cuántas personas hay en _____ familia? ¿Es grande o pequeña _____ familia? ¿Tienes muchos primos? ¿Dónde viven _____ primos?

(Workbook, Exercise J)
(Quiz 4)

Pronunciación   Las consonantes *b, v*

There is no difference in pronunciation between a **b** and a **v** in Spanish. The **b** or **v** sound is somewhat softer than the sound of an English *b*. When making the **b, v** sound in Spanish, the lips barely touch.

ba	be	bi	bo	bu
bajo	bebé	bien	botella	burrito
trabaja	escribe	biología	recibo	bueno
sábado		rubio		abuelo

(Tape Activities 16–17)

va	ve	vi	vo	vu
va	ve	viudo	vosotros	vuelo
vamos	avenida	vive	favor	vuestro
	nueve	televisión		
	verano	revista		
	primavera	viento		
		invierno		

Trabalenguas y dictado

El joven vive en la avenida Vigo.
El bebé escribe en la revista.
El joven rubio ve el burro en la televisión.
Benito trabaja con Bárbara en la clase de biología.

Nota _____

   v de «vaca»   *b* de «burro»

Since it is difficult to determine whether a word is spelled with a **b** or a **v**, Spanish speakers will sometimes ask ¿*v* de «vaca» o *b* de «burro»?

conversación

¿Cuántos hermanos tienes?   (Tape Activity 18)

Ejercicio   Contesten. *(Answer.)*

1. ¿Cuántos hermanos tiene Tadeo?
2. ¿Cuántos años tiene su hermano?
3. ¿Cuántos años tiene su hermana?
4. ¿Quién es el bebé de la familia?
5. ¿Cuántos años tiene él?

Additional personalization: **¿Eres el (la) bebé de tu familia?**
¿Quién es el (la) bebé de la familia?
¿Cuántos años tiene?
Y tú, ¿cuántos años tienes?

Options for **Conversación:**
1) Class can practice it orally.
2) Students can present it to class.
3) Students can work in pairs at their seats.
4) Students can read the conversation.
5) Answers to the questions can be written.

126

Lectura cultural

La familia hispana

La familia tiene mucha importancia en la sociedad hispánica. Cuando un joven hispano habla de su familia, por lo general, no habla solamente* de sus padres y de sus hermanos. Habla también de sus abuelos, de sus tíos y de sus primos. En fin,* habla de todos sus parientes. Los padrinos* también son como miembros de la familia.

Muchas veces los abuelos viven con sus hijos y sus nietos—sobre todo* si un abuelo o una abuela es viudo o viuda.*

Aquí tenemos los nombres de varios miembros de una familia hispana. Los nombres también reflejan la importancia que tiene la familia de una persona.

el marido	la mujer
Arturo Guzmán Echeverría	María Cristina Blanco Robles

Option:
You may wish to present only the first part of the Lectura and explain to students the Hispanic custom for taking names.

---

solamente *only*   *En fin* *In brief*   *padrinos* *godparents*   *sobre todo* *especially, above all*   *viuda(o)* *widow(er)*

Toda la familia asiste a la boda, Ciudad de México

El marido tiene dos apellidos.* El apellido Guzmán es el apellido de su padre.
El apellido Echeverría es el apellido de su madre. Su mujer es María Cristina
Blanco Robles. Blanco es el apellido de su padre y Robles es el apellido de su madre.
Muchas veces la señora cambia* su nombre después del matrimonio.* Después del
matrimonio con el señor Guzmán Echeverría, ella toma el nombre María Cristina
Blanco de Guzmán. Mantiene* el apellido de su padre y toma también el apellido de
su marido.

El señor Guzmán Echeverría y su mujer María Cristina Blanco de Guzmán
tienen una hija—Alicia Guzmán Blanco. Ella tiene el apellido de su padre y el
apellido del padre de su madre—su abuelo materno.

Ejercicio Contesten. *(Answer.)*

1. ¿Qué tiene la familia en la sociedad hispánica?
2. Cuando un joven hispano habla de su familia, ¿habla solamente de sus padres
   y de sus hermanos?
3. ¿De quiénes habla?
4. Muchas veces, ¿viven los abuelos con sus hijos y sus nietos?

---

*apellidos   *last names, surnames*   *cambia   *changes*   *matrimonio   *marriage*
*Mantiene   *She keeps*

A Lesson Test is provided in the Test Package.

Actividades

(Tape Activities—**Segunda parte**)

(optional)

1 Preguntas personales

Tell about your family. Give the following information:

- ¿Cuántas personas hay en tu familia?
- ¿Cuántos hermanos tienes?
- ¿Cuántos años tienen ellos?
- ¿Cuántos años tienes tú?
- ¿Dónde viven Uds.?
- ¿Tienen Uds. un perro o un gato?
- ¿Tienes muchos primos?
- ¿Dónde viven ellos?

2

Write a story about your favorite cousin or friend. Tell who he/she is, where he/she lives, describe the person, tell where he/she goes to school, tell some of the things he/she does.

> *Mi primo(a) o amigo(a) favorito(a)...*

3

Prepare your own family tree using the Hispanic system for taking last names. Use the blank family tree below as a guide.

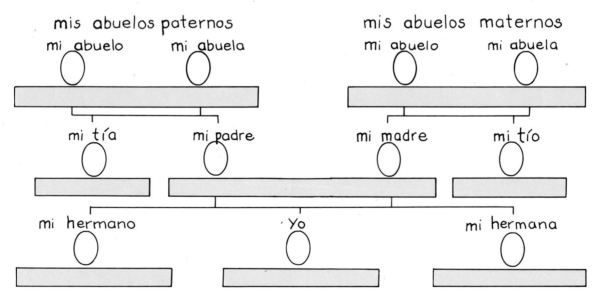

mis abuelos paternos
mi abuelo   mi abuela

mis abuelos maternos
mi abuelo   mi abuela

mi tía   mi padre   mi madre   mi tío

mi hermano   Yo   mi hermana

129

Revista

Abuelito con su
nieta en Santiago de
Compostela, España

Abuelita con su nieta
en Quito, Ecuador

Recuerdo del Bautizo

El bautizo
- ¿Qué día tiene lugar el bautizo de Yolanda Sofía?
- ¿Dónde tiene lugar?
- ¿Quiénes son los padres de Yolanda Sofía?
- Y los padrinos, ¿son ellos marido y mujer?

Yolanda Sofía

Nació:
el 2 de Octubre de 1981

Se Bautizó:
el 2 de Octubre de 1982
en el Templo de Belén

Cusco

Padres:

Emilio Meza Gonzales

Carmela Salazar de Meza

Padrinos:

Francisco Ugarte Gamarra

María Dolores Astete de Ugarte

Una familia mexicano-americana asiste
al bautizo de los gemelos en el sudoeste
de los Estados Unidos.

Toda la familia y todos los amigos
asisten al matrimonio en Madrid.
Llegan a la iglesia.

patricia fregoso olvera
y
joaquín de la cueva macías

nos uniremos en matrimonio con la
bendición de dios y de nuestros padres

eva martha
carlos
y
ana maría

el próximo día tres de mayo a las
doce treinta horas, en la iglesia de
san jerónimo. calle san jerónimo s/n,
oficiando la ceremonia el r. p. luis
gonzález morfín, s. j.

cuernavaca, mor. 1975

Aquí tenemos una invitación a una boda.
• ¿De quiénes anuncia el matrimonio?
• ¿Quiénes son los padres?
• ¿Qué día tiene lugar la boda?
• ¿En qué iglesia tiene lugar?
• ¿Dónde está la iglesia?
• ¿Está en México Cuernavaca?

¿Cuál es la fecha
del día del padre?

Junio 19, Día del Padre
camisa
Manhattan
INTERNATIONAL

131

10 Los hispanos en los EE. UU.

(Tape Activity 1)

Vocabulario

contento(a)

triste

enfermo(a)

nervioso(a)

cansado(a)

la fiebre

la gripe

el catarro

el dolor de cabeza

la cama

el hospital

la consulta del médico

Ejercicio 1 ¿Cómo está?
Contesten según el dibujo.

1. ¿Está contenta o está triste la muchacha?

2. ¿Está contento o está triste el muchacho?

3. ¿Está enfermo o está bien el muchacho?

4. ¿Está enferma o está bien la muchacha?

5. ¿Está nervioso o está tranquilo el muchacho?

Ejercicio 2 El pobre Juanito está enfermo.

Aquí está el pobre Juanito. Él está enfermo.

1. ¿Tiene la gripe Juanito?
2. ¿Tiene fiebre?
3. ¿Tiene dolor de cabeza?
4. ¿Está en cama?
5. ¿Está en el hospital?

(Tape Activity 2)

Ejercicio 3 Y tú, ¿estás de buen humor o estás de mal humor?

¿Estás de buen humor o estás de mal humor cuando . . . (Tape Activity 3)

1. estás enfermo(a)?
2. estás contento(a)?
3. estás nervioso(a)?
4. tienes catarro?
5. tienes la gripe?
6. tienes fiebre?
7. tienes dolor de cabeza?

Expresiones útiles

When Spanish speakers wish to express concern over something unpleasant they have just heard, they will often say:

¡Ay de mí!
¡Qué lástima!
¡Qué pena!

Ejercicio 4 ¡Ay de mí!

Sigan el modelo. (Tape Activity 4)

Estoy triste.
¡Ay de mí! ¡Qué lástima!

1. Estoy enfermo(a).
2. Estoy nervioso(a).
3. Tengo la gripe.
4. Tengo fiebre.
5. Tengo dolor de cabeza.

(Workbook, Exercises A–C)

(Quiz 1)

Estructura

Ser y estar

Origen y colocación

In Spanish there are two verbs that mean *to be*. They are **ser** and **estar**. These verbs have very distinct uses. The verb **ser** is used to express origin, where something or someone is from.

> **La muchacha es de Cuba.**
> **La guitarra es de España.**

The verb **estar** is used to express location, where something or someone is located.

> **Los alumnos están en la escuela.**
> **La televisión está en la sala.**

It is very important to remember that the verb **estar** is used for both a temporary location and a permanent location.

> **Madrid está en España.**
> **La casa está en la calle Velázquez.**

Ejercicio 1 ¿De dónde es?
Contesten. (Tape Activity 5)

Exercises 1–8 are learning exercises. Exercises 9–11 are testing exercises.

1. ¿Es de Cuba el muchacho?
2. ¿Es de Colombia la muchacha?
3. ¿Es de Guatemala el joven?
4. ¿Es de Puerto Rico la joven?
5. ¿Es de España la guitarra?
6. ¿Es de Puerto Rico la profesora?
7. ¿Son de México las fresas?
8. ¿Son de Venezuela las películas?

Ejercicio 2 ¿De dónde es su familia?
Preguntas personales

1. ¿De dónde es su abuelo?
2. ¿De dónde es su abuela?
3. ¿De dónde es su padre?
4. ¿De dónde es su madre?
5. ¿De dónde es Ud.?

Ejercicio 3 ¿Dónde está el apartamento?
Contesten. (Tape Activity 6)

1. ¿Está en España Madrid?
2. ¿Está la calle Velázquez en Madrid?
3. ¿Está el apartamento en la calle Velázquez?
4. ¿Está el apartamento en un edificio alto?
5. ¿Está en la planta baja el apartamento?
6. ¿Está también el hospital en la calle Velázquez?
7. ¿Está el médico en el hospital?
8. ¿Está la consulta del médico en el hospital?

Expansion:
After going over this exercise, have students say it or write it in their own words.

Ejercicio 4 ¿En qué clase estás?
Preguntas personales

1. ¿Estás en la escuela ahora?
2. ¿En qué clase estás?
3. ¿Estás con tus amigos?
4. ¿Dónde está tu escuela?
5. ¿Dónde está tu casa?

Ejercicio 5 ¿De dónde es y dónde está ahora?
Contesten según la oración.

1. **Rosita es de Puerto Rico pero ahora está en España.**
   ¿De dónde es Rosita?
   ¿Dónde está Rosita ahora?
2. **Jesús es de España pero ahora está en México.**
   ¿De dónde es Jesús?
   ¿Dónde está él ahora?
3. **Inés es de Colombia pero ahora está en los Estados Unidos.**
   ¿De dónde es Inés?
   ¿Dónde está ella ahora?

Expansion:
Have students make up sentences about people they know, stating where they are from originally and where they are now.

(Workbook, Exercises D–F)
(Tape Activity 7)

Característica y condición

The verb **ser** is used to express a characteristic that does not change.

> **María es muy sincera.**
> **El edificio es muy alto.**

The verb **estar** is used to express a temporary condition.

> **Juanito está enfermo.**
> **Los muchachos están cansados.**

Ejercicio 6 ¿Quién es así?

Make up a sentence using the name of a person you know who has the particular characteristic listed below.

1. alto(a)
2. moreno(a)
3. rubio(a)
4. simpático(a)
5. divertido(a)
6. sincero(a)
7. atlético(a)
8. inteligente
9. fuerte
10. popular

Ejercicio 7 ¿Cómo es?
Contesten.

(Tape Activity 8)

1. ¿Es interesante el periódico?
2. ¿Es buena la película?
3. ¿Es popular el deporte?
4. ¿Es fácil el español?
5. ¿Es grande la escuela?

Ejercicio 8 ¿Cómo está?
Contesten según el dibujo.

1. ¿Cómo está?

3. ¿Cómo está?

5. ¿Cómo está?

2. ¿Cómo está?

4. ¿Cómo está?

6. ¿Cómo está?

Ejercicio 9 ¿*Ser* o *estar*?
(Tape Activity 9)

Formen oraciones según los modelos.

el médico / inteligente
El médico es inteligente.

Juanito / enfermo
Juanito está enfermo.

1. el libro / interesante
2. la joven / contenta
3. los muchachos / atléticos
4. el señor / enfermo
5. la ciudad / grande

6. el edificio / alto
7. mi amigo / cansado
8. Elena / triste
9. la tienda / elegante
10. el apartamento / pequeño

(Workbook, Exercises G–H)

Ejercicio 10 Los alumnos están en la escuela.
Completen con *ser* o *estar*.

1. Los alumnos _____ en la escuela.
2. La profesora de español _____ de Cuba.
3. Ella _____ muy simpática.
4. Ella _____ en la escuela ahora.
5. Su casa _____ en Chicago.
6. Los libros que _____ en la clase _____ de España.

Ejercicio 11 Un amigo muy bueno
(Tape Activity 10)

Completen con *ser* o *estar*.

Juanito _____ un amigo muy bueno. Él _____ muy atlético. _____ muy inteligente también. Y además _____ sincero y simpático. Siempre _____ de buen humor. Él _____ muy divertido. Pero hoy él no _____ de buen humor. Él _____ de mal humor. _____ muy cansado. Tiene dolor de cabeza y _____ enfermo. Él tiene la gripe. _____ en casa. Él _____ en cama.

136

La casa de Juanito _____ en la calle once en Chicago. Juanito no _____ de Chicago. Él _____ de Nueva York pero ahora su familia _____ en Chicago. Sus padres no _____ de Nueva York. Sus padres _____ de Cuba y sus abuelos _____ de España. Juanito tiene una familia internacional. Pero ahora todos _____ en Chicago y _____ muy contentos. Su apartamento _____ muy bonito. _____ en el tercer piso de un edificio muy alto.

(Workbook, Exercise 1) (Quiz 2) (Tape Activity 11)

Expansion:
1) Have students retell the story of Juanito in their own words.
2) Have students make up as many original questions about Juanito as they can.

Los adjetivos de nacionalidad

Many adjectives of nationality end in either **-o** or **-e.** Adjectives of nationality that end in either **-o** or **-e** follow the same pattern as any other **-o** or **-e** adjective. Note that those that end in **-o** have *four* forms and those that end in **-e** have *two* forms.

el muchacho cubano	los muchachos cubanos
la muchacha cubana	las muchachas cubanas
el muchacho canadiense	los muchachos canadienses
la muchacha canadiense	las muchachas canadienses

However, there are many adjectives of nationality that end in a consonant. Unlike other adjectives that end in a consonant, adjectives of nationality ending in a consonant have *four* forms rather than two. Observe the following:

el muchacho español	los muchachos españoles
la muchacha española	las muchachas españolas

Adjectives of nationality that end in **-s** or **-n** have a written accent in the masculine singular. The accent is dropped in all other forms.

francés	franceses
francesa	francesas
inglés	ingleses
inglesa	inglesas
alemán	alemanes
alemana	alemanas

Ejercicio 12 ¡Claro que es español!
Contesten.

1. ¿Es español el libro?
2. ¿Son españoles los profesores?
3. ¿Es española la película?
4. ¿Son españolas las señoras?

Ejercicio 13 ¿De qué nacionalidad es?
Completen.

1. Carlos es _____. **español**
2. Teresa y Carmen son _____. **mexicano**
3. Ellos son _____. **argentino**
4. Isabel es _____. **portugués**
5. Las alumnas son _____. **francés**
6. Los señores son _____. **irlandés**
7. Ella es _____. **americano**
8. Él es _____. **inglés**

(Workbook, Exercise J)

Have each class member give his/her own nationality. You may wish to teach the expression **Yo soy de origen** _____. This expression is used again in the **Lectura** of this lesson.

Ejercicio 14 ¿De dónde es?
Sigan el modelo. (Tape Activity 12)

Hans es de Alemania.
Es verdad. Hans es alemán.

1. Jesús es de España.
2. Los jóvenes son de México.
3. Colette es de Francia.
4. Ellos son de Alemania.
5. Los vestidos son de Inglaterra.
6. Los muchachos son de Cuba.
7. Elena es de Irlanda.
8. Ellos son de Portugal.   (Quiz 3)

Pronunciación   ## Las consonantes *s, c, z*

The consonant **s** is pronounced the same as the *s* in the English word *sing*.

sa	se	si	so	su
sala	enseña	sí	peso	sur
casa	clase	así	sopa	Susana
saca	serio	necesita	sobrino	
ensalada		simpático	nervioso	

(Tape Activities 13–14)

The consonant **c** in combination with **e** or **i** (**ce, ci**) is pronounced the same as an **s** in all areas of Latin America. In many parts of Spain, **ce** and **ci** are pronounced like a *th* as in the English word *thin*.

The consonant **z** in combination with **a, o,** or **u** (**za, zo, zu**) is also pronounced the same as an **s** throughout Latin America. In many areas of Spain, **za, zo,** and **zu** are pronounced like a *th*.

If you use the Latin American pronunciation, you will have to be very careful when you spell words that contain an **s**, a **c**, or a **z**.

za	ce	ci	zo	zu
cabeza	cena	ciudad	almuerzo	(zumo)
	necesita	ciudadano		
	francés	recibe		
		cocina		
		ciencia		
		fácil		
		difícil		

Trabalenguas y dictado

Susana cena en la cocina en casa.
El sobrino de Susana es sincero.
Toman el almuerzo a las doce y diez.
Cecilia tiene dolor de cabeza.

Ejercicio Completen según la conversación.

Roberto no _____ muy bien. Él _____ enfermo. Él _____ muy cansado y tiene _____ de cabeza. Cree que _____ fiebre. Mañana él tiene que ir al _____. Probablemente tiene la gripe.

Lectura cultural

norte

nordeste

este

oeste

sur

sudoeste

Los hispanos en los Estados Unidos

Hoy hay más de* doce millones de personas que viven en los Estados Unidos que son de origen hispano. Por eso, el español es un idioma* muy importante. Es el idioma de millones de personas en nuestro país y de millones más en España, México, Centroamérica, Sudamérica y el Caribe.

¿Quiénes son los hispanos que viven aquí en los Estados Unidos? Pues, hay muchos grupos. Algunos* son recién llegados.* Otros viven aquí desde antes de la llegada* de los *Pilgrims*. En el sudoeste y en Texas y California hay millones de mexicano-americanos. Muchos de ellos viven en ciudades que tienen nombres españoles como Laredo, El Paso, Santa Fe, Los Ángeles, San Francisco. Vemos su influencia en la arquitectura, en la comida y en palabras como «adobe, patio, rodeo, vista y taco».

Desde mil novecientos diecisiete los puertorriqueños son ciudadanos* de los Estados Unidos. Hay millones de puertorriqueños en las grandes ciudades del nordeste.

Un grupo de recién llegados son los cubanos. Hay muchos cubanos en Miami y también en ciudades del nordeste como Union City y West New York, New Jersey.

Hoy llegan nuevos* grupos. Hay muchos dominicanos, salvadoreños, guatemaltecos y nicaragüenses que viven en varias partes de los Estados Unidos. Es verdad que hay muchos grupos. Pero tienen mucho en común. Todos están orgullosos* de sus tradiciones, de su cultura y, sobre todo, de su idioma—el español.

Ejercicio ¿Verdadero o falso?

1. Hay millones de personas de origen hispano que viven en los Estados Unidos.
2. El español es el idioma de muchas personas en muchos continentes.
3. Todas las personas de origen hispano en los Estados Unidos son recién llegados.
4. Hay millones de mexicano-americanos en las grandes ciudades del nordeste.
5. Muchas ciudades del sudoeste, de Texas y de California tienen nombres españoles.
6. La palabra «patio» es una palabra de origen inglés.
7. Los cubanos son ciudadanos de los Estados Unidos desde 1917.
8. Todos los cubanos que viven en los Estados Unidos viven en Miami o en las afueras de Miami.
9. Hay millones de puertorriqueños en las grandes ciudades del nordeste.
10. Hoy llegan a los Estados Unidos otros grupos de personas de origen hispano.

Expansion: Ask students if they live in an area that has a large ethnic population. What group is it?

A Lesson Test is provided in the accompanying Test Package.

***más de** *more than*   ***idioma** *language*   ***Algunos** *Some*   ***recién llegados** *recent arrivals*   ***desde antes de la llegada** *since before the arrival*   ***ciudadanos** *citizens* ***nuevos** *new*   ***orgullosos** *proud*

Actividades

1

(optional)

Here is a map of the United States. See if you can guess how many names of the states listed below are of Spanish origin.

- Illinois
- Nevada
- Massachusetts
- Florida
- Colorado

- Arizona
- Washington
- Montana
- New York

2

Make up five possible reasons in Spanish for each of the following.

Yo estoy cansado(a) porque . . .

Yo estoy triste porque . . .

Yo estoy contento(a) porque . . .

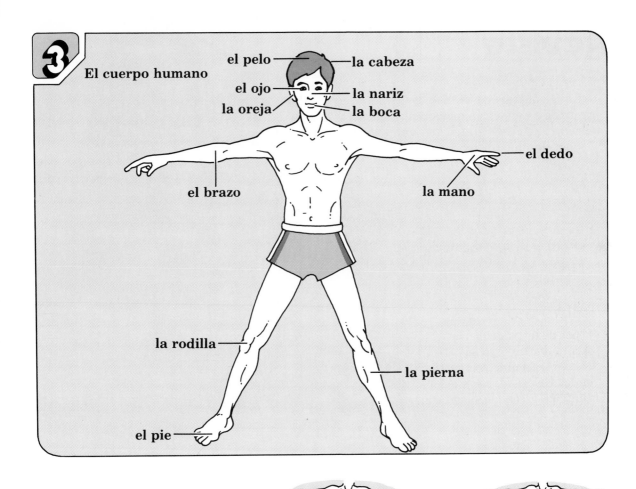

3 El cuerpo humano

el pelo — la cabeza
el ojo — la nariz
la oreja — la boca
el brazo
el dedo
la mano
la rodilla
la pierna
el pie

ojos azules   ojos castaños   brazos largos   brazos cortos

- ¿Tienes el pelo rubio, castaño o negro?
- ¿Tienes ojos castaños o azules?
- ¿Tienes una nariz larga o corta?

- ¿Tienes una boca grande o pequeña?
- ¿Tienes los brazos largos o cortos?

Have students give a complete description of themselves or a good friend.

4 ¡Aquí tenemos un monstruo!

- ¿Es alto o bajo?
- ¿Es grande o pequeño?
- ¿De qué color son los ojos?
- ¿Cómo es la nariz?
- Y la boca, ¿cómo es?
- ¿Cómo son los brazos? ¿Y los pies? ¿Y las piernas?

143

En el sudoeste de los Estados Unidos hay mucha gente de ascendencia mexicana. La señora Villegas enseña una clase bilingüe en una escuela de Texas. ¿En qué idiomas enseña la señora Villegas?

Jackie Navarro es una joven de origen cubano. Ahora Jackie vive en Miami. ¿En qué otra parte de los EE. UU. vive mucha gente de ascendencia cubana?

El cinco de mayo hay celebraciones y desfiles en las ciudades del sudoeste de los EE. UU. ¿Por qué celebran los mexicano-americanos el cinco de mayo?

Cado año en la Ciudad de Nueva York hay un desfile en la Quinta Avenida en honor de los ciudadanos puertorriqueños de la ciudad.

El señor Nathan Quiñones es un ex-profesor de español. El señor Quiñones es de ascendencia puertorriqueña. Hoy él es el canciller de todas las escuelas de la ciudad de Nueva York—el sistema escolar más grande de nuestro país.

Aquí tenemos otras personas famosas que son de origen hispano. ¿Sabes quiénes son?

Kathleen Ortega es de origen mexicano. ¿Quién es ella?

Hernán Badillo es de origen puertorriqueño. ¿Quién es él?

Gloria Rojas es de origen puertorriqueño también. ¿Quién es ella?

145

11 El cumpleaños

Transparencies can be used for the initial presentation of vocabulary.
Reminder: A vocabulary list is provided in the Teacher's Resource Kit.

vocabulario

(Tape Activity 1)

En la tienda de ropa para caballeros

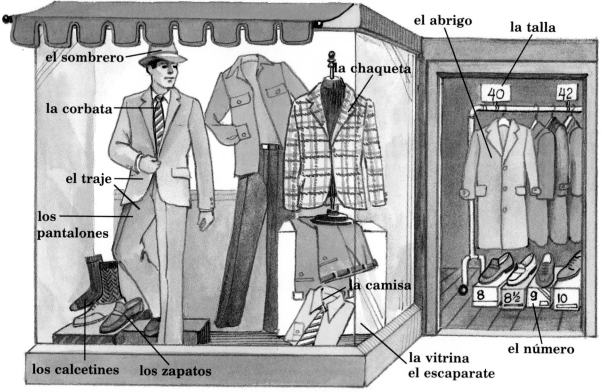

- el abrigo
- la talla
- el sombrero
- la chaqueta
- la corbata
- 40
- 42
- el traje
- los pantalones
- la camisa
- 8
- 8½
- 9
- 10
- los calcetines
- los zapatos
- la vitrina
- el escaparate
- el número

(Tape Activity 2)

Ejercicio 1 ¿Qué venden en una tienda de ropa para señores?

1.

2.

3.

4.

5.

6.

En la tienda de ropa para señoras

el sombrero

el suéter

la falda

las medias

el vestido

la blusa

la manga corta

la manga larga

los zapatos (de tacón alto)

Ejercicio 2 ¿Qué venden en una tienda de ropa para señoras?

1.

2.

3.

4.

5.

6.

Ejercicio 3 ¿Cómo es la ropa?
Contesten.

1. ¿Tiene mangas largas
   o mangas cortas la blusa?

2. ¿Tiene mangas largas
   o mangas cortas la camisa?

3. ¿Tiene rayas la camisa?

5. ¿Cuál es el número de los zapatos?

4. ¿Tienen tacones altos o bajos los zapatos?

6. ¿Cuál es la talla del traje?

(Tape Activity 6)

Roberto está en la tienda de ropa. **Va a** comprar **un regalo** para Clarita.

Mañana Clarita va a **cumplir** quince **años.** Es su **cumpleaños.**

La familia va a **dar una fiesta.** Van a **invitar** a sus amigos.

(Tape Activity 7)

Ejercicio 4 ¿Cuántos años va a cumplir Clarita?
Contesten.

1. ¿Cuántos años va a cumplir Clarita?
2. ¿Cuándo va a cumplir quince años?
3. ¿Cuándo es su cumpleaños?
4. ¿Quién está en la tienda de ropa?
5. ¿Qué va a comprar Roberto?
6. ¿Para quién va a comprar un regalo?
7. ¿Va a dar la familia de Clarita una fiesta?
8. ¿Van a invitar a sus amigos a la fiesta?

Los colores

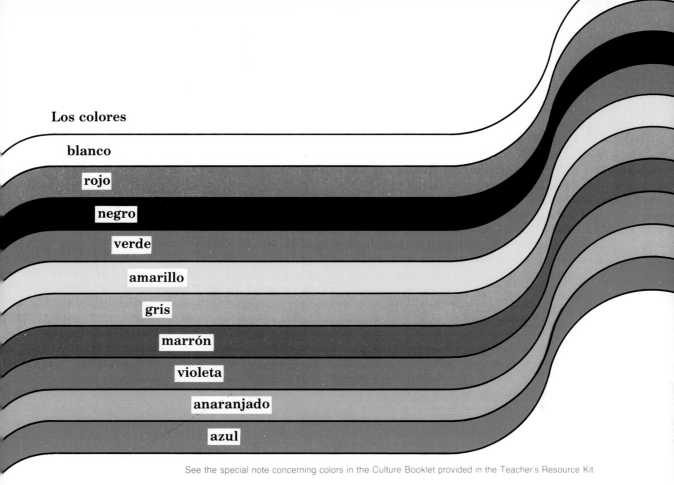

blanco

rojo

negro

verde

amarillo

gris

marrón

violeta

anaranjado

azul

See the special note concerning colors in the Culture Booklet provided in the Teacher's Resource Kit.

Ejercicio 5 ¿De qué color es?
Contesten.

1. ¿De qué color son los calcetines?
2. ¿De qué color es la blusa?
3. ¿De qué color es la corbata?
4. ¿De qué color es el suéter?
5. ¿De qué color es la falda?
6. ¿De qué color es la camisa?

(Quiz 1)

Estructura

Ir a con el infinitivo

The expression **ir a** followed by the infinitive is used to express what *is going to* happen in the near future.

> **Elena va a cumplir quince años.**
> **Sus padres van a dar una fiesta.**
> **Yo voy a ir a la fiesta.**

The **ir a** + *infinitive* construction corresponds to the English *to be going to*.

Ejercicio 1 Clarita va a cumplir quince años.
Contesten.

1. ¿Va a cumplir quince años Clarita?
2. ¿Van a dar una fiesta sus padres?
3. ¿Van a invitar a sus amigos?
4. ¿Van a comer durante la fiesta?
5. ¿Vas a ir a la fiesta?
6. ¿Vas a comprar un regalo para Clarita?
7. ¿Vas a comprar una blusa?
8. ¿Vas a ir a la tienda con Roberto?
9. ¿Van Uds. a mirar la ropa en el escaparate?

Ejercicio 2 Después de las clases . . .
Sigan el modelo.

Después de las clases, voy a casa.
Después de las clases, voy a ir a casa.

1. Preparo una merienda.
2. Tomo la merienda con mis amigos.
3. Luego miramos la televisión.
4. Vemos una película en la televisión.
5. Luego, Pablo va a casa.
6. Él estudia.
7. Carmen y yo vamos a la tienda.
8. Compramos un regalo para Clarita.
9. Sus padres dan una fiesta.
10. Nosotros asistimos a la fiesta.

La *a* personal

(Workbook, Exercises C–D)
(Tape Activities 8–10)
(Quiz 2)

Compare the sentences in each column.

Miro la televisión.
Veo la película.

Miro a Juanita.
Veo a la muchacha.

Note that the verbs in the first column are followed by a thing. The verbs in the second column are followed by a person. Whenever the direct object of a verb is a person, it must be preceded by the preposition **a**. This is called the **a personal** and it has no English equivalent.

There is only one exception to this rule and that is with the verb **tener**. The **a personal** never follows the verb **tener**.

> **Tengo dos amigos.**   **Tengo muchos primos.**

Ejercicio 3　¿Qué ves o a quién ves?
Contesten.

1. ¿Miras el escaparate?
2. ¿Miras al empleado?
3. ¿Escuchas el disco?
4. ¿Escuchas a la profesora?

5. ¿Ves la camisa?
6. ¿Ves al muchacho?
7. ¿Recibes un regalo?
8. ¿Recibes a tus amigos?

Ejercicio 4　¿Qué? ¿A quién?
Completen según el dibujo.

El español es fácil.

1. Juan mira _____.

3. Elena ve _____.

5. El profesor enseña _____.

2. Tadeo escucha _____.

4. Carmen ve _____.

6. Clarita recibe _____.

Pronunciación　　Las consonantes *c, q*

We have already learned that **c** in combination with **e** or **i** (**ce, ci**) is pronounced like an **s**. The consonant **c** in combination with **a, o,** or **u** (**ca, co, cu**) has a hard **k** sound.

(Workbook, Exercises E–F)
(Tape Activities 11–12)
(Quiz 3)

ca	**co**	**cu**
casa	color	cubano
cama	como	escucha
camisa	cocina	película
saca	come	secundaria
toca	taco	cuaderno
escaparate	blanco	cumpleaños

(Tape Activities 13–14)

Since **ce, ci** have the soft **s** sound, **c** changes to **qu** when it combines with **e** or **i** (**que, qui**) in order to maintain the hard **k** sound.

que	**qui**
que	quien
chaqueta	química
parque	aquí
pequeño	quince

Trabalenguas y dictado

La chaqueta aquí en el escaparate es blanca.
Carmen come una comida cubana en casa.
Chico escucha discos cubanos en el parque.
¿Quién come comida rica aquí en el parque?

Expresiones útiles

Very often in English if we wish to be polite, instead of saying to someone *I want,* we can soften our request by saying *I would like.* There is an equivalent for this polite expression in Spanish. It is **Quisiera** followed by whatever it is that you would like.

As the person hands you what you would like, he/she will frequently say **Aquí tiene Ud. ...** followed by whatever he/she is handing you.

conversación
(Tape Activity 15)

En una tienda de ropa

Empleado	¿Sí, señor?
Enrique	Quisiera una camisa blanca, por favor.
Empleado	Sí, señor. ¿De mangas largas o de mangas cortas?
Enrique	De mangas cortas, por favor.
Empleado	¿Y qué talla necesita Ud.?
Enrique	Treinta y ocho, por favor.
Empleado	Aquí tiene Ud. una camisa blanca a rayas azules y aquí tiene otra sin rayas.
Enrique	Quisiera la camisa sin rayas, por favor.
Empleado	De acuerdo. ¿Algo más, señor?
Enrique	No, nada más, gracias. ¿Cuánto es?
Empleado	Quinientos pesos, señor.

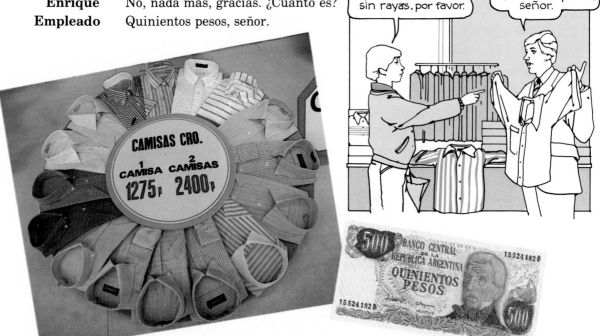

Ejercicio Contesten.

1. ¿Adónde va Enrique?
2. ¿Qué va a comprar Enrique?
3. ¿Va a comprar una camisa de mangas cortas o de mangas largas?
4. ¿Qué talla necesita Enrique?
5. ¿Compra él la camisa a rayas azules?
6. ¿Compra él la camisa sin rayas?
7. ¿Necesita algo más?
8. ¿Cuánto es la camisa?

(Workbook, Exercise F)
(Tape Activity 16)

Ropa de Señora

Vestidos/Trajes

Estados Unidos	8	10	12	14	16	18	20
España	36	38	40	42	44	46	48

Medias

Estados Unidos	8	8½	9	9½	10	10½
España	6	6½	7	7½	8	8½

Zapatos

Estados Unidos	03	04	05	06	07	08	09	10
España	36	37	38	39	41	42	43	44

Ropa de Caballero

Trajes/Abrigos

Estados Unidos	36	38	40	42	44	46
España	46	48	50	52	54	56

Camisas

Estados Unidos	14	14½	15	15½	16	16½	17	17½	18
España	36	37	38	39	41	42	43	44	45

Zapatos

Estados Unidos	5	6	7	8	8½	9	9½	10	11
España	38	39	41	42	43	43	44	44	45

Calcetines

Estados Unidos	9½	10	10½	11	11½
España	38/39	39/40	40/41	41/42	42/43

153

La quinceañera

In addition to reinforcing the structure points of this lesson, this **Lectura** reintroduces many of the regular verbs.

Hoy es un día muy importante en la vida* de Clarita Gómez Guzmán. Hoy ella cumple quince años. Sus padres van a dar una fiesta en honor de sus quince años. Es una costumbre hispánica.

Llegan los invitados.* Llegan los abuelos, los tíos, los primos, y claro, llegan los padrinos también. Los padres invitan a todos los parientes. Invitan también a los amigos de Clarita. Pero, como de costumbre,* la fiesta no es solamente para los jóvenes. Es para toda la familia.

Durante* la fiesta todos hablan, cantan, bailan* y comen. Y todos tienen regalos para Clarita. Ella recibe discos, libros, blusas, una falda, blue jeans y T-shirts.

Los padrinos casi siempre dan un regalo especial en honor de los quince años de su ahijada.* De sus padrinos Clarita recibe un collar de perlas.* Ella está muy contenta. Clarita agradece* mucho a sus padrinos, a sus parientes y a sus amigos.

Ejercicio   Contesten.

1. ¿Cuántos años tiene Clarita Gómez Guzmán?
2. ¿Quiénes van a dar una fiesta?
3. ¿Quiénes llegan a la fiesta?
4. ¿A quiénes invitan los padres a la fiesta?
5. ¿Es solamente para los jóvenes la fiesta?
6. ¿Qué tienen todos los invitados?
7. ¿Qué regalos recibe Clarita?
8. ¿Quiénes dan un regalo especial?
9. ¿Qué recibe Clarita de sus padrinos?
10. ¿A quiénes agradece Clarita?

(Workbook, Exercise G)

---

*vida *life*   *invitados *guests*   *como de costumbre *as customary*   *Durante *During*
*bailan *they dance*   *ahijada *goddaughter*   *collar de perlas *pearl necklace*
*agradece *thanks*

Actividades

1 (optional)

Prepare a list for a complete outfit of clothing for a woman. Prepare another list for a complete outfit of clothing for a man.

Ropa de Señora | Ropa de Caballero

1.
2.
3.
4.
5.

1.
2.
3.
4.
5.

2 Give your favorite color for the following items of clothing.

1. pantalones

2. una chaqueta

3. una camisa

4. una blusa

5. una falda

6. un vestido

3 Read or act out the following conversation. Then change **una camisa blanca** to **un par de zapatos** and change the underlined words as necessary.

— Quisiera una camisa blanca, por favor
— Sí, señor(ita). ¿De mangas cortas o de mangas largas?
— De mangas cortas, por favor.
— ¿Y qué talla necesita Ud.?
— Treinta y ocho, por favor. ¿Y cuánto es la camisa que está en el escaparate?
— Mil pesos.
— ¿Tiene Ud. mi talla?
— Sí, señor(ita).
— Muy bien. Quisiera la camisa que está en el escaparate.

4 Entrevista

• En los Estados Unidos, ¿hay a veces una fiesta especial en honor del cumpleaños de una muchacha?
• Por lo general, ¿cuántos años tiene la muchacha?
• ¿Van sus amigos a la fiesta?
• ¿Van todos sus parientes a la fiesta también?
• ¿Es la fiesta para los jóvenes o es para toda la familia?
• ¿Van sus padrinos a la fiesta?
• ¿Recibe la muchacha un regalo especial de sus padrinos?

157

Revista

*Hoy que cumples 15 años...
Debo declararte!...*

Aquí tenemos una tarjeta
del Perú.
¿Quién va a recibir esta
tarjeta de cumpleaños?
¿Es para un muchacho o
para una muchacha?

Hoy Teresa Guzmán
cumple quince años
en la Ciudad de México.
¿Lleva ella un vestido
elegante a la fiesta en
su honor?

Es una tienda elegante de ropa para caballeros en Bogotá, Colombia. ¿Qué ves en el escaparate de la tienda?

Es una tienda de ropa para señoras en la Calle Preciados en Madrid. ¿Qué ves en el escaparate?

Si tienes que comprar un regalo para una quinceañera, ¿a qué tienda vas a ir?

quinceañeras

Inés Raquel Leopoldo Rivera cumplio los 15 el pasado dos de mayo. Sus padres, Felipe e Hipólita, le obsequiarán con un viaje a Tampa, Florida. Reside en Flamboyán Gardens, Bayamón.

Lisa Noemi Rosas celebró el 8 de abril la llegada de sus 15. Su familia le ofreció una cena y mas tarde, hará un viaje a Suiza...

159

12 El fútbol

(Tape Activity 1)

vocabulario

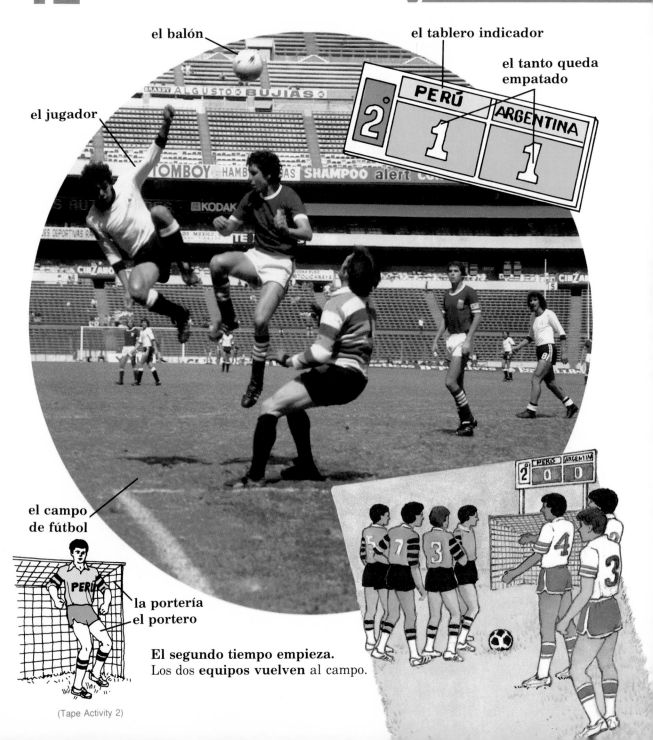

el balón

el tablero indicador

el tanto queda empatado

PERÚ 2° 1

ARGENTINA 1

el jugador

el campo de fútbol

la portería
el portero

El segundo tiempo empieza.
Los dos **equipos vuelven** al campo.

(Tape Activity 2)

la cabeza

la mano

el pie

González **mete un gol.**
El portero no **puede parar** el balón.
González **marca un tanto.**

Perú **gana el partido.**
Argentina **pierde.**

Los jugadores **juegan** al fútbol.
Un jugador **lanza** el balón con **el pie.**

Ejercicio 1   Juegan al fútbol.
Contesten.

1. ¿Están en el campo de fútbol
   los dos equipos?
2. ¿Empieza el primer tiempo o el
   segundo tiempo?
3. ¿Cuántos equipos hay en el campo?
4. ¿Tiene un jugador el balón?

5. ¿Lanza el balón con el pie?
6. ¿Para el balón el portero?
7. ¿Mete un gol el jugador?
8. ¿Marca un tanto?
9. ¿Qué equipo gana?
10. ¿Qué equipo pierde?

Ejercicio 2   ¿Cuántos, cómo, quiénes, qué, dónde?
Formen una pregunta según el modelo.

Expansion: Have students make up as many original questions
as they can using each of these interrogative words.

Hay *once* jugadores en el equipo de fútbol.
*¿**Cuántos** jugadores hay en el equipo de fútbol?*

1. Hay *dos* equipos en el campo.
2. Un equipo es *muy bueno.*
3. *Los jóvenes* juegan al fútbol.

4. Un jugador lanza *el balón* con el pie.
5. El portero está *cerca de la portería.*

Ejercicio 3   Un juego de fútbol
Completen.

1. El _____ indicador indica el tanto.
2. El _____ guarda la portería.
3. Cuando empieza el segundo tiempo,
   los jugadores _____ al campo.
4. Un jugador _____ el balón con
   el pie y _____ un gol.

5. Mete un gol y _____ un tanto.
6. Argentina no gana.
   Argentina _____.

(Workbook, Exercises A–B)
(Tape Activities 3–4)
(Quiz 1)

Expansion: Have students discuss their school's football team.

εstructura

El presente de los verbos de cambio radical *e → ie*

The verbs **empezar, comenzar** (*to begin*), **querer** (*to want*), **perder** (*to lose*), and **preferir** (*to prefer*) are called stem-changing verbs. This means that the stem of the infinitive (**quer-er, prefer-ir**) will change. Observe the following.

Infinitive	empezar	querer	preferir
yo	empiezo	quiero	prefiero
tú	empiezas	quieres	prefieres
él, ella, Ud.	empieza	quiere	prefiere
nosotros, -as	empezamos	queremos	preferimos
(vosotros, -as)	(empezáis)	(queréis)	(preferís)
ellos, ellas, Uds.	empiezan	quieren	prefieren

Note that all stem-changing verbs have regular endings.

The **-e** of the infinitive stem (**quer-er**) changes to **-ie** in all forms of the present tense except **nosotros** (and **vosotros**).

Note too that the verbs **empezar, comenzar, querer,** and **preferir** are often followed by an infinitive. The verbs **empezar** and **comenzar** take the preposition **a** when followed by an infinitive.

Ellos empiezan a jugar.

The verbs **querer** and **preferir** are immediately followed by the infinitive.

Prefieren ganar.   **No quieren perder.**

Ejercicio 1   Empezamos a jugar y queremos ganar.
Contesten con *nosotros*.

1. ¿Empiezan Uds. a jugar?
2. ¿Empiezan Uds. a las dos?
3. ¿Quieren Uds. meter un gol?
4. ¿Quieren Uds. ganar el partido?
5. ¿Pierden Uds. a veces?
6. ¿Prefieren Uds. jugar en el parque o en la calle?
7. ¿Prefieren Uds. jugar con un equipo bueno o con un equipo malo?

(Tape Activity 5)

Ejercicio 2   El segundo tiempo empieza.
Contesten.

1. ¿Empieza el segundo tiempo?
2. ¿Empiezan a jugar los jugadores?
3. ¿Prefieren ganar los dos equipos?
4. ¿Quieren marcar muchos tantos?
5. ¿Quiere González meter un gol?
6. ¿Quiere parar el balón el portero?
7. ¿Pierde el equipo de González?

162   (Workbook, Exercise C)

Ejercicio 3 Lo que prefiero yo.
Preguntas personales

1. ¿Prefieres jugar al fútbol o al béisbol?
2. ¿Prefieres jugar en el partido o prefieres mirar el partido y ser espectador(a)?
3. ¿Siempre quieres marcar muchos tantos?
4. ¿Quieres ganar?
5. ¿Pierdes a veces?

Ejercicio 4 ¿Quién va a ganar?
Completen con el verbo indicado.

Elena _____ (querer) jugar al fútbol. Yo _____ (querer) jugar al béisbol. Y
tú, ¿_____ (preferir) jugar al fútbol o _____ (preferir) jugar al béisbol? Si tú
_____ (querer) jugar al béisbol, tú y yo ganamos y Elena _____ (perder). Pero si tú
_____ (querer) jugar al fútbol, tú y Elena ganan y yo _____ (perder).
 Cuando yo _____ (querer) leer, Eduardo _____ (querer) escuchar discos. Yo
_____ (empezar) a leer y él _____ (empezar) a escuchar discos. Eduardo, ¿por qué
_____ (empezar) tú a escuchar discos cuando yo _____ (querer) leer?

Ejercicio 5 Nosotros preferimos . . . pero él prefiere . . .
Completen con *preferir* y el infinitivo.

Nosotros _____  pero nuestro amigo _____.

Nosotros preferimos leer pero nuestro amigo prefiere jugar al fútbol.

1. Nosotros _____  pero nuestro amigo _____.

2. Nosotros _____  pero nuestro amigo _____.

3. Nosotros _____ pero nuestro amigo _____.

Ejercicio 6 Yo quiero una cosa y mis amigos prefieren otra.
Escriban con *nosotros*.

 Yo quiero ir a la carnicería porque prefiero comprar la carne allí y no en el
supermercado. Mi amigo prefiere comprar todo en el supermercado. Él cree que yo
pierdo mucho tiempo porque voy de una tienda a otra.

 Nosotros . . .

(Workbook, Exercises D–F)
(Tape Activities 6–7)

El presente de los verbos de cambio radical o → ue

The verbs **volver** (*to return*), **poder** (*to be able*), and **dormir** (*to sleep*) are also stem-changing verbs. Note that the **-o** of the infinitive changes to **-ue** in all conjugated forms except **nosotros** (and **vosotros**).

o → ue

Infinitive	volver	poder	dormir
yo	vuelvo	puedo	duermo
tú	vuelves	puedes	duermes
él, ella, Ud.	vuelve	puede	duerme
nosotros, -as	volvemos	podemos	dormimos
(vosotros, -as)	(volvéis)	(podéis)	(dormís)
ellos, ellas, Uds.	vuelven	pueden	duermen

Note that the **u** of the verb **jugar** also changes to **ue** in all forms except **nosotros** (and **vosotros**).

Infinitive	jugar
yo	juego
tú	juegas
él, ella, Ud.	juega
nosotros, -as	jugamos
(vosotros, -as)	(jugáis)
ellos, ellas, Uds.	juegan

In Spain the verb **jugar** is always followed by the preposition **a.** However, the preposition is omitted in many countries of Latin America.

Juego al fútbol.   **Juego fútbol.**

Ejercicio 7 Nosotros jugamos al fútbol.
Contesten con *nosotros.*

1. ¿Juegan Uds. al fútbol?
2. ¿Pueden Uds. jugar en el patio de la escuela?
3. ¿Vuelven Uds. a casa después del partido?
4. ¿Duermen Uds. después de un partido de fútbol?

Ejercicio 8 En la clase de educación física
Preguntas personales

1. ¿Juegas al fútbol en la clase de educación física?
2. ¿Juega la clase en el gimnasio?
3. ¿Pueden Uds. jugar en el patio de la escuela?
4. Después del partido de fútbol, ¿vuelven Uds. a la escuela?

Ejercicio 9 No puedo jugar ahora.

Completen.

Eduardo   Yo _____ (jugar) mucho al fútbol. ¿_____ (Jugar) tú mucho también?

Tomás   Sí, yo _____ (jugar) mucho pero no _____ (poder) jugar ahora.

Eduardo   ¿Por qué no _____ (poder) jugar ahora?

Tomás   Yo no _____ (poder) porque tengo un amigo que _____ (volver) hoy de México.

Eduardo   ¿A qué hora _____ (volver) él?

Tomás   Él _____ (volver) a las dos y yo _____ (querer) estar en casa.

Eduardo   Ok, entonces, ¿por qué no _____ (jugar) (nosotros) mañana?

Tomás   ¡Buena idea! Y mi amigo Carlos _____ (poder) jugar también.

(Workbook, Exercises G–J)
(Tape Activities 8–9)
(Quiz 2)

Pronunciación   Las consonantes *j, g*

The Spanish **j** sound does not exist in English. In Spain the **j** sound is quite guttural (coming from the throat). It is similar to the sound German speakers make when they say *ach*. In Latin America the **j** sound is much softer. It is somewhat similar to the English *h* in the words *hat* or *hot*.

ja	**je**	**ji**	**jo**	**ju**
Jaime	Jesús	Méjico	José	jugar
hija	traje	mejicano	hijo	jugador
jabón			joven	juego
				junio
				julio

(Tape Activities 10–11)

Note that **g** in combination with **e** or **i** (**ge, gi**) has the same sound as the **j**. For this reason, you must pay particular attention to the spelling of words that have **je, ji, ge,** or **gi.**

ge	**gi**
gente	gigante
general	Gijón
	gimnasio

Trabalenguas y dictado

Los jóvenes juegan en el gimnasio.
El hijo de Jaime es jugador de fútbol.
La gente trabaja en Gijón.
El hijo joven de José trabaja en junio en Gijón.

The consonant **g** has two sounds. As explained above, **g** in combination with **e** or **i** (**ge, gi**) is pronounced like a **j. G** in combination with **a, o,** or **u** (**ga, go, gu**) is similar to the **g** sound in the English word *go*, but it is somewhat softer. To maintain this sound with **e** or **i,** a silent or unpronounced **u** is added (**gue, gui**).

ga	**go**	**gu**
gana	juego	(gusano)
juega	amigo	segundo
amiga	pago	
paga	luego	
llega	domingo	

gue	**gui**
(guerra)	guitarra

Trabalenguas y dictado

La amiga llega y luego toca la guitarra.
Gómez juega bien y gana el juego.

Expresiones útiles

A very useful word in Spanish is **ya.** The most literal meaning of **ya** is *already.*

Ya tenemos muchos.

The word **ya** can convey some other meanings. For example, in the English expression *I'm coming right now,* **ya** would also be used. Note, however, that Spanish speakers use another verb in this expression.

¡Ya voy!

Ya can also mean *now* in such expressions as *Now I understand, Now I get it.*

Ya entiendo.

(Tape Activity 12)

Los muchachos juegan al fútbol, Unidad Independencia, México

conversación

¿Quieres jugar al fútbol?

Anita	¡Carmen, Carmen!
Carmen	¡Ya voy! ¿Qué quieres?
Anita	¿Quieres jugar al fútbol?
Carmen	Sí, ¿cuándo? ¿Ahora?
Anita	Sí, ahora.
Carmen	¿Puede jugar también mi amiga, Elena? Ella juega muy bien.
Anita	¡Ay, no! ¡Qué pena! Ya tenemos once jugadoras. Pero ella puede jugar mañana si quiere.
Carmen	Está bien.

(Tape Activity 14)

Ejercicio   Contesten.

1. ¿A qué van a jugar las muchachas?
2. ¿Cuándo van a jugar?
3. ¿Quiere jugar Carmen?
4. ¿Puede jugar Elena?
5. ¿Cómo juega ella?
6. ¿Por qué no puede jugar Elena?
7. ¿Puede jugar mañana si quiere?

167

El fútbol hispanoamericano

(Tape Activity 15)

Un deporte muy popular en todos los países hispánicos es el fútbol. El fútbol que juegan en España y en Latinoamérica no es como el fútbol norteamericano. Los jugadores no pueden tocar° el balón con las manos. Tienen que usar los pies o la cabeza.

En un equipo de fútbol hay once jugadores. Cuando empieza el partido los dos equipos siempre quieren ganar. Pero no es posible. Solamente un equipo puede ganar. El otro tiene que perder. Hay solamente una excepción. A veces el tanto queda empatado.

Estamos en el estadio° del General Sánchez. Los dos equipos están en el campo.° Quedan° solamente dos minutos en el segundo tiempo. El tanto está empatado en cero. González tiene el balón. Lanza el balón con los pies. ¿Entra el balón en la portería o no? El portero Ochoa quiere parar el balón pero no puede. González mete un gol. Marca un tanto. En los últimos dos minutos su equipo gana: uno a cero.

° **tocar** *to touch*   ° **estadio** *stadium*   ° **campo** *field*   ° **Quedan** *Remain*

Ejercicio **Escojan.** (Tape Activity 16)

1. ¿Dónde es popular el fútbol?
   a. No es un deporte popular.
   b. En todos los países hispanos.
   c. Solamente en los Estados Unidos.

2. ¿Es el fútbol hispano como el fútbol norteamericano?
   a. No. Hay solamente once jugadores en el equipo.
   b. No. Los jugadores tienen que lanzar el balón.
   c. No. Los jugadores no pueden tocar el balón con las manos.

3. ¿Cuántos jugadores hay en un equipo de fútbol?
   a. Hay dos.
   b. Hay once.
   c. En el fútbol no hay equipos.

4. ¿Cuántos equipos juegan en un partido de fútbol?
   a. Dos.
   b. Once.
   c. No hay equipos.

5. ¿Qué quiere cada equipo?
   a. Quiere ganar.
   b. Quiere perder.
   c. Quiere empatar el tanto.

6. El tanto queda empatado.
   a. Es verdad. Está en cero a cero.
   b. Es verdad. Está en cero a uno.
   c. Es verdad. Está en uno a once.

7. ¿Cuántos tiempos hay en un partido de fútbol?
   a. Uno.
   b. Dos.
   c. Cuatro.

   (Workbook, Exercises K–O)

8. ¿Mete un gol González?
   a. Sí, el balón entra en la portería.
   b. Sí, el portero para el balón.
   c. Sí, lo mete en el balón.

A Lesson Test is provided in the accompanying Test Package.

169

Actividades

1 Entrevista

(optional)

- ¿Eres muy aficionado(a) a los deportes?
- ¿Eres muy aficionado(a) al fútbol?
- ¿En qué escuela estudias?
- ¿Es popular el fútbol en tu escuela?
- ¿Tiene tu escuela un equipo?
- ¿Es bueno el equipo?
- ¿Ganan muchos partidos?
- ¿Cuántos jugadores hay en el equipo?
- ¿Juegas con el equipo?
- Si no juegas al fútbol, ¿juegas a otro deporte? ¿Cuál es?

2

Speak with a friend and tell him/her all the things you want to do either now or in the future.

3

Select a captain of one of your school's teams and tell all you can about him/her.

4

Say all you can about the illustration below.

170

5 Otros deportes

el vólibol

el tenis

el golf

el básquetbol

el béisbol

el atletismo

el ciclismo

el esquí

el jai alai

el boxeo

la natación

el esquí acuático

¿Cuál es tu deporte favorito? ¿Por qué?
¿Qué deportes practicas? ¿Prefieres los
deportes de equipo o los deportes
individuales?

Revista

ATLETICO MADRILEÑO

Juegan al básquetbol durante los juegos panamericanos. ¿Juegas tú al básquetbol?

¿Cuál es el deporte del argentino, Guillermo Vilas?

¿Cuál es el deporte de la mexicano-americana Nancy López?

El atleta Alberto Salazar es de origen cubano.

Juegan al vólibol en el patio de una escuela en Quebradillas, Puerto Rico. ¿Pueden Uds. jugar al vólibol en el patio de su escuela?

Muchos jóvenes españoles coleccionan fotografías de sus futbolistas favoritos. Cada ciudad grande tiene su equipo. ¿Tienen todas las ciudades grandes de los EE. UU. un equipo de fútbol?

OLMO
F.C. Barcelona

HUGO SÁNCHEZ
At. de Madrid

AMARILLA
Real Zaragoza

¿Queda empatado el tanto entre México y Australia?

Mundial Juvenil de Fútbol

México y Australia 1-1 en jornada inaugural

Repaso

¿Quieres jugar?

Tomás   Hola, Clarita. ¿Cómo estás?

Clarita   Estoy bien, gracias.

Tomás   ¿Quieres jugar al fútbol?

Clarita   Sí. ¡Cómo no!

Tomás   ¿Y dónde está tu hermano? Él puede jugar también.

Clarita   No, no puede. Está en casa. Tiene que estudiar. Mañana tiene examen.

Ejercicio 1   Contesten.

1. ¿Con quién habla Tomás?
2. ¿Cómo está Clarita?
3. ¿A qué quiere jugar Clarita?
4. ¿Dónde está su hermano?
5. ¿Puede él jugar también?
6. ¿Por qué no puede jugar?

Los verbos de cambio radical

Review the following forms of stem-changing verbs. Note that the infinitive stem changes in all forms except **nosotros** (and **vosotros**).

$$e \rightarrow ie$$

Infinitive	empezar	querer	preferir
yo	empiezo	quiero	prefiero
tú	empiezas	quieres	prefieres
él, ella, Ud.	empieza	quiere	prefiere
nosotros, -as	empezamos	queremos	preferimos
(vosotros, -as)	(empezáis)	(queréis)	(preferís)
ellos, ellas, Uds.	empiezan	quieren	prefieren

$$o \rightarrow ue$$

Infinitive	volver	poder	dormir
yo	vuelvo	puedo	duermo
tú	vuelves	puedes	duermes
él, ella, Ud.	vuelve	puede	duerme
nosotros, -as	volvemos	podemos	dormimos
(vosotros, -as)	(volvéis)	(podéis)	(dormís)
ellos, ellas, Uds.	vuelven	pueden	duermen

Note that the verb **tener** is a stem-changing verb that also has an irregular **yo** form.

Infinitive	tener
yo	tengo
tú	tienes
él, ella, Ud.	tiene
nosotros, -as	tenemos
(vosotros, -as)	(tenéis)
ellos, ellas, Uds.	tienen

Ejercicio 2 Completen con la forma apropiada del verbo indicado.

¡Qué expectación! _____ (Empezar) el segundo tiempo. El tanto queda empatado. Nuestro equipo _____ (tener) que ganar. Nosotros no _____ (poder) perder. ¡Ay! ¡Cómo yo _____ (querer) meter un gol y marcar un tanto! Si nuestro equipo _____ (perder), no vamos a ser los campeones. Nuestro equipo no _____ (poder) perder. Nosotros _____ (querer) ganar y _____ (tener) que ganar. ¡A la victoria! Nuestro equipo _____ (tener) que ganar el campeonato.

Los verbos *ser* y *estar*

The verb **ser** is used to express

1. place of origin—where someone or something is from

   Marisa es de Bogotá.
   Los zapatos son de México.

2. a permanent characteristic

   María es sincera.
   El edificio es alto.

The verb **estar** is used to express

1. location—permanent or temporary

   Bogotá está en Colombia.
   Los alumnos están en la escuela.

2. a temporary condition

   El pobre Juanito está enfermo.
   Estamos cansados.

Ejercicio 3 Preguntas personales

1. ¿De dónde eres?
2. ¿Dónde estás ahora?
3. ¿Dónde está tu casa?
4. ¿De dónde son tus padres?
5. ¿Cómo estás hoy?
6. ¿Cuáles son algunas de tus características? ¿Cómo eres?

Ejercicio 4 Completen con *ser* o *estar*.

Carlos _____ un muchacho muy simpático. Él _____ muy serio pero _____ también muy divertido. Por lo general, él _____ de buen humor. Pero hoy, no. Él _____ de mal humor. ¿Por qué? Él _____ enfermo. Tiene catarro. ¿Dónde _____ Carlos ahora? Ahora él _____ en la consulta del médico. El médico le examina a Carlos. El médico de Carlos _____ muy bueno. Él _____ de México.

A complete Unit Self-test (self-correcting) appears in the Workbook.
Two Unit tests (one written, one oral) are provided in the accompanying Test Package.

175

Lectura cultural

opcional

Una serenata

Son las seis de la mañana en Guanajuato, México. Teresa duerme. Hay un ruido° en la calle. El ruido despierta° a Teresa. Ella todavía° está cansada pero va a la ventana.° ¿Y qué ve? En la calle ella ve a un grupo de amigos. ¿Por qué están los amigos en la calle a las seis de la mañana? Pues, hoy es el cumpleaños de Teresa. Sus amigos le dan una serenata en honor de su cumpleaños. Ellos cantan y tocan la guitarra. Cantan «Las mañanitas». Para Teresa el día de fiestas y celebraciones comienza con un poco de música.

° **serenata** *serenade*   ° **ruido** *noise*   ° **despierta** *wakes up*   ° **todavía** *still*
° **ventana** *window*

Ejercicio   Contesten.

1. ¿Dónde vive Teresa?
2. ¿Qué hay en la calle?
3. ¿Qué despierta a Teresa?
4. ¿A qué hora despierta a Teresa el ruido?
5. ¿Adónde va ella?
6. ¿Qué ve ella en la calle?
7. ¿Qué día es hoy?
8. ¿Por qué cantan y tocan la guitarra sus amigos?

177

Lectura cultural

opcional

la plaza de toros

El matador torea.

el redondel

el toro

pobre	Una persona que no tiene dinero es pobre.
rico	Una persona que tiene mucho dinero es rica.
hambre	Tengo hambre. Tengo que comer algo.
el (la) huérfano(a)	Un(a) niño(a) que no tiene padres es huérfano(a).
la naranja	una fruta de color naranja

Manolo

Es el año 1932. En un pueblo pequeño de Andalucía, Palma del Río, nace* un niño.

Mi nombre es Manolo. Mi familia vive en una de las típicas casas blancas de Andalucía. Es una casa pequeña. En la casa hay mucha pobreza* y la vida es difícil. Hay cuatro niños en mi familia. Todos pasamos hambre.* A veces podemos comer unas migas* de pan. Con frecuencia visitamos el convento para ver si las monjas* tienen un panecillo* o un poco de aceite.* Mi madre trabaja en casa. Cuida de los niños.* Mi padre es un hombre bueno. Siempre busca* trabajo. Él trabajo como una bestia en los campos. Gana* poco dinero pero trabaja mucho.

---

* **nace** *is born*   * **pobreza** *poverty*   * **pasamos hambre** *feel hungry*   * **migas** *crumbs*
* **monjas** *nuns*   * **panecillo** *roll (bread)*   * **aceite** *olive oil*   * **Cuida de los niños** *She takes care of the children*   * **busca** *looks for*   * **Gana** *He earns*

En 1936 empieza la guerra.* Es la Guerra Civil española. En la guerra nadie*
gana. Todos pierden. Y nosotros también perdemos. Perdemos a nuestro padre. Mi
padre no tiene ideas políticas pero tiene que ir a la cárcel.* Mi madre siempre visita
a mi padre en la prisión. Pero un día, ella no puede ir. Va mi hermana, Angelita.
Ella está vestida de* negro. Mi madre está muerta.* Mi padre está triste y también
está enfermo. Unos años después, él puede salir de la cárcel. Quiere volver al
pueblo donde está enterrada* mi madre. Pero no puede. Está muy enfermo y muere*
en Córdoba. No puede terminar (completar) el viaje a casa.

Ahora soy huérfano. No tengo dinero. Tengo que buscar trabajo. Trabajo en los
campos como mi padre. Pero no quiero trabajar en los campos. Quiero ser matador.
De noche voy a la finca* de una de las familias ricas de mi pueblo. En la finca
tienen toros. Empiezo a torear. El señor llama* a la policía y no puedo torear más.
   Un día hay una corrida humilde en mi pueblo. Soy yo el torero. Es un éxito*
tremendo. Tengo muchas ilusiones. Pero otra vez la tragedia. Como no tengo dinero,
no puedo comer. Robo* unas naranjas y voy a la cárcel. Tengo que salir de mi
pueblo.

---

*__guerra__ *war*   *__nadie__ *no one*   *__cárcel__ *jail*   *__vestida de__ *dressed in*
*__muerta__ *dead*   *__enterrada__ *buried*   *__muere__ *dies*   *__finca__ *farm*   *__llama__ *calls*
*__éxito__ *success*   *__Robo__ *I rob*

Voy a Madrid sin una peseta. Busco trabajo. Busco pesetas. Busco comida.
Cuando estoy cansado tengo que dormir en la calle. Un domingo hay una corrida en
Madrid. Yo voy a la plaza. No soy el torero pero quiero ser el torero. Entro en el
redondel y empiezo a torear. Otra vez llega la policía y yo voy a la cárcel.

Después de muchos años de pobreza y de hambre, tengo suerte.* En un café,
hablo con el señor Rafael Sánchez, el director de muchos matadores. Con la ayuda*
de Rafael, tengo la oportunidad de torear en la famosa plaza de Madrid. Es el
veinte de mayo de mil novecientos sesenta
y cuatro. Es un éxito tremendo. Empieza
a cambiar* mi suerte. Hoy soy el matador
más famoso de España. Soy el ídolo de
toda la nación y soy millonario.
Ya no toreo. Ahora ruedo* películas.
Pero no puedo olvidar* los días
de mi pobreza. Ayudo mucho
a los pobres que todavía hay
en España.

Soy el Cordobés.

*suerte *luck*   *ayuda *help*   *cambiar *to change*   *ruedo *I shoot (film)*
*olvidar *forget*

180

Ejercicio Escojan.

1. ¿Dónde nace Manolo?
   a. Él nace en Madrid, la capital de España.
   b. Él nace en una ciudad grande en el norte de España.
   c. Él nace en un pueblo pequeño de Andalucía.

2. ¿Cómo es la casa de la familia de Manolo?
   a. Es una casa pequeña y blanca.
   b. Es una casa de piedra con techo de paja.
   c. Es una casa particular en las afueras de la ciudad.

3. ¿Cómo es la familia de Manolo?
   a. Es una familia rica.
   b. Es una familia muy pobre.
   c. Es una familia contenta.

4. ¿Trabaja mucho el padre de Manolo?
   a. Sí, trabaja como una bestia y gana mucho dinero.
   b. Sí, trabaja mucho pero no gana mucho dinero.
   c. No, su padre no trabaja.

5. ¿Cuándo va su padre a la cárcel?
   a. Va cuando nace Manolo.
   b. Va cuando muere la madre de Manolo.
   c. Va durante la Guerra Civil española.

6. ¿Por qué no vuelve el padre a casa?
   a. No puede salir de la cárcel.
   b. No quiere volver.
   c. Muere en Córdoba.

7. ¿Quiere trabajar en los campos Manolo?
   a. Sí, quiere trabajar como su padre.
   b. Sí, quiere trabajar en la finca de una de las familias ricas.
   c. No, quiere ser matador.

8. ¿Por qué va Manolo a la cárcel?
   a. Porque roba dinero.
   b. Porque tiene ideas políticas.
   c. Porque roba unas naranjas.

9. Cuando Manolo sale de su pueblo, ¿adónde va?
   a. Va a Madrid.
   b. Va a una finca en Córdoba.
   c. No puede salir de su pueblo.

10. ¿Qué es Manolo hoy?
    a. Él es millonario.
    b. Él es el director de un café.
    c. Él es un señor pobre.

Appendix

Los números

Cardinal numbers

1 uno
2 dos
3 tres
4 cuatro
5 cinco
6 seis
7 siete
8 ocho
9 nueve
10 diez
11 once
12 doce
13 trece
14 catorce
15 quince
16 dieciséis
17 diecisiete
18 dieciocho
19 diecinueve
20 veinte
21 veintiuno
22 veintidós
23 veintitrés
24 veinticuatro
25 veinticinco
26 veintiséis
27 veintisiete
28 veintiocho
29 veintinueve
30 treinta
31 treinta y uno
32 treinta y dos
33 treinta y tres
34 treinta y cuatro
35 treinta y cinco
36 treinta y seis
37 treinta y siete
38 treinta y ocho
39 treinta y nueve
40 cuarenta
50 cincuenta
60 sesenta
70 setenta
80 ochenta
90 noventa

100 ciento (cien)
105 ciento cinco
113 ciento trece
117 ciento diecisiete
122 ciento veintidós
134 ciento treinta y cuatro
148 ciento cuarenta y ocho
160 ciento sesenta
200 doscientos
250 doscientos cincuenta
277 doscientos setenta y siete
300 trescientos
400 cuatrocientos
500 quinientos
600 seiscientos
700 setecientos
800 ochocientos
900 novecientos
1000 mil
1004 mil cuatro
1015 mil quince
1031 mil treinta y uno
1492 mil cuatrocientos noventa
   y dos
1861 mil ochocientos sesenta
   y uno
1970 mil novecientos setenta
2000 dos mil
10.000 diez mil
40.139 cuarenta mil ciento treinta
   y nueve
100.000 cien mil
785.026 setecientos ochenta
   y cinco mil veintiséis
1.000.000 un millón
50.000.000 cincuenta millones

Ordinal numbers

primero(a)
segundo(a)
tercero(a)
cuarto(a)
quinto(a)
sexto(a)
séptimo(a)
octavo(a)
noveno(a)
décimo(a)

Las horas

1:00 Es la una.
2:00 Son las dos.
3:00 Son las tres.
4:00 Son las cuatro.
5:00 Son las cinco.
6:00 Son las seis.
7:00 Son las siete.
8:00 Son las ocho.
9:00 Son las nueve.
10:00 Son las diez.
11:00 Son las once.
12:00 Son las doce.
3:15 Son las tres y cuarto.
2:45 Son las tres menos cuarto.
4:30 Son las cuatro y media.
5:30 Son las cinco y media.
2:10 Son las dos y diez.
1:50 Son las dos menos diez.
1:10 Es la una y diez.
12:50 Es la una menos diez.
1:15 Es la una y cuarto.
1:30 Es la una y media.

Los días

lunes
martes
miércoles
jueves
viernes
sábado
domingo

Los meses

enero
febrero
marzo
abril
mayo
junio
julio
agosto
septiembre
octubre
noviembre
diciembre

Los verbos

Regular verbs

present   **hablar**

to speak
hablo
hablas
habla
hablamos
(habláis)
hablan

comer

to eat
como
comes
come
comemos
(coméis)
comen

escribir

to write
escribo
escribes
escribe
escribimos
(escribís)
escriben

Irregular verbs

present   **dar**

to give
doy
das
da
damos
(dais)
dan

estar

to be
estoy
estás
está
estamos
(estáis)
están

ir

to go
voy
vas
va
vamos
(vais)
van

salir

to leave, to go out
salgo
sales
sale
salimos
(salís)
salen

ser

to be
soy
eres
es
somos
(sois)
son

tener

to have
tengo
tienes
tiene
tenemos
(tenéis)
tienen

Present tense of stem-changing verbs

First class stem-changing verbs

-ar *verbs*

e → ie	*o → ue*
sentar[1]	**mostrar**[2]
to seat	*to show*
siento	muestro
sientas	muestras
sienta	muestra
sentamos	mostramos
(sentáis)	(mostráis)
sientan	muestran

-er *verbs*

e → ie	*o → ue*
perder[3]	**volver**[4]
to lose	*to return*
pierdo	vuelvo
pierdes	vuelves
pierde	vuelve
perdemos	volvemos
(perdéis)	(volvéis)
pierden	vuelven

Second class

-ir *verbs*

e → ie	*o → ue*
preferir	**morir**[5]
to prefer	*to die*
prefiero	muero
prefieres	mueres
prefiere	muere
preferimos	morimos
(preferís)	(morís)
prefieren	mueren

[1] *cerrar, comenzar, empezar,* and *pensar* are similar
[2] *acostar* and *costar* as well as *jugar (u → ue)* are similar
[3] *defender* and *entender* are similar
[4] *llover* is similar
[5] *dormir* is similar

The following Spanish-English and English-Spanish Vocabularies contain all the words and expressions that appear in this Spanish text. The numbers or letters after each entry indicate the lesson in which the word or expression is first presented. Note that the following abbreviations are used throughout: *A* to *G* refers to **Lección preliminar A** to **G** and *LCO* refers to the **Lectura cultural opcional.**

Spanish-English Vocabulary

A

a to, at, by *3*
  a casa at home *6*
  a eso de about *8*
  a pie on foot *LCO*
el abrigo coat *11*
abril April *E*
la abuela grandmother *9*
el abuelo grandfather *9*
  los abuelos
    grandparents *9*
aburrido, -a boring *2*
el aceite oil *LCO*
además moreover, besides
  3
adiós good-bye *B*
¿adónde? where? *6*
adorable adorable *9*
aficionado, -a fond of *3*
afuera outside *8*
  las afueras outskirts,
    environs *8*
agosto August *E*
el agua water *7*
  el agua mineral mineral
    water *7*
la ahijada goddaughter *11*
el ahijado godson *11*
ahora now *7*
el aire air *LCO*
  al aire libre outdoor
    LCO
  el mercado al aire
    libre open-air (outdoor)
    market *LCO*
alemán, -ana German *10*
el álgebra (*f*) algebra *F*
algo something, anything
  7
algunos, -as some *10*
el alimento food *7*
  los alimentos
    enlatados canned
    foods *7*
el almuerzo lunch *8*
alto, -a tall, high *1*

de tacón alto
  high-heeled *11*
la alumna student *1*
el alumno student *1*
amarillo, -a yellow *11*
americano, -a American
  1
la amiga girl friend *2*
el amigo boyfriend *2*
anaranjado, -a orange *11*
andaluz, -za of or from
  Andalucía *LCO*
antes (de) before *10*
el año year *9*
  cumplir . . . años to
    turn . . . years old *11*
  tener . . . años to
    be . . . years old *9*
el apartamento apartment
  8
el apellido last name,
  surname *9*
aprender to learn *8*
el apunte note *5*
aquí here *9*
argentino, -a Argentinean
  5
la arquitectura architecture
  10
el arte art *5*
así so *A*
la asignatura (school) subject
  5
asistir to attend *8*
atlético, -a athletic *3*
el atletismo track *12*
la avenida avenue *8*
¡ay! ay!, alas! *1*
  ¡ay de mí! woe is me!,
    gosh! *1*
la ayuda help *LCO*
azul blue *11*

B

bailar to dance *11*
bajo, -a short *1*

el balón ball (soccer) *12*
el basquetbol basketball *12*
bastante rather,
  somewhat; enough *4*
el bebé baby *9*
beber to drink *8*
el béisbol baseball *12*
la bestia beast *LCO*
bien well *A*
el bife beef *LCO*
la biología biology *F*
blanco, -a white *11*
la blusa blouse *11*
la boca mouth *10*
bonito, -a pretty *7*
la botella bottle *7*
el boxeo boxing *12*
el brazo arm *10*
bueno, -a good *A*
  buenas noches good
    night *A*
  buenas tardes good
    afternoon *A*
  buenos días good
    morning *A*
el burrito rolled flour tortilla
  stuffed with chunks of beef
  D
buscar to look for, to
  search for *LCO*

C

el caballero gentleman *11*
  la tienda de ropa para
    caballeros men's
    clothing store *11*
la cabeza head *10*
  el dolor de cabeza
    headache *10*
cada each *12*
el café café; coffee *6*
la cafetería cafeteria *8*
la caja cash register; box *7*
los calcetines socks *11*
el cálculo calculus *5*
la calidad quality *7*

el calor heat *G*
    hacer calor to be hot (weather) *G*
la calle street *8*
la cama bed *10*
    cambiar to change *9*
la camisa shirt *11*
el campo field; country *8*
    el campo de fútbol soccer field *12*
    canadiense Canadian *10*
la canasta basket *LCO*
    cantar to sing *5*
la cantidad quantity *8*
la capacidad capacity *8*
la capital capital *3*
la cárcel jail *LCO*
el cariño affection *4*
la carne meat *7*
la carnicería butcher shop, meat market *7*
    caro, -a expensive *7*
la carta letter *8*
la casa home, house *6*
    a casa (to) home *6*
    en casa at home *6*
    casi almost *7*
    castaño, -a brown *11*
el catarro cold *10*
    catorce fourteen *C*
la celebración celebration *LCO*
la cena dinner *8*
    cenar to have dinner *8*
    cerca (de) near *LCO*
el cerdo pig *7*
    la chuleta de cerdo pork chop *7*
    cero zero *12*
el ciclismo bicycle racing *12*
    cien, ciento one hundred *C*
la ciencia science *5*
    las ciencias domésticas home economics *5*
    cinco five *C*
    cincuenta fifty *C*
la ciudad city *8*
el, la ciudadano, -a citizen *10*
    cívico, -a civic *5*
    la educación cívica civics *5*
    ¡claro! of course! *5*
    ¡claro que sí! of course! *5*

la clase class *F, 5*
    clásico, -a classical *6*
el, la cliente customer, client *6*
la cocina kitchen *6*
el colegio high school *1*
    colombiano, -a Colombian *2*
el color color *11*
el collar necklace *11*
el comedor dining room *8*
    comenzar (ie) to begin *12*
    comer to eat *8*
la comida meal *8*
    como like, as; since *5*
    ¿cómo? how? *1*
    ¡cómo no! of course! *5*
    completar to complete *LCO*
la composición composition *8*
la compra purchase *7*
    ir de compras to go shopping *7*
    comprar to buy *7*
    comprender to understand *8*
    común common *10*
    con with *4*
la consulta office *10*
    la consulta del médico doctor's office *10*
    contento, -a happy *10*
el contrario contrary, opposite *8*
    al contrario on the contrary *8*
el convento convent *LCO*
la corbata tie *11*
la cortesía courtesy *D*
    corto, -a short *11*
la corrida bullfight *LCO*
    corriente current; common *10*
    costar (ue) to cost *7*
la costumbre custom, tradition *11*
    de costumbre as customary, as usual *11*
el cuaderno notebook *5*
    ¿cuál? which? *E*
    cuando when *G*
    ¿cuándo? when? *G*
    ¿cuánto? how much? *D*
    cuarenta forty *C*
    cuarto, -a fourth *8*

    cuatro four *C*
    cuatrocientos four hundred *C*
    cubano, -a Cuban *2*
el cuerpo body *10*
el cuidado care *1*
    ¡pero, cuidado! but be careful! *1*
    cuidar (de) to care for, to take care of *LCO*
la cultura culture *10*
el cumpleaños birthday *11*
    cumplir to fulfill *11*
    cumplir . . . años to turn . . . years old *11*
el curso course *5*

CH

la chaqueta jacket *11*
la chuleta chop *7*
    la chuleta de cerdo pork chop *7*

D

    dar to give *7*
    dar un paseo to take a walk *LCO*
    de from; of *2*
    de buen humor in a good mood *10*
    de costumbre as customary, as usual *11*
    de la mañana A.M. *F*
    de la tarde P.M. *F*
    de mal humor in a bad mood *10*
    de nada you're welcome *D*
    ¿de quién? whose? *4*
    de tacón alto high-heeled *11*
    débil weak *3*
el dedo finger *10*
    delante (de) in front of *LCO*
el deporte sport *3*
    derecho, -a right; straight *8*
el desayuno breakfast *8*
    descansar to rest *LCO*
el descubrimiento discovery *E*
    desde since *10*
    después (de) after *6*

el día day *A*
   buenos días good morning *A*
   todo el día all day *6*
   todos los días every day *7*
diario, -a daily *5*
el dibujo drawing, picture *9*
diciembre December *E*
diecinueve nineteen *C*
dieciocho eighteen *C*
dieciséis sixteen *C*
diecisiete seventeen *C*
diez ten *C*
difícil difficult *4*
el dinero money *7*
el, la director, -ra director *LCO*
el disco record *6*
divertido, -a fun, amusing *2*
doce twelve *C*
el dolor pain, ache *10*
   el dolor de cabeza headache *10*
doméstico, -a domestic *5*
   las ciencias domésticas home economics *5*
domingo Sunday *E*
dominicano, -a Dominican, of or from the Dominican Republic *10*
¿dónde? where? *4*
dormir (ue) to sleep *12*
dos two *C*
doscientos two hundred *C*
durante during *11*
duro, -a hard *6*

E

la edad age *9*
el edificio building *8*
la educación education *F*
   la educación cívica civics *5*
   la educación física physical education *5*
el ejemplo example *6*
   por ejemplo for example *6*
   el the *1*
   él he *1*
   ella she *1*

ellas they *3*
ellos they *3*
empatar to tie *12*
empezar (ie) to begin *12*
el, la empleado, -a employee *7*
en in *1*
   en casa at home *6*
   en fin in brief; finally *9*
la enchilada enchilada (filled tortilla) *D*
enero January *E*
enfermo, -a sick *7*
enlatado, -a canned *7*
   los alimentos enlatados canned foods *7*
la ensalada salad *8*
enseñar to teach *5*
enterrado, -a buried *LCO*
entonces then; so *3*
entrar to enter *12*
el equipo team *12*
el escaparate display window *11*
escribir to write *8*
escuchar to listen to *6*
la escuela school *1*
español, -a of or from Spain *4*
el español Spanish *4*
especial special *11*
especializado, -a specialized *7*
el, la espectador, -ra spectator *12*
el esquí ski *12*
   el esquí acuático water skiing *12*
el estadio stadium *12*
estar to be *7*
el este east *10*
estudiar to study *5*
excelente excellent *7*
la excepción exception *12*
el éxito success *LCO*
   tener éxito to be successful *LCO*

F

fácil easy *4*
la facultad school (of a university) *8*
la falda skirt *11*
la falta lack *LCO*
la familia family *8*

fantástico, -a fantastic *2*
el favor favor *D*
   por favor please *D*
favorito, -a favorite *5*
febrero February *E*
la fecha date *E*
feo, -a ugly *2*
la fiebre fever *10*
la fiesta party *11*
fijo, -a fixed *LCO*
el fin end *9*
   en fin in brief; finally *9*
la finca ranch, farm *LCO*
la física physics *5*
   la educación física physical education *5*
francés, -esa French *5*
la frecuencia frequency *LCO*
   con frecuencia frequently *LCO*
la fresa strawberry *7*
fresco, -a cool *G*
   hacer fresco to be cool (weather) *G*
el frío cold *G*
   hacer frío to be cold *G*
la fruta fruit *7*
la frutería fruit store, fruit market *7*
fuerte strong *3*
el fútbol soccer *12*
   el campo de fútbol soccer field *12*

G

ganar to win; to earn *12*
la gasolinera gas station *6*
el, la gato, -a cat *9*
la generalidad generality *8*
generoso, -a generous *4*
la gente people *7*
la geografía geography *5*
la geometría geometry *5*
el gimnasio gymnasium *12*
el gol goal *12*
   meter (marcar) un gol to score a goal *12*
el golf golf *12*
gracias thank you *D*
la gramática grammar *9*
grande large, big *3*
la gripe cold, grippe *10*
gris gray *11*

el grupo group *10*
  guapo, -a handsome, good-looking *2*
  guardar to guard *12*
  guatemalteco, -a Guatemalan, of or from Guatemala *10*
la guerra war *LCO*
la guitarra guitar *5*

H

la habichuela bean *7*
  hablar to talk *5*
  hacer to do; to make *G*
    hacer buen tiempo to be nice (weather) *G*
    hacer calor to be hot (weather) *G*
    hacer fresco to be cool (weather) *G*
    hacer frío to be cold (weather) *G*
    hacer mal tiempo to be bad (weather) *G*
    hacer sol to be sunny *G*
    hacer viento to be windy *G*
el hambre (*f*) hunger *LCO*
  pasar hambre to feel hungry *LCO*
  hasta until; even *B*
    hasta la vista so long, good-bye *B*
    hasta luego so long, see you later *B*
    hasta pronto see you soon *B*
  hay there is, there are *7*
  no hay de qué you're welcome *D*
el helado ice cream *8*
la hermana sister *3*
el hermano brother *3*
  higiénico, -a hygienic *7*
    el papel higiénico toilet paper *7*
la hija daughter *9*
el hijo son *9*
  los hijos children *9*
  hispánico, -a Hispanic *6*
  hispano, -a Hispanic *9*
  hispanoamericano, -a Spanish-American *10*
la historia history *F*
  hola hello *2*

el hombre man *B*
el honor honor *11*
la hora hour; time *F*
  ¿a qué hora? at what time? *F*
  ¿qué hora es? what time is it? *F*
el hospital hospital *10*
el hotel hotel *13*
  hoy today *E*
el, la huérfano, -a orphan *LCO*
  humilde humble *LCO*
el humor humor, wit; mood *10*
  de buen humor in a good mood *10*
  de mal humor in a bad mood *10*

I

la idea idea *LCO*
el idioma language *10*
el ídolo idol *LCO*
la ilusión illusion *LCO*
la importancia importance *9*
  importante important *8*
la independencia independence *E*
el indicador indicator *12*
  el tablero indicador scoreboard *12*
  indicar to indicate *12*
el, la indio, -a Indian *LCO*
la influencia influence *10*
  inglés, -esa English *F*
  inteligente intelligent *2*
  interesante interesting *2*
  internacional international *10*
el invierno winter *G*
el, la invitado, -a guest *11*
  invitar to invite *11*
  ir to go *7*
    ir a to be going to *11*
    ir de compras to go shopping *7*
  irlandés, -esa Irish *10*
  italiano, -a Italian *19*

J

el jabón soap *7*
  el jabón en polvo soap powder, powdered soap *7*

joven young *6*
jueves Thursday *E*
el, la jugador, -ra player *12*
  jugar (ue) to play *12*
julio July *E*
junio June *E*

K

el kilo(gramo) kilogram *7*

L

la the *1*
el lago lake *LCO*
  lanzar to throw *12*
  largo, -a long *11*
  las the *3*
la lástima pity, shame *10*
  ¡qué lástima! what a pity!, what a shame! *10*
la lata tin can *7*
el latín Latin *5*
la leche milk *7*
la lechería dairy store *7*
la lechuga lettuce *7*
  leer to read *8*
la legumbre vegetable *7*
  lejos far *LCO*
la lengua language *LCO*
el libro book *8*
  ligero, -a light *8*
la limonada lemonade *D*
  listo, -a ready; smart *1*
  los the *3*
  luego then *6*
    hasta luego so long, see you later *B*
  lunes Monday *E*

LL

la llegada arrival *10*
  llegar to arrive *6*
  llevar to carry; to wear *LCO*

M

la madre mother *9*
  madrileño, -a of or from Madrid *8*
el maíz corn *LCO*
  malo, -a bad *5*
la manga sleeve *11*

la **mano** hand *10*
mantener to keep *9*
la **mañana** morning *7*
de la mañana A.M. *F*
las **mañanitas** short musical piece (Mexican song usually sung at birthday celebrations) *LCO*
marcar to score *12*
marcar un tanto to score a point *12*
el **marido** husband *9*
martes Tuesday *E*
marzo March *E*
marrón brown *11*
más more *7*
más de more than *10*
el **matador** bullfighter *LCO*
las **matemáticas** mathematics *5*
el **matrimonio** marriage *9*
mayo May *E*
la **mayoría** majority *8*
las **medias** stockings *11*
el, la **médico, -a** doctor *10*
la **consulta del médico** doctor's office *10*
medio, -a half, medium, middle *7*
el **mediodía** noon *6*
al mediodía at noon *6*
el **menú** menu *D*
el **mercado** market *7*
el mercado al aire libre open-air (outdoor) market *LCO*
la **merienda** light afternoon meal, snack; picnic *6*
meter to put, to place *12*
meter (marcar) un gol to score a goal *12*
mexicano, -a Mexican *1*
mi my *9*
mí me *1*
¡ay de mí! woe is me!, gosh! *1*
el, la **miembro, -a** member *9*
miércoles Wednesday *E*
la **miga** crumb *LCO*
mil one thousand *C*
el **millón** million *10*
el, la **millonario, -a** millionaire *LCO*
mineral mineral *7*
el agua mineral mineral water *7*

el **minuto** minute *12*
mirar to look at, to watch *6*
mismo, -a same *7*
el **modelo** model, example *10*
moderno, -a modern *LCO*
la **monja** nun *LCO*
el **monstruo** monster *10*
la **montaña** mountain *LCO*
moreno, -a dark-haired; brown, brunette *1*
morir (ue) to die *LCO*
la **muchacha** girl *1*
el **muchacho** boy *1*
mucho a lot, much *5*
muerto, -a dead *LCO*
la **mujer** woman; wife *9*
la **música** music *F*
muy very *2*

N

nacer to be born *LCO*
la **nación** nation *LCO*
la **nacionalidad** nationality *4*
nada nothing
de nada you're welcome *D*
la **naranja** orange *11*
la **nariz** nose *10*
la **natación** swimming *12*
necesitar to need *7*
negro, -a black *11*
nervioso, -a nervous *10*
el, la **nicaragüense** Nicaraguan, of or from Nicaragua *10*
la **nieta** granddaughter *9*
el **nieto** grandson *9*
el, la **niño, -a** child *LCO*
los niños children *LCO*
no no; not *1*
¡cómo no! of course! *5*
no hay de qué you're welcome *7*
la **noche** night *F*
buenas noches good night *A*
el **nombre** name *9*
el **nordeste** northeast *10*
el **norte** north *10*
norteamericano, -a of or from North America *10*
nosotros, -as we *4*
la **nota** (class) grade, mark *5*

novecientos nine hundred *C*
noventa ninety *C*
la **novia** fiancée *1*
noviembre November *E*
el **novio** fiancé *1*
nuestro, -a our *9*
nueve nine *C*
nuevo, -a new *10*
el **número** number, (shoe) size *11*
la **nutrición** nutrition *LCO*

O

octubre October *E*
ochenta eighty *C*
ocho eight *C*
ochocientos eight hundred *C*
el **oeste** west *10*
el **ojo** eye *10*
olvidar to forget *LCO*
once eleven *C*
la **oportunidad** opportunity *8*
la **oración** sentence *10*
la **oreja** ear *10*
orgulloso, -a proud *10*
el **origen** origin *10*
el **otoño** autumn *G*
otro, -a other, another *7*
otra vez again *LCO*
¡oye! hey!, listen! *2*

P

el **padre** father *9*
los padres parents *9*
el **padrino** godfather *9*
los padrinos godparents *9*
pagar to pay (for) *7*
el **país** country *8*
la **paja** straw *LCO*
la **palabra** word *10*
el **pan** bread *7*
la **panadería** bakery *7*
el **panadero** baker *7*
el **panecillo** bread roll *LCO*
los **pantalones** pants, trousers *11*
la **papa** potato *8*
el **papel** paper *7*
el papel higiénico toilet paper *7*
para for; in order to *4*

parar to stop *12*

pardo, -a brown *11*

el pariente relative *9*

el parque park *LCO*

la parte part *10*

particular private, particular *8*

la casa particular private house *8*

el partido game (sports) *12*

pasar to spend, to pass (time) *LCO*

pasar hambre to feel hungry *LCO*

el paseo walk, stroll *8*

dar un paseo to take a walk, to stroll *LCO*

el pastel pastry *7*

la pastelería pastry shop *7*

paterno, -a paternal *9*

el patio patio *12*

la película film *8*

el pelo hair *10*

la pena pain, grief *10*

¡qué pena! what a pity! *10*

pequeño, -a small *3*

perder (ie) to lose *12*

perdón pardon, excuse me *7*

el periódico newspaper *8*

la perla pearl *11*

pero but *1*

¡pero, cuidado! but be careful! *1*

la persona person *2*

el perrito little dog, puppy *9*

el perro dog *9*

la pescadería fish store, fish market *7*

el pescado fish *7*

la peseta peseta, monetary unit of Spain *LCO*

el peso peso, monetary unit of several Latin American countries *7*

el pie foot *10*

a pie on foot *LCO*

la piedra stone *LCO*

la pierna leg *10*

el piso floor, story (of a building), apartment *8*

la planta floor *8*

la planta baja ground floor *8*

la plaza public square *LCO*

la plaza de toros bullring *LCO*

pobre poor *10*

la pobreza poverty *LCO*

poco little, few *LCO*

poder (ue) to be able *12*

la policía police force *LCO*

político, -a political *LCO*

el polvo powder; dust *7*

el jabón en polvo soap powder, powdered soap *7*

popular popular *2*

por for *6*

por consiguiente consequently *8*

por ejemplo for example *6*

por favor please *D*

por la mañana in the morning *7*

por lo general generally *8*

¿por qué? why? *7*

¡por supuesto! of course! *5*

por teléfono on the phone *6*

porque because *LCO*

la portería gate, goal area *12*

el, la portero, -a goalie *12*

portugués, -esa Portuguese *10*

posible possible *5*

postal postal *4*

la tarjeta postal postcard *4*

el precio price *7*

preferir (ie) to prefer *12*

preparar to prepare *6*

la primaria elementary school *6*

primario, -a primary, elementary *2*

la primavera spring *G*

primero, -a first *E*

el primer tiempo first half (sports) *12*

el, la primo, -a cousin *9*

la prisión prison *LCO*

privado, -a private *2*

probablemente probably *10*

el problema problem *LCO*

el producto product *7*

el, la profesor, -ra teacher, professor *5*

pronto soon

hasta pronto see you soon *B*

público, -a public *2*

el pueblo town *8*

puertorriqueño, -a Puerto Rican *10*

pues well . . . then *3*

el puesto stand, stall (market) *LCO*

Q

¡qué! what!; how! *1*

no hay de qué you're welcome *D*

¡qué lástima! what a pity! *10*

¡qué pena! what a shame! *10*

¡qué suerte! what luck! *1*

¿qué? what? *4*

¿qué tal? how are things? *A*

¿qué tiempo hace? what is the weather? *G*

quedar to remain *12*

querer (ie) to want *12*

querido, -a dear *4*

¿quién? who? *1*

¿de quién? whose? *4*

la química chemistry *5*

quince fifteen *C*

la quinceañera the fifteen-year old (girl) *11*

quinientos five hundred *C*

R

la raya stripe, line *11*

recibir to receive *8*

recién recently, newly *10*

recién llegado newcomer *10*

el redondel bullring *LCO*

reflejar to reflect *9*

el refresco refreshment *LCO*

el regalo gift *11*

regatear to bargain *LCO*

el regateo bargaining *LCO*

la región region *LCO*

remar to row *LCO*

remoto, -a remote *LCO*

el restaurante restaurant *D*

la **revista** magazine *8*
rico, -a rich *LCO*
robar to rob, to steal *LCO*
rodar (ue) to shoot film *LCO*
la **rodilla** knee *10*
rojo, -a red *11*
el **rollo** roll *7*
la **ropa** clothing, clothes *11*
la tienda de ropa para caballeros men's clothing store *11*
rubio, -a blond(e) *1*
el **ruido** noise *LCO*

S

sábado Saturday *E*
sacar to get (a grade); to pull out, to take out *5*
la **sala** living room *6*
la **salud** health *7*
el **saludo** greeting *A*
salvadoreño, -a Salvadoran, of or from El Salvador *10*
secundario, -a secondary *1*
segundo, -a second *8*
el segundo tiempo second half (sports) *12*
seis six *C*
seiscientos six hundred *C*
el **semestre** semester *5*
el **señor** sir, Mr., gentleman *A*
la **señora** Ms., Mrs., madam *A*
la **señorita** Miss, Ms. *A*
septiembre September *E*
ser to be *2*
la **serenata** serenade *LCO*
serio, -a serious *2*
sesenta sixty *C*
setecientos seven hundred *C*
setenta seventy *C*
sí yes *1*
¡claro que sí! of course! *5*
siempre always *LCO*
siete seven *C*
simpático, -a nice *2*
simple simple *20*
sin without *LCO*

sincero, -a sincere *2*
sobre on, above *9*
sobre todo especially, above all *9*
la **sobrina** niece *9*
el **sobrino** nephew *9*
social social *LCO*
la **sociedad** society *9*
el **sol** sun *G*
hacer sol to be sunny (weather) *G*
solamente only *9*
el **sombrero** hat *11*
la **sopa** soup *8*
su his, her, their, your *9*
el **suburbio** suburb *8*
el **sudoeste** southwest *10*
la **suerte** luck *1*
tener suerte to be lucky *LCO*
el **suéter** sweater *11*
el **supermercado** supermarket *7*
el **sur** south *10*

T

el **tablero** board *12*
el tablero indicador scoreboard *12*
el **tacón** heel *11*
de tacón alto high-heeled *11*
tal such *A*
¿qué tal? how are things? *A*
la **talla** size (clothing) *11*
también also *1*
tan so *LCO*
el **tanto** score *12*
meter (marcar) un tanto to score *12*
tarde late *6*
la **tarde** afternoon *F*
buenas tardes good afternoon *A*
de la tarde P.M. *F*
la **tarjeta** card *4*
la tarjeta postal postcard *4*
el **techo** roof *LCO*
el **teléfono** telephone *6*
la **televisión** television *6*
tener to have *9*
tener . . . años to be . . . years old *9*
tener que to have to *9*

tener suerte to be lucky *LCO*
el **tenis** tennis *12*
tercero, -a third *8*
terminar to end *6*
la **tía** aunt *9*
el **tiempo** time *12;* weather *G*
hacer buen tiempo to be nice (weather) *G*
hacer mal tiempo to be bad (weather) *G*
el primer tiempo first half (sports) *12*
¿qué tiempo hace? what is the weather? *G*
el segundo tiempo second half (sports) *12*
la **tienda** store *7*
la tienda de ropa clothing store *11*
la tienda de ropa para caballeros men's clothing store *11*
la tienda de ropa para señoras women's clothing store *11*
el **tío** uncle *9*
típico, -a typical *LCO*
tocar to play (a musical instrument) *5;* to touch *12*
todavía still, yet *LCO*
todo, -a all, everything *5*
sobre todo especially, above all *9*
todo el día all day *6*
todos everyone *2*
todos los días every day *7*
tomar to take *5*
tonto, -a foolish, dumb *1*
torear to fight bulls *LCO*
el **torero** bullfighter *LCO*
el **toro** bull *LCO*
la plaza de toros bullring *LCO*
la **tortilla** type of pancake made from corn *LCO*
la **tostada** open crisp corn tortilla topped with beans, ground beef, lettuce *D*
trabajar to work *6*
el **trabajo** work *LCO*
la **tradición** tradition *10*
la **tragedia** tragedy *LCO*
el **traje** suit *11*

tranquilo, -a peaceful, tranquil *10*

trece thirteen *C*

treinta thirty *C*

tremendo, -a tremendous *LCO*

tres three *C*

trescientos three hundred *C*

la trigonometría trigonometry *5*

triste sad *10*

tu your *9*

tú you *2*

U

Ud. you (sing. polite) *5*

Uds. you (pl. polite) *4*

último, -a last *12*

un, uno, -a a, one *C*

la universidad university *8*

unos, -as some *LCO*

usar to use *12*

V

varios, -as various *9*

veinte twenty *C*

veinticinco twenty-five *C*

veinticuatro twenty-four *C*

veintidós twenty-two *C*

veintinueve twenty-nine *C*

veintiocho twenty-eight *C*

veintiséis twenty-six *C*

veintisiete twenty-seven *C*

veintitrés twenty-three *C*

veintiuno twenty-one *C*

vender to sell *LCO*

la ventana window *LCO*

ver to look at, to watch, to see *8*

el verano summer *G*

la verdad truth *2*

verde green *11*

vestido, -a dressed *LCO*

el vestido dress *11*

la vez time *LCO*

    a veces at times *6*

    muchas veces many times *8*

    otra vez again *LCO*

la vida life *11*

el viento wind *G*

    hacer viento to be windy *G*

viernes Friday *E*

violeta purple *11*

visitar to visit *LCO*

la vista view, sight

    hasta la vista so long, good-bye *B*

la vitrina display window *11*

la viuda widow *9*

el viudo widower *9*

vivir to live *8*

el volibol volleyball *12*

volver (ue) to return *12*

vuestro, -a your *9*

Y

y and *A*

ya already; now *12*

yo I *2*

Z

el zapato shoe *11*

English-Spanish Vocabulary

A

a un, uno, -a *1*
able: to be able poder (ue) *12*
about a eso de (*time*) *8*
above sobre *9*
  above all sobre todo *9*
ache el dolor *10*
  headache el dolor de cabeza *10*
adorable adorable *9*
affection el cariño *4*
after después (de) *6*
afternoon la tarde *6*
  good afternoon buenas tardes *A*
again otra vez *LCO*
age la edad *9*
air el aire *LCO*
algebra el álgebra (*f*) *F*
all todo, -a *5*
  all day todo el día *6*
  above all sobre todo *9*
almost casi *7*
already ya *12*
also también *1*
always siempre *LCO*
American americano, -a *1*
amusing divertido, -a *2*
and y *A*
Andalucía (of or from) andaluz, -za *LCO*
another otro, -a *7*
apartment el apartamento *8*
April abril *E*
architecture la arquitectura *10*
Argentinean argentino, -a *5*
arrival la llegada *10*
to arrive llegar *6*
art el arte *5*
as como *5*
at a *7*
  at home en casa *8*
  athletic atlético, -a *3*
to attend asistir *8*
August agosto *E*
aunt la tía *9*
autumn el otoño *G*
avenue la avenida *8*

B

baby el bebé *9*
bad malo, -a *5*
  to be bad weather hacer mal tiempo *G*
baker el panadero *7*
bakery la panadería *7*
ball el balón, la pelota *12*
to bargain regatear *LCO*
bargaining el regateo *LCO*
baseball el béisbol *12*
basket la canasta *LCO*
to be ser *2*; estar *7*
  to be able poder (ue) *12*
  to be bad weather hacer mal tiempo *G*
  to be born nacer *LCO*
  to be cold (weather) hacer frío *G*
  to be cool (weather) hacer fresco *G*
  to be hot (weather) hacer calor *G*
  to be lucky tener suerte *LCO*
  to be nice (weather) hacer buen tiempo *G*
  to be successful tener éxito *LCO*
  to be sunny (weather) hacer sol *G*
  to be windy hacer viento *G*
  to be ... years old tener ... años *9*
beast la bestia *LCO*
bed la cama *10*
beef el bife *LCO*
before antes (de) *10*
to begin comenzar (ie) *12*; empezar (ie) *12*
besides además *3*
big grande *3*
biology la biología *F*
birthday el cumpleaños *11*
black negro, -a *11*
blond(e) rubio, -a *1*
blouse la blusa *11*
blue azul *11*
board el tablero *12*
  scoreboard el tablero indicador *12*
boat (small) el barquito *LCO*
book el libro *8*
boring aburrido, -a *2*
born: to be born nacer *LCO*
bottle la botella *7*

box la caja *7*
boy el muchacho *1*
bread el pan *7*
  bread roll el panecillo *LCO*
breakfast el desayuno *8*
brother el hermano *3*
brown castaño, -a; de color café; marrón; moreno, -a; pardo, -a *11*
brunet(te) moreno, -a *1*
building el edificio *8*
bullfight la corrida *LCO*
bullfighter el matador *LCO*; el torero *LCO*
bullring la plaza de toros *LCO*; el redondel *LCO*
buried enterrado, -a *LCO*
but pero *1*
  but be careful! ¡pero, cuidado! *1*
butcher shop la carnicería *7*
to buy comprar *7*

C

café el café *8*
cafeteria la cafetería *8*
calculus el cálculo *5*
can la lata *7*
Canadian canadiense *10*
canned enlatado, -a *7*
  canned foods alimentos enlatados *7*
capacity la capacidad *8*
capital la capital *8*
card la tarjeta *4*
  postcard la tarjeta postal *4*
care: to take care of cuidar de *LCO*
to carry llevar *LCO*
cash register la caja *7*
cat el, la gato, -a *9*
celebration la celebración *LCO*
to change cambiar *9*
chemistry la química *5*
child el, la niño, -a *LCO*
  children los niños *LCO*
chop la chuleta *7*
  pork chop la chuleta de cerdo *7*

citizen el, la ciudadano, -a
10
city la ciudad *8*
civic cívico, -a *5*
civics la educación cívica *5*
civil civil *LCO*
class la clase *F*
clothes la ropa *11*
  clothing store la tienda de
  ropa *11*
coast la costa *9*
coat el abrigo *11*
coffee el café *8*
coincidence la coincidencia
LCO
cold el catarro, la gripe *10*
cold el frío *G*
  to be cold (weather) hacer
  frío *G* **(person)** tener frío
Colombian colombiano, -a *2*
color el color *8*
common común *10*
to complete completar *LCO*
composition la composición
8
consequently por
  consiguiente *8*
contrary el contrario *8*
  on the contrary al
  contrario *8*
convent el convento *LCO*
cool fresco, -a *G*
  to be cool (weather) hacer
  fresco *G*
corn el maíz *LCO*
to cost costar (ue) *7*
country el campo; el país *8*
course el curso *5*
course: of course! ¡claro!,
  ¡claro que sí!, ¡cómo no!, ¡por
  supuesto! *5*
courtesy la cortesía *D*
cousin el, la primo, -a *9*
crumb la miga *LCO*
Cuban cubano, -a *10*
culture la cultura *10*
current corriente *10*
custom la costumbre *11*
  as customary de costumbre
  11
customer el, la cliente *LCO*

D

daily diario, -a *5*
dairy store la lechería *7*
to dance bailar *11*

date la fecha *E*
daughter la hija *9*
day el día *6*
  all day todo el día *6*
  every day todos los días *7*
dead muerto, -a *LCO*
dear querido, -a *4*
December diciembre *E*
to die morir (ue) *LCO*
difficult difícil *4*
dining room el comedor *8*
dinner la cena *8*
director el, la director, -ra
LCO
discovery el descubrimiento
E
display window el
  escaparate, la vitrina *11*
to do hacer *G*
doctor el, la médico, -a *10*
  doctor's office la consulta
  del médico *10*
dog el perro *9*
  little dog el perrito *9*
domestic doméstico, -a *5*
Dominican dominicano, -a
10
drawing el dibujo *9*
dress el vestido *11*
dressed vestido, -a *LCO*
to drink beber *8*
during durante *11*

E

each cada *12*
ear la oreja *10*
to earn ganar *12*
east el este *10*
easy fácil *4*
to eat comer *8*
education la educación *F*
  physical education la
  educación física *5*
eight ocho *C*
  eight hundred ochocientos
  C
eighteen dieciocho *C*
eighty ochenta *C*
eleven once *C*
employee el, la empleado, -a
7
enchilada la enchilada *D*
end el fin *9*
to end terminar *6*
English el inglés *F*
enough bastante *4*

to enter entrar *12*
environs las afueras *8*
especially sobre todo *9*
even hasta *B*
everyone todos, -as *2*
everything todo, -a *5*
example el ejemplo *6;* el
  modelo *10*
  for example por ejemplo *6*
excellent excelente *7*
exception la excepción *12*
excuse me perdón *7*
expensive caro, -a *7*
eye el ojo *10*

F

facility la facilidad *8*
faculty la facultad *8*
family la familia *8*
fantastic fantástico, -a *2*
farewell la despedida *B*
farm la finca *LCO*
father el padre *9*
favor el favor *D*
favorite favorito, -a *5*
February febrero *E*
fever la fiebre *10*
few poco, -a *LCO*
fiancé el novio *1*
fiancée la novia *1*
field el campo *8*
  soccer field el campo de
  fútbol *12*
fifteen quince *C*
  fifteen-year old (girl) la
  quinceañera *11*
fifty cincuenta *C*
film la película *8*
to film rodar (ue) *LCO*
finally en fin *9*
first primero, -a *E*
  first half (of a game) el
  primer tiempo *12*
fish el pescado *7*
  fish store (market) la
  pescadería *7*
five cinco *C*
  five hundred quinientos
  C
fixed fijo, -a *LCO*
floor (of a building) el piso
  8; la planta *8*
  ground floor la planta baja
  8
fond (of) aficionado, -a (a) *3*

food   el alimento   *7*
  canned foods   los alimentos
    enlatados   *7*
foolish   tonto, -a   *1*
foot   el pie (*human*)   *12*
  on foot   a pie   *LCO*
for   por   *6;* para   *4*
  for example   por ejemplo   *6*
  for that reason   por eso   *10*
to forget   olvidar   *LCO*
forty   cuarenta   *C*
four   cuatro   *C*
  four hundred   cuatrocientos
    C
fourteen   catorce   *C*
French   francés, -esa   *5*
frequency   la frecuencia
  LCO
frequently   con frecuencia
  LCO
Friday   viernes   *E*
friend   el, la amigo, -a   *B*
from   de   *2*
front: in front of   delante de
  LCO
fruit   la fruta   *7*
  fruit store   la frutería   *7*
to fulfill   cumplir   *11*
funny   divertido, -a   *2*

G

game   el partido   *12*
gas station   la gasolinera
  6
generality   la generalidad   *8*
generally   por lo general   *8*
generous   generoso, -a   *4*
gentleman   el señor   *A;* el
  caballero   *11*
geometry   la geometría   *5*
German   alemán, -ana   *10*
get: to get a grade   sacar una
  nota   *5*
gift   el regalo   *11*
girl   la chica   *1;* la muchacha
  1
to give   dar   *7*
to go   ir   *7*
  to be going to   ir a   *11*
  to go shopping   ir de
    compras   *7*
goal   el gol   *12*
  goal area   la portería   *12*
goalie   el, la portero, -a   *12*
goddaughter   la ahijada   *11*
godfather   el padrino   *9*

godparents   los padrinos   *9*
godson   el ahijado   *11*
good   bueno, -a   *A*
  good afternoon   buenas
    tardes   *A*
  good morning   buenos días
    A
  good night   buenas noches
    A
good-bye   hasta la vista, adiós
  B
grammar   la gramática   *9*
granddaughter   la nieta   *9*
grandfather   el abuelo   *9*
grandmother   la abuela   *9*
grandparents   los abuelos   *9*
grandson   el nieto   *9*
gray   gris   *11*
green   verde   *11*
greeting   el saludo   *A*
grief   la pena   *10*
grippe   la gripe   *10*
group   el grupo   *10*
Guatemalan   guatemalteco, -a
  10
guest   el, la invitado, -a   *11*
guitar   la guitarra   *5*
gymnasium   el gimnasio   *12*

H

half   medio, -a   *7*
  first half (sports)   el primer
    tiempo   *12*
  second half   el segundo
    tiempo   *12*
hand   la mano   *12*
handsome   guapo, -a   *2*
happy   contento   *10*
hard   duro, -a   *6*
hat   el sombrero   *11*
to have   tener (ie)   *9*
  to have to   tener que   *9*
he   él   *1*
head   la cabeza   *10*
  headache   el dolor de
    cabeza   *10*
health   la salud   *7*
heat   el calor   *G*
heel   el tacón   *11*
  high-heeled   de tacón alto
    11
hello   hola, buenos días   *A*
help   la ayuda   *LCO*
here   aquí   *9*
high   alto, -a   *1*
  high-heeled   de tacón alto   *11*

high school   el colegio   *1*
his   su   *9*
Hispanic   hispánico, -a   *6;*
  hispano, -a   *10*
history   la historia   *F*
home   la casa   *6*
  at home   a casa   *6;* en casa
    8
honor   el honor   *11*
hospital   el hospital   *10*
to be hot (weather)   hacer
  calor   *G*
hour   la hora   *F*
house   la casa   *6*
  private house   la casa
    particular   *8*
how?   ¿cómo?   *1*
  how are things?   ¿qué tal?
    A
  how much?   ¿cuánto?   *D*
humble   humilde   *LCO*
humor   el humor   *10*
hundred   cien, ciento   *C*
hunger   el hambre (*f*)   *LCO*
  to feel hungry   pasar
    hambre   *LCO*
husband   el marido   *9*

I

I   yo   *2*
ice cream   el helado   *8*
idea   la idea   *LCO*
idol   el ídolo   *LCO*
illusion   la ilusión   *LCO*
importance   la importancia
  9
important   importante   *8*
in   en   *1*
  in order to   para   *4*
independence   la
  independencia   *E*
Indian   el, la indio, -a   *LCO*
to indicate   indicar   *12*
influence   la influencia   *10*
intelligent   inteligente   *2*
interesting   interesante   *2*
international   internacional
  10
to invite   invitar   *11*
Irish   irlandés, -esa   *10*
Italian   italiano, -a   *10*

J

jacket   la chaqueta   *11*
jail   la cárcel   *LCO*

January enero *E*
July julio *E*

K

to **keep** mantener *9*
  kilogram el kilo(gramo) *7*
  kitchen la cocina *6*

L

  lack la falta *LCO*
  lady la señora *A*
  lake el lago *LCO*
  language el idioma *10*; la
    lengua *LCO*
  large grande *3*
  last último, -a *12*
    last name el apellido *9*
  late tarde *6*
  Latin el latín *5*
to **learn** aprender *8*
  lemonade la limonada *D*
  letter la carta *8*
  lettuce la lechuga *7*
  life la vida *11*
  light (not heavy) ligero, -a *8*
  like como *5*
to **listen to** escuchar *6*
    listen! ¡oye! *2*
  little poco *LCO*
to **live** vivir *8*
  living room la sala *6*
  long largo, -a *11*
to **look at** mirar *6*
to **look for** buscar *LCO*
to **lose** perder (ie) *12*
  luck la suerte *1*
    good luck! ¡buena suerte!
    1
    what luck! ¡qué suerte! *1*
  lucky: to be lucky tener
    suerte *LCO*
  lunch el almuerzo *8*

M

  Madrid (of or from)
    madrileño, -a *LCO*
  magazine la revista *8*
  majority la mayoría *8*
to **make** hacer *G*
    to make (films) rodar (ue)
    LCO
  March marzo *E*
  mark (school) la nota *5*
  market el mercado *7*

outdoor market el mercado
  al aire libre *LCO*
marriage el matrimonio *9*
marvel la maravilla *LCO*
mathematics las matemáticas
  5
May mayo *E*
me mí *1*
meal la comida *8*
meat la carne *7*
  meat market la carnicería
  7
medium medio, -a *7*
member el, la miembro, -a *9*
menu el menú *D*
Mexican mexicano, -a *1*
middle medio, -a *7*
milk la leche *7*
million el millón *10*
millionaire el, la millonario, -a
  LCO
mineral mineral *7*
  mineral water el agua
  mineral *7*
minute el minuto *12*
Miss la señorita *A*
model el modelo *10*
modern moderno, -a *LCO*
Monday lunes *E*
money el dinero *7*
mood el humor *10*
  in a bad mood de mal
  humor *10*
  in a good mood de buen
  humor *10*
more más *7*
  more than más de *10*
moreover además *3*
morning la mañana *7*
  good morning
    (day) buenos días *A*
  in the morning por la
  mañana *7*
mother la madre *9*
mountain la montaña *LCO*
mouth la boca *10*
Mr. el señor *A*
Mrs. la señora *A*
Ms. la señora, la señorita *A*
much mucho *5*
music la música *F*
my mi *9*

N

name el nombre *9*
  last name el apellido *9*

nation la nación *LCO*
nationality la nacionalidad
  4
near cerca (de) *LCO*
necklace el collar *11*
to **need** necesitar *7*
nephew el sobrino *9*
nervous nervioso, -a *10*
never nunca *16*
new nuevo, -a *10*
newcomer el, la recién
  llegado, -a *10*
newspaper el periódico *8*
Nicaraguan nicaragüense
  10
nice simpático, -a *2*
  to be nice (weather) hacer
  buen tiempo *G*
night la noche *F*
  good night buenas noches
  A
nine nueve *C*
  nine hundred novecientos
  C
nineteen diecinueve *C*
ninety noventa *C*
no no *1*
noon el mediodía *6*
  at noon al mediodía *6*
north el norte *10*
North American
  norteamericano, -a *10*
northeast el nordeste *10*
not no *1*
note el apunte *5*
to **note** notar *LCO*
notebook el cuaderno *5*
November noviembre *E*
now ahora *LCO*; ya *12*
number el número *11*
nun la monja *LCO*

O

ocean el océano *LCO*
October octubre *E*
of de *2*
  of course! ¡claro!, ¡claro que
  sí!, ¡cómo no!, ¡por supuesto!
  5
office la consulta *10*
  doctor's office la consulta
  del médico *10*
on sobre *9*
one uno, -a *C*
  one hundred cien, ciento
  C

only solamente 9
open abierto, -a LCO
opportunity la oportunidad 8
opposite contrario, -a LCO
orange anaranjado, -a 11
origin el origen LCO, 10
orphan el, la huérfano, -a LCO
other otro, -a 7
our nuestro, -a, -os, -as 9
outdoor al aire libre LCO
  outdoor market el mercado al aire libre LCO
outside afuera 8
outskirts las afueras 8
oxygen el oxígeno LCO
  oxygen mask la máscara de oxígeno LCO

P

pain el dolor 10
pants los pantalones 11
paper el papel 7
  toilet paper el papel higiénico 7
pardon perdón 7
parents los padres 9
park el parque LCO
part la parte 10
party la fiesta 11
pastry el pastel 7
  pastry shop la pastelería 7
paternal paterno 9
to pay (for) pagar 7
peaceful tranquilo, -a 10
peak el pico LCO
pearl la perla 11
pedestrian el peatón LCO
pencil el lápiz LCO
people la gente 8
person la persona 2
physical education la educación física 5
physics la física 5
picture el cuadro 13; el dibujo 9
piece el pedazo
  small piece el pedacito LCO
pig el cerdo 7
pity la lástima 10
  what a pity! ¡qué lástima!; ¡qué pena! 10
to place meter 12
to play jugar (ue) 12

to play (a musical instrument) tocar 5
player el, la jugador, -ra 12
plaza la plaza LCO
please por favor D
police (force) la policía LCO
political político -a LCO
poor pobre 10
popular popular 2
pork el cerdo 7
  pork chops las chuletas de cerdo 7
Portuguese portugués, -esa 10
possible posible 5
postal postal 4
postcard la tarjeta postal 4
potato la papa 8
poverty la pobreza LCO
powder el polvo 7
  soap powder el jabón en polvo 7
to prefer preferir (ie) 12
to prepare preparar 6
pretty bonito, -a 7
price el precio 7
primary primario, -a 2
prison la prisión LCO
private particular 8; privado, -a 2
  private house la casa particular 8
probably probablemente 10
problem el problema LCO
product el producto 7
professor el, la profesor, -ra 5
promenade el paseo 8
proud orgulloso, -a 10
public público, -a 2
Puerto Rican puertorriqueño, -a 10
puppy el perrito 9
purple violeta 11
to put meter 12

Q

quality la calidad 7
quantity la cantidad 8

R

ranch la finca LCO
rather bastante 4
to read leer 8
ready listo, -a 1

to receive recibir 8
recently recién 10
record el disco 6
red rojo, -a 11
to reflect reflejar 9
refreshment el refresco LCO
region la región LCO
relative el, la pariente 9
to remain quedar 12
remote remoto, -a LCO
to rent alquilar LCO
to rest descansar LCO
to return volver (ue) 12
rich rico, -a LCO
right derecho 8
to rob robar LCO
roll el rollo 7
roof el techo LCO
room el cuarto
  dining room el comedor 8
  living room la sala 6
to row remar LCO

S

sad triste 10
salad la ensalada 8
Salvadoran (of or from El Salvador) salvadoreño, -a 10
same mismo, -a 7
Saturday sábado E
school la escuela 1
  elementary school la primaria 5
  secondary school el colegio 1
science la ciencia 5
score el tanto 12
to score marcar, meter 12
  to score a goal marcar (meter) un gol 12
  to score a point marcar un tanto 12
scoreboard el tablero indicador 12
to search buscar LCO
second segundo, -a 8
  second half (of a game) el segundo tiempo 12
secondary secundario, -a 1
  secondary school el colegio 1
to see ver 8
  see you later hasta luego B
  see you soon hasta pronto B

to sell vender *LCO*
semester el semestre *5*
sentence la oración *10*
September septiembre *E*
serenade la serenata *LCO*
serious serio, -a *2*
seven siete *C*
  seven hundred setecientos *C*
seventeen diecisiete *C*
seventy setenta *C*
shame la lástima *10*
  what a shame! ¡qué lástima! *10*
she ella *1*
shirt la camisa *11*
shoe el zapato *11*
to shop ir de compras *7*
short bajo, -a *1*; corto, -a *11*
sick enfermo, -a *7*
since desde *10*
sincere sincero, -a *2*
to sing cantar *5*
sir el señor *A*
sister la hermana *3*
six seis *C*
  six hundred seiscientos *C*
sixteen dieciséis *C*
sixty sesenta *C*
size (shoe) el número *11*; **(clothing)** la talla *11*
ski el esquí *12*
skirt la falda *11*
to sleep dormir (ue) *12*
sleeve la manga *11*
small pequeño, -a *3*
smart listo, -a *1*
so así *A*
  so then entonces *3*
so tan *LCO*
so long hasta la vista *B*; hasta luego *B*
soap el jabón *7*
  soap powder el jabón en polvo *7*
soccer el fútbol *12*
  soccer field el campo de fútbol *12*
society la sociedad *9*
socks los calcetines *11*
some algunos, -as *10*; unos, -as *LCO*
something algo *7*
somewhat bastante *4*
son el hijo *9*
soup la sopa *8*
south el sur *10*

southwest el sudoeste *10*
Spain (of or from) español, -la *4*
Spanish el español *F*
Spanish-American hispanoamericano, -a *10*
special especial *11*
specialized especializado, -a *7*
spectator el, la espectador, -ra *12*
to spend (time) pasar *LCO*
sport el deporte *3*
spring la primavera *G*
square la plaza *LCO*
stadium el estadio *12*
stand (market) el puesto *LCO*
station la estación
  gas station la gasolinera *6*
to steal robar *LCO*
still todavía *LCO*
stockings las medias *11*
stone la piedra *LCO*
to stop parar *12*
store la tienda *6*
  clothing store la tienda de ropa *11*
  men's clothing store la tienda de ropa para caballeros *11*
  women's clothing store la tienda de ropa para señoras *11*
story (of a building) el piso *8*
straight derecho *8*
straw la paja *LCO*
strawberry la fresa *7*
street la calle *8*
stripe la raya *11*
strong fuerte *3*
student el, la alumno, -a *1*
to study estudiar *5*
subject la asignatura *5*
suburb el suburbio *8*
success el éxito *LCO*
successful: to be successful tener éxito *LCO*
such tal *A*
suit el traje *11*
summer el verano *G*
sun el sol *G*
Sunday domingo *F*
sunny: to be sunny (weather) hacer sol *G*

supermarket el supermercado *7*
surname el apellido *9*
sweater el suéter *11*

T

taco (filled and fried tortilla) el taco *D*
to take tomar *5*
  to take a walk dar un paseo *LCO*
  to take care of cuidar de *LCO*
  to take out sacar *5*
to talk hablar *5*
tall alto, -a *1*
to teach enseñar *5*
team el equipo *12*
telephone el teléfono *6*
television la televisión *6*
ten diez *C*
tennis el tenis *12*
tent la tienda *6*
thank you gracias *D*
to thank agradecer *11*
the la, el *1*; las, los *3*
their su *9*
then entonces *3*; luego *6*
  well ... then pues *3*
there: there is, there are hay *7*
therefore por eso *10*
they ellas, ellos *3*
thing (little) la cosita *LCO*
to think opinar *LCO*; pensar (ie) *LCO*
third tercero, -a *8*
thirteen trece *C*
thirty treinta *C*
thousand mil *C*
three tres *C*
  three hundred trescientos *C*
to throw lanzar *12*
Thursday jueves *E*
tie la corbata *11*
to tie (score) empatar *12*
time la hora *F*; la vez *LCO*
  at times a veces *6*
  at what time? ¿a qué hora? *F*
  short time el rato *LCO*
  what time is it? ¿qué hora es? *F*
tin can la lata *7*
tired cansado, -a *10*

Index